CRIB DEATH:

THE SUDDEN INFANT DEATH SYNDROME

The Judgment of Solomon, a ceiling fresco by Raphael, about 1509 to 1511. Reproduced, by permission, from Marcel Brion's *Bible in Art*, Phaidon Press (London), 1956. The fresco depicts the first recorded SIDS victim on the floor; the surviving infant was to be divided by the sword, to resolve the dispute over who was the true mother. The true mother relinquished her claim, to spare the child; Solomon thereupon awarded her the child. The dead infant was reported as "overlain."

CRIB DEATH:
THE SUDDEN INFANT DEATH SYNDROME

Warren G. Guntheroth, M.D.

Professor of Pediatrics
Head, Division of Pediatric Cardiology
University of Washington School of Medicine
Seattle, Washington

FUTURA PUBLISHING COMPANY
Mount Kisco, New York
1982

Copyright © 1982
Futura Publishing Company, Inc.

Published by
Futura Publishing Company, Inc.
295 Main Street,
Mount Kisco, New York 10549

L.C. #: 82-70102
ISBN #: 087-993-175-2

Dedication

I dedicate this book to the living children

Acknowledgements

Since there is no way that a monograph such as this can be accomplished "at work," the evenings and weekends at home become dedicated to that purpose. I feel a continued, deep gratitude that my wife, Ellie, has tolerated my commitment to the task; even more important, over the years she has helped build my physical and emotional "cave," so necessary for warmth and quiet—and recovery from wounds—that allow the next day's excursion.

In the past three years, Jon Jacky, Ph.D., worked closely with me and helped educate me about many aspects of cardiopulmonary physiology. Our loyal and efficient secretary, Caye Nollette, has been a great help and comfort. Even my climbing buddy, Edwin Emery, has sacrificed some good opportunities for new peaks to allow me to finish some urgent parts of this manuscript.

Finally, I honestly attribute the entire enterprise to Steven Korn, who suggested this monograph and persisted until I was willing to make the commitment.

Preface

I became interested in sudden and unexpected deaths during my general pediatric residency in Boston Children's Hospital. It was at this hospital that Dr. Sydney Farber had discovered two instances of undiagnosed septicemia in 1934; it was a well-established routine that any infant dead on arrival at our hospital received a post-mortem blood culture, in addition to a thorough autopsy. By the mid-50's, it was apparent that very few of these victims of Sudden Infant Death Syndrome (SIDS) had bacterial infection, and I became intrigued by Stowen's suggestion that, in the absence of anatomic disorders that could explain death, a reflex mechanism was the probable cause. Not long after I arrived in Seattle in 1957, the infant of a friend was found dead in the morning, and the death was described in the local papers as due to suffocation by bed clothes. I wrote the coroner in King County, who was not a physician, and his response was positive, and I felt encouraged. In 1958 I joined the faculty at the University of Washington School of Medicine as a pediatric cardiologist, but my first "lobbying" effort with my Chairman, Dr. Robert Aldrich, was for permission to give a lecture to the entire medical school class on crib death. (It was annoying many years later to have all medical school faculty castigated by Curran (1972) who argued that the problem of SIDS was not "palatable to the American medical research community," and that "little, if any, instruction is given in the problem in medical schools").

During my residency, and after I began to take care of children with congenital heart disease at the University Hospital in Seattle, I was struck by a few cases in which an infant with a mild respiratory disease would be discovered apneic in the emergency room or on the hospital ward, who could be resuscitated with fairly simple external ventilation. When our medical school was directed to hold a conference on the subject of SIDS by the State Legislature (a novel but effective approach), I recommended the invitation of Geoffrey Dawes, to ensure that the subject of reflexes might be considered, in a group that was otherwise going to consist of only pathologists, immunologists, and virologists. In talking with Dr. Dawes via a trans-Atlantic call, he indicated some surprise about the invitation since he did not regard himself as an expert, and confessed that he had never heard of the disorder. Fortunately for us, he consented to come, and has helped the field immensely since that time.

I did not begin laboratory research on the subject of SIDS for several years, in spite of funds available nationally, simply because I had no testable hypothesis, an essential for good research (in contrast to descriptive studies with no particular hypothesis which could be compared to the catching, sorting, and labeling of butterflies). Crib death was not the kind of problem that can be approached by a team of engineers with a large amount of money, comparable to the Space Program. My laboratory for animal experiments was funded by a grant from the National Heart Institute, dedicated to research on shock and the control of the venous system. In those days, the granting agencies did not mind whether you stuck closely to the original proposal, but did require evidence of productivity, reflected in innovative publications. During some shock experiments, we observed an agonal phenomenon of apnea, bradycardia, and a brief elevation of blood pressure. This appeared to be a reflex, and we felt that it was likely an expression of the cerebral ischemic pressor response originally described by Cushing at the turn of the century. We were impressed with the similarity of this reflex to the dive reflex, or as it is also called, the oxygen-conserving reflex. Our first experiment that was directly related to SIDS then was to look for the dive reflex in infant monkeys, to test the hypothesis that Wolf had proposed, that SIDS was due to "an inappropriate dive reflex" which terminated in some sort of lethal cardiac arrhythmia. We also tested for obligatory nasal breathing, implicated by Shaw as a cause of SIDS. This work was begun about 1970 and was published in 1972. The single most striking feature of that study to me, as a cardiologist, was that the cardiovascular system behaved blamelessly, and in a truly conservative manner, and could not be implicated as the lethal weakness. Since there are really only two final pathways to death, apnea and asystole, our attention became increasingly directed toward the apnea. (In a statistical phrase, there is only one degree of freedom for the terminal mechanism).

Although a cardiologist, one of my earliest interests in research was of certain aspects of the control of ventilation, culminating in a new hypothesis for the cause of hyperpneic spells in the tetrad of Fallot. This interest led to a thorough reading of the literature of control of ventilation, which several years later became very useful to me in looking at the question of apnea as a mechanism of death in crib death. However, the actual discovery that led to one of our basic articles on ventilation, concerning hypoxic apnea and gasping, was a result of serendipity. We were attempting to determine if petechiae were specific in reflecting the cause of death. Landing had suggested the need for such a study in 1969, and we planned to begin with the successful animal model of Handforth, published in 1959. His method of producing petechiae was to be used for our control group, since we assumed that 100% of those animals would have petechiae. His method was airway occlusion. It was a considerable surprise when *none* of the animals killed in that manner had petechiae, and it was only after several days of experiments and a careful re-reading of his original protocol, that we discovered the secret was to release the airway after the animal had stopped breathing. Much to our surprise, the anesthetized rat would, after approximately one minute, gasp, and begin to breathe regularly again. Since the word "gasp" was not even listed in the medical dictionaries of that year, we spent several years studying that phenomenon, as well as the strange phenomenon that allowed the animal to be stable but apneic for up to a minute, in spite of very high CO_2 and very low O_2.

In summary, my interest in ventilation control plus the background of cardiology, I believe qualifies me for an examination of the various theories proposed as causing sudden infant death. I first wrote a review at the request of the Editorial Board of the *American Heart Journal*, published in 1977. Not long afterward, Mr. Steven Korn, Publisher of Futura Publishing Company, asked if I would write a monograph. I was interested, but felt that it would be a neglect of my research to undertake such a task, and declined. He continued to write at about six-month intervals to inquire politely whether I had changed my mind. Paradoxically, the event that permitted me to undertake the project finally was the failure to be funded by the National Institute of Child Health and Development. (We proposed to determine the means of death in animals that were subjected to maternal deprivation, and examine for any similarity of those deaths to the autopsy findings of SIDS.)

The organization of this monograph caused me considerable thought and some dissatisfaction. The problem was that chronology alone did not suffice, since frequently the rebuttal to an hypothesis came three or four years later, and the relationship might be lost in a chronological approach. A pathology approach was not satisfactory alone, for no other reason than there are simply no lethal post-mortem findings, by definition, in SIDS. Epidemiology based on dead infants would clearly have the same difficulties, although the kind of information obtained would be different. Approaching the subject from the point of view of theories of cause was of particular interest, but that alone would be unsatisfactory, and inevitably biased. Consequently, I decided on the format of beginning with an overview, in chronologic order, followed by discussion of the post-mortem findings, the epidemiology, the clinical and physiological characteristics of near-miss SIDS, and then discussing the cardiac and respiratory theories. Then, although all final pathways are either cardiac or pulmonary, contributing disorders had to be considered, and these are discussed in a separate chapter. Finally, of course, was the chapter on management, and some comments about the future and research. There is inevitably redundancy in that method of organizing, but I wished each chapter to stand alone, for optimal utility.

Since I had been in attendance at the three conferences on SIDS held in the United States and Canada, and because of continued reading of the literature, I had a good starting point for a book. In addition, I instituted a Medlars, computerized literature search. This generated an incredible number of references, which required almost two months of full-time reading, prior to beginning the manuscript. Although the final monograph includes almost five hundred references, this represents actually a fraction of the total publications. In my selection I gave consideration to priority, and to truly novel ideas, and to reports that were quantitative. The Medlars was updated in January, 1982.

One of the most difficult problems for me was dealing with certain statements and actions of colleagues, some of them personal friends. Their methods were not acceptable to me as a scientist, nor as an advocate of children. Their intentions were and are honorable, but I do not believe that ends justify means. Lysenkoism is not only intellectually dishonest, it ultimately must fail, since the truth can be obscured for awhile, but not forever, no matter how distasteful it may be. In the area of SIDS, the doctrine at the root of much current controversy is the phrase "SIDS cannot be prevented." The original beneficiary of this doctrine was presumably the bereaved parent; the hope was to make them feel guiltless. In order to preserve that party-line, near-miss infants were labeled as a separate entity, prolonged apnea, or in the newest release, "infantile apnea." Although home monitors were vigorously resisted by that wing of the medical community, the resistance has buckled, and many parents, including the recent past President of the National Foundation for SIDS have used a monitor, and are active in monitoring programs. Fortunately, the current objection to linking the two will do no harm, as long as the infants who present as a near-miss are adequately treated, regardless of what they are called. However, there are now over four hundred cases of near-miss that have been reported from around the world in the medical literature, and they all have had apnea. There are no more than one or two subjects who have been "near-miss" with a cardiac arrhythmia; as suggested above, there is only one degree of freedom, which means that apnea is at least the final pathway for SIDS, and no amount of sophistry will change that.

Perhaps the best hope comes from the enlightened parents, who are the intended beneficiaries of the benighted paternalism exhibited by many of our physicians in this field. The parents have still a profound concern for other bereaved parents, but are moving forward into prevention of SIDS, and judging from the large number of home apnea-monitoring programs springing up around the country, primarily with initiative from parent groups, the priorities are being restored toward the well-being of the infant as first priority. These parents are not foolish enough to believe that home monitors *cause* anxiety, but that a near-miss, or an earlier child with SIDS, is all that it takes for any normal parents to feel anxious about their child. To do something to prevent that seems most reasonable, and suggestions that prayer alone will suffice would be more appropriate coming from a faith-healer than from a pediatrician.

I apologize for these, and later, harsh words, but this is not simply an intellectual polemic; lives of infants are at stake. One of the earliest writers on this subject, Templeman in 1892, was accused of insensitivity, but no one can doubt his devotion to the cause of reducing infant mortality. For this reason I hope I will be forgiven by those who are mentioned unfavorably in the text that follows.

When friends and colleagues learned that I was writing a book on SIDS, they smiled and asked what *I* believe is the cause of SIDS. For those too impatient to read the entire text, I present here a synopsis of my understanding of the cause of sudden infant death. Apnea, particularly sleep apnea, is a universal phenomenon, which is usually of brief duration, and harmless. In the adult, prolonged apnea results in arousal, and the patient is only aware of insomnia. I believe that failure to arouse is the crucial element in SIDS. The infant during fetal life did not have to breathe, in spite of very low oxygen concentration in the blood, and had no cause for alarm. It appears that a degree of maturation is required for the infant to develop the mechanisms of arousal, or mechanisms that permit resumption of breathing once apnea has commenced, and that vulnerability lasts for the first five or six months of life. The first month appears to be spared, largely because of the persistence of an effective gasp mechanism, which comes into play at extremely low oxygen concentrations, and is capable of resuscitating the infant at birth and for the first three or four weeks, but not thereafter. Many contributing factors have been found, but no one of them is universal; the single most common factor, however, is the presence of a relatively mild infection, usually upper respiratory, but on some occasions, enteric. The other epidemiologic characteristics of the mother and infant are entirely non-specific, and prove only that factors that increase the vulnerability of the infant will also increase the chance of dying of SIDS.

Warren G. Guntheroth, M.D.
Seattle, Washington

Table of Contents

Chapter I

Overview of SIDS

Crib death has a history of more than two thousand years, and many names. The British refer to it as "cot death," and in the First International Conference on this disorder it was called simply "sudden death in infants" (Wedgwood and Benditt, 1963). After the Second International Conference in 1969, the "official" term in the United States and Canada has been Sudden Infant Death Syndrome. (Bergman et al, 1970). However, the British Conference of 1970 preferred the title "Sudden and Unexpected Deaths in Infancy" (Camps and Carpenter, 1972). The British title is more informative, although the American title is more widely used at the present, and with the term "syndrome" added, the title can mean precisely what we choose it to mean (Humpty Dumpty, in *Alice Through the Looking Glass*). Fortunately, there is more agreement on the definition of the entity than there is upon the title, and that definition is sudden and unanticipated death in an infant, excluding the neonatal period, with no recognized lethal disorder. In the 1969 Conference, the diagnosis of SIDS was to be restricted to those infants in whom an autopsy had ruled out any other cause of death, an important requirement for credible research on the subject, but an unreasonable requirement for death certificates or general medical use. Although "infant" is derived from "non-speaking," and might apply for the first year of life, there is a concensus that the syndrome occurs with rare exceptions in the age group of one month to six months of

1

life. The presence of mild disorders, such as ordinary upper respiratory infection, does not disqualify the diagnosis of SIDS, since that illness is not ordinarily lethal, although it might cause minor post-mortem changes. It is essential to admit at the outset of any discussion of this syndrome that there are many lethal diseases which leave no diagnostic markers on post-mortem examination. The desire to dispel a mysterious and threatening aura around these crib deaths led to an exaggeration of the specificity of this disorder, and has permitted continued speculation about rare lethal disorders having a substantial role in this common problem, simply because that rare disorder left no unique post-mortem changes. The diagnosis of SIDS is a diagnosis by exclusion, but the means of exclusion are imperfect, and at best the diagnosis is one that is *compatible* with the disorder, never uniquely diagnostic.

The earliest explanation of unexpected infant deaths was accidental suffocation by the mother or wet-nurse, and the first example in the world's literature is in First Kings (Chapter 3, Verse 19) ". . . and this woman's child died in the night; because she overlaid it." The other occupants of the bed were an infant of similar age, with his mother. The surviving infant was subsequently claimed by the bereaved mother, but Solomon restored the infant to the true mother who volunteered to relinquish the infant to avoid Solomon's proposal to give half of the remaining infant to each mother, implemented by the sword. Little has been noted of the attitude that was inherent in Solomon's recommendation, but it seems clear that infanticide was not considered to be a criminal or moral issue, let alone overlaying. Until the early Christian Church began to oppose infanticide, there was no punishment for overlaying. The first record of punishment is around 700 A.D. when the Roman Catholic Church imposed punishment for either infanticide or overlaying, but the punishment was not a civil matter, and even infanticide was a relatively minor sin. The mention of overlaying and infanticide in the same context reflects the difficulty in determining which was the "true" cause of death. Because of this difficulty, there was increasing punitiveness toward both over the next centuries. In fourteenth century records of an English church, overlaying was declared to be a venial sin, since even though unintentional, negligence was inferred (Savitt, 1979). References to overlaying appear in the sixteenth and seventeenth centuries in England and Italy, and in Plymouth Colony, where the situation was described simply as "stifling," a term free of any implication of intent. In the seventeenth century the first preventative measures were introduced in Florence with a device called the arcuccio, a wooden and iron arch that would prevent suffocation in the event that the mother rolled over the infant during her sleep. The ecclesiastical punishment thereupon escalated, so that a nurse whose infant died of "smothering" due to failure to use the device, was excommunicated. The penalties were more severe for unwed mothers who were more suspect of infanticide. The invention reached England in the eighteenth century; a drawing appeared in the "Art of Nursing" in 1733 and Savitt found reference to its use in Italy as late as 1890.

As infanticide became a concern of the civil courts, the awful ambiguity of infant death began to receive attention from the medical profession. This coincided with the emergence of clinical and pathologic correlations. In the late eighteenth century enlargement of the thymus gland was thought to play a direct role in the death of these infants. Initially, it was postulated that the gland impinged directly on the trachea or on the blood supply to the head, or in some way interfered with the function of the heart and lung. The term "thymic asthma" gained acceptance in Europe and the United States during the nineteenth century, although many communities continued to skeptically attribute most infant deaths to suffocation, accidental or intentional. The presence of a large thymus must indeed have been surprising to the early anatomists, since infants dying of chronic disease would have a shrunken thymus, and therefore more similar to the adult's involuted thymus. Since there was no other explanation for death, as we have noted in the definition of SIDS, it seemed quite plausible to attribute these unexplained and sudden deaths to the thymus in some way. It was obviously an attractive alternative to the accusation of infanticide or culpable negligence.

The medical literature of the nineteenth century began to contain increasingly accurate descriptions of the phenomenon. In 1834, Fearn described under the title "Sudden and Unexplained Death in Children" two infants who died at six and five months of age with nearly identical post-mortem findings. His description in *Lancet* has scarcely been improved upon in the past century and one-half: "I found nothing unusual in the cavity of the skull—no engorgement of the vessels—no sanguinous or serous effusion. The viscera of the belly were in every respect of healthy appearance, and there was nothing in the stomach to indicate that it had come by its death unfairly. In the chest, however, I found, upon the surface of the thymus gland, numerous spots of extravasated blood, similar spots upon the surface of the lower and back parts of each lung, and many patches of ecchymosis upon the margin of the right ventricle of the heart, and along the course of the trunk of the coronary vein. There was no engorgement, however, of the pulmonary vessels, of the coronaries, or of the vessels of the thymus." Since the second child had been in bed alone, Dr. Fearn concluded that it could not possibly have been suffocated by overlaying, and he questioned whether overlaying was indeed a cause of death in either infant. The similarity of the two cases led him to conclude that death may have occurred from a "sudden and violent action of the heart."

The American literature contains one of the earliest and most incisive attacks on the theory of thymic asthma. Lee in 1842 pointed out that normal infants had a large thymus, and that those clinical disorders that were attributed to thymic asthma were, in fact, ". . . spasm of the glottis, bronchitis, pneumonia, etc., and not the result of a new disease." In

Germany in 1858, Friedleben published a monograph also "debunking" the concept of a lethally enlarged thymus.

Perhaps because of the continued aspersions of neglect, if not forthright accusations of infanticide, some in the medical profession persisted in attempts to explain the continuing phenomenon of sudden and unexpected deaths in infants by other means. Paltauf (1889) rekindled interest in the thymus as an explanation for sudden death in infants with the elegant diagnosis of "status thymico-lymphaticus." Although based on nothing more substantive than concepts disproved fifty years earlier, the impressive title for the disease seemed to overwhelm the opposition, and the term survived throughout the world and into the 1940's; believers included even Osler (1905). Although undoubtedly well-intentioned, it must be noted that this theory directly led to "prophylactic" irradiation of the thymus gland in infants in the 1930's and even the 40's, which has subsequently been shown to cause carcinoma of the thyroid.

The ongoing debate as to cause was of itself evidence that the problem of sudden and unexpected death in infants was a very widespread phenomenon. Savitt (1975) found a remarkable similarity of the age distribution of two hundred twenty-six cases of "smothering, suffocation, and overlaying" in Virginia between 1853 and 1860 to that of a distribution of SIDS in King County, Washington, in 1965–1967 (Bergman et al, 1972). The occurrence of sudden, unexplained deaths in infants was a significant problem in Dundee, Scotland, causing a police surgeon (Templeman, 1892) to publish what appears to be an epic example of insensitivity; he asserted that the "principle causes producing the great mortality from overlaying are, (1) ignorance and carelessness of mothers, (2) drunkenness, (3) overcrowding, and (4) according to some observers, illegitimacy and the life insurance of infants." He concluded that infanticide was not likely, but did advocate prosecution of the parents of dead infants for negligence. On reading carefully, an underlying motive was clearly the saving of infant lives rather than societal revenge. In fact, his description of the living conditions of the lower classes in an industrial city at the end of the nineteenth century reveal genuine sympathy as well as unprecedented perceptivity. His report constitutes the first systematic epidemiologic study of SIDS, based on two hundred fifty-eight cases. He reported the higher incidence of infant deaths at night, in the winter months, and in the first three months of life. He found a greater prevalence among the poorer classes and illegitimate infants. Templeman's autopsy description was also quite accurate: ". . . in about half of the cases examined small punctiform hemorrhages were observed beneath the pleura and pericardium. The larynx, trachea, and bronchi were as a rule congested, and contained some frothy, often blood-stained mucus." Although he concluded that overlaying was the cause of SIDS, his analysis of the epidemiology and pathology of SIDS has been improved only slightly in the ensuing ninety years.

The first humane explanation of sudden, unexpected death in infants that is supportable in light of modern knowledge was that of a specific respiratory ailment as cause (Brouardel, 1895). The role of infection was suggested again by Farber in 1934, as a fulminating bacterial infection. These infants were thought to die so quickly that the post-mortem changes did not accurately reflect the lethal septicemia. Farber speculated that a larger percentage of SIDS cases might be proven to be septicemia if careful post-mortem cultures were obtained. (Although plausible in theory, and the recommendation laudable, the suspicion has not been confirmed. Paradoxically, an infant with septicemia is no longer classified as SIDS if septicemia is proven). The major importance of Farber's contribution was that the two cases he reported had originally been attributed to suffocation.

In 1938, histologic evidence of respiratory infections was found in nineteen of thirty cases of sudden infant death, without specific bacterial infection being implicated (Goldbloom and Wigglesworth, 1938). An increasing number of papers from that time forward began to find more evidence of respiratory infections and a reciprocal decrease in the number of autopsies certified as "suffocation" (Werne and Garrow, 1947). At about the same time, however, other areas of the country showed an increasing number of infant deaths due to suffocation, with a reciprocal decline in deaths certified as "status thymico-lymphaticus" (Abramson, 1944; Werne and Garrow, 1947). By the 1940's, taking an infant to bed with the mother was no longer a common practice, and the "suffocation" was attributed to bed clothes, or to the posture of the infant. Fortunately, Woolley in 1945 proved that healthy infants could scarcely be suffocated unintentionally by bed clothes or posture, and that infants demonstrated a remarkable ability to escape by changing their position. For most well-read physicians, that study spelled the end to the diagnosis of accidental suffocation for sudden infant death, although the wide-spread utilization of non-medical coroners kept "suffocation" appearing in newspapers and in vital statistics up to the present time.

The first modern epidemiologic report on SIDS was published by Adelson and Kinney in 1956, on one hundred twenty-six cases. To Templeman's findings they added that there are more SIDS victims that are male than female, more black than white, and more prematurely born than full-term. Of particular significance, more than half of the dead infants had been exposed to a respiratory infection in the ten days prior to death, and actually had a history of mild symptoms. In Sheffield, over 90% of the infants were found to have had symptoms beginning forty-eight hours or more before death when careful follow-up inquiry was conducted (Emery, 1959), but there was no longer the tendency for most deaths to occur on the weekend as occurred in Dundee sixty years earlier (Templeman, 1892).

As infection began to be considered a common finding in SIDS, some pathologists began to wonder about the disparity between death and the extent of histopathology attributable to the infection. In 1953, Adelson speculated about a reflex inhibition of vital functions in sudden death in adults, and postulated a "vagocardiac" lethal effect. Stowens (1957) proposed a more massive, lethal reflex. He cited the presence of small hemorrhages, emphysema, and pulmonary edema as evidence of bronchospasm, followed by a cardiac arrest or some other lethal arrhythmia. He found no evidence of inflammation, and denied that these patients died as a result of an infectious disease.

An abnormal function of a respiratory reflex was proposed in 1959 by Handforth. Although Stowens had considered laryngospasm, he felt that the evidence favored bronchospasm because of the post-mortem findings of local emphysema and pulmonary edema. Handforth was struck by the post-mortem distribution of petechiae on the lungs, heart, and thymus. He asserted that these petechiae were characteristic of autopsies of subjects who had asphyxiated. He strengthened the argument by producing petechiae in rats by obstructing the airway. (We shall return to this subject later, but suffice it to say that Handforth did *not* leave the airway obstructed, but allowed the animals to recover from the episode of hypoxia before they were killed.) Handforth, lacking an anatomic, fixed airway obstruction at autopsy, postulated that laryngospasm had occurred, secondary to a relatively minor respiratory infection in the infant. We should note that Handforth presented the first animal model for the study of SIDS.

The 1960's saw a crescendo of new theories attempting to explain SIDS. Milk hypersensitivity was suggested by Parish et al (1960). Evidence of hyperimmunization in infants to cow's milk was presented, and a guinea pig model demonstrated an anaphylactic type of death as a probable mechanism. Although there have been several studies subsequently that find in a population of SIDS victims a greater preponderance of babies who drink cow's milk than breast milk, several independent studies have shown no difference from normal in the immune level to cow's milk protein in SIDS victims. In the 60's, the evidence for viral infections increased (Gold et al, 1961); some concern about low levels of gammaglobulin as a contributing factor were expressed earlier (Spain et al, 1954). In 1961 Adelson, who was probably the first to institute systematic, community-wide surveys of infant deaths, warned of the regrettable frequency of homicide in infants, some of whom had been reported as crib death. He urged an autopsy as a routine, with careful consideration of possible infanticide.

As is frequently the case in science, a new syndrome was discussed in 1962, not as an explanation for SIDS, but as an interesting neurological disorder. Severinghaus and Mitchell (1962) described Ondine's curse, occurring in adults with brainstem lesions, in whom apnea occurred with the onset of sleep. Ondine was a sea nymph in a play by Jean Giraudaux, in love with an unfaithful mortal. His punishment was that all of his vital functions would continue only if he consciously willed them to; consequently, sleep would be lethal. (There is a similar German myth by La Motte-Fouque, but that particular Undine did not have such an imaginative curse as sleep apnea.) Sleep apnea as an explanation for sudden infant death was not suggested for several years.

Choanal atresia was described in 1962, not as a major contributor to the overall population of crib death, but as a treatable cause of dyspnea, cyanosis, and occasionally death in the newborn (Canby, 1962). Again, it was several years later that nasal obstruction by various means was implicated as a major factor in SIDS.

Electrolyte disorders, resulting from dietary deficiencies, was suggested by Maresch in 1962; although this possibility, with differing specific electrolytes, recurs over the years, there is no confirmation that this is important except in isolated cases.

In 1963 an international conference on sudden infant death was held in Seattle (Wedgwood and Benditt, 1963). This conference was the result of political activity by lay persons in the state of Washington who felt that crib death was a medical problem that had been neglected, and through their efforts, an appropriation was made by the State Legislature to fund a meeting of experts on the subject. The majority of the participants were pathologists, which was reasonable at the time since this was a disease thought to be uniformly fatal. When the meeting was organized, I was able to invite Geoffrey Dawes to discuss cardiopulmonary reflexes in the infant, in the hope of finding a specific reflex that could be implicated. It had been my experience that on occasion an infant would be discovered in the hospital, or at home by a parent, in a state of apnea and cyanosis, with marked bradycardia, who could be resuscitated, and who would thereafter remain quite normal (Guntheroth, 1963). Obviously, the hope was that the syndrome had a reversible state, and with better knowledge, diagnosis during life could be made, and preventive measures taken. Although most in the British contingent to the Seattle conference were convinced that the sudden death in infants was an anaphylactic reaction to cow's milk, there was obvious skepticism from others including Dawes, since Gold had earlier reported no increase in milk antibodies (1961), and two other American groups supported Gold's findings.

A modest addition to the epidemiology of SIDS was made at the 1963 meeting. Landing estimated the incidence at 10–15,000 per year in the United States. He concluded that any relationship to virus infection was non-specific, i.e., not related to any particular virus. The discussants agreed that the increased prevalence in lower socioeconomic groups did not prevent the occurrence in the upper levels. Adelson reviewed his superb pathological studies on infants, including the characteristic features of pulmonary petechiae, although he denied any specific role for mechanical suffocation. He reported the random position of the child when found dead, and that most cases, but not all, presumably occurred during sleep. He stated that, although 60% of the victims had been judged by their parents to have had either a respiratory infection or diarrhea, viral isolation was successful in only one-fourth of the subjects by Gold and colleagues.

Dr. Valdes-Dapena presented a very thorough epidemiological and pathologic report on two hundred cases of SIDS. She reported that hypogammaglobulinemia had not been found; in fact, the level of gammaglobulin was actually higher in SIDS than in her control population. She found 31% of the patients were premature by gestation and many of them were underweight. There was a tendency for clustering of the deaths in poor neighborhoods, recalling Templeman's 1892 report.

After the first Conference on SIDS, a wider range of theories as to cause began to appear. Still, there were and are only two final pathways to death for any age group, apnea and cardiac arrest. Four infants who were observed to die after several episodes of apnea, cyanosis, and bradycardia were reported by Stevens (1965). The attacks were attributed to an acute respiratory infection, and the author proposed an important role as a trigger for these infections, precipitating apnea and resulting in sudden infant death syndrome. Wolf in 1966 postulated an inappropriate dive reflex in SIDS, with apnea secondary to saliva or vomitus stimulating the trigeminal nerve region of the face. He postulated that the terminal arrhythmia might be ventricular fibrillation, due to some abnormality of the reflex or of the control systems at that age. Frasier and Froggat (1966) suggested that SIDS might be primarily a cardiac arrhythmia and mentioned two syndromes known to produce sudden death in older subjects. These subjects have a prolonged Q-T interval on electrocardiogram, and have syncope, and ultimately death, following exertion or situations evoking strong emotions. Both of these disorders are genetically determined; Jervell and Lange-Nielsen syndrome is a recessive disorder associated with hereditary deafness (1957), and Romano-Ward syndrome is inherited in a dominant fashion, and is not associated with deafness (1963, 1964). In 1967 we reported (Church et al, 1967) that premature infants, found to be at increased risk for SIDS in several studies, would demonstrate episodes of marked sinus bradycardia and junctional escape rhythm when recorded with a Holter-type tape recorder. These arrhythmias were found with deep sleep, in addition to gastrointestinal stimulation. We speculated that this might indicate an instability of the autonomic nervous system in these premature infants. In 1968, James described some histologic changes in the region of the atrioventricular node, occurring at an age that might create an instability that could lead to death. However, James and others agreed that these changes were a part of the normal remodeling process of that tissue.

At about this time, there was a renewed suggestion that poor mothering skills might contribute (Carpenter and Shaddick, 1965), and that activities such as cigarette smoking by the mother were associated, at least statistically (Steele and Langworth, 1966). Valdes-Dapena carefully warned that even intentional homicide was difficult to rule out at autopsy (1967). Two physicians went further: Towbin (1967) suggested spinal injury as evidence of abuse, and Asch (1968) pointed out the relatively substantial incidence of maternal post-partum depression, and suggested that many infants diagnosed as SIDS were actually cases of infanticide. Towbin's speculation was refuted only two years later (Harris and Adelson, 1969).

In 1968, Shaw proposed one of the most simple and initially plausible explanations of SIDS, taking into account the common history of a respiratory infection and the age distribution of SIDS. He pointed out that infants are born as obligate nasal breathers, so that obstruction of the nasopharynx by swelling or mucus could result in death by asphyxiation.

In 1969 the second international conference on SIDS was held in Seattle (Bergman et al, 1970). Improved data was presented on the epidemiology, although little was qualitatively new. Bergman insisted that sleep was almost invariably the state during which SIDS occurred, although the evidence was largely circumstantial. The Conference agreed that lower socioeconomic class and low birth weight produced an increased risk of SIDS, but as is the case for so many correlates of SIDS, the relationship was by no means specific, and frequently insensitive, for prediction. Houstek pointed out an important positive correlation between the incidence of SIDS and *all* infant mortality. (This relationship may well account for the correlations with socioeconomic class and birth weight, as a general indicator of the vulnerability of an infant to all diseases, and not SIDS alone.) I suggested that sleep apnea should be considered as a precipitating event, since prematures frequently showed this disorder and were at increased risk for SIDS. During sleep, the respiratory drive diminishes in all individuals, and at the least would create a lowered resistance to apnea during the sleep state. Monitoring was suggested as a possible step in prevention, if a near-miss infant was found (Guntheroth, 1970). Bergman pointed out that two of approximately twenty infants admitted to his hospital as "abortive crib deaths" subsequently succumbed, and at autopsy were diagnosed as sudden infant death.

At the second conference on SIDS, a lively debate on the specificity of petechiae began, which has continued more or less to the present. Beckwith argued that petechiae were observed on the surface of the lung and the intrathoracic portion of the thymus, but not on the abdominal viscera or on the cervical (non-thoracic) part of the thymus. He inferred that the petechiae were due to a highly negative intrathoracic pressure, secondary to airway obstruction. Marshall disagreed on the basis of his experience with deaths due to known airway obstruction, and postulated that petechiae meant an increase in capillary pressure. Nevertheless, several participants in the conference concluded that laryngospasm was a likely final pathway, precipitated by an infection of the respiratory tract.

The British held a symposium in 1970 on "Sudden and Unexpected Death in Infancy (Cot Deaths)" (Camps and Carpenter, 1972). The subject was reviewed thoroughly, but few new hypotheses emerged. The conference, however, had a different emphasis from the Seattle Conference of the year before. There was skepticism expressed by Camps about the meaning of petechiae found at autopsy. Carpenter reviewed surveys of cot death for the United Kingdom, finding similar evidence of infection, post-mortem findings, time of the year, time of the day, and the overall incidence as had been reported by American researchers. He confirmed a higher prevalence of unwed mothers of SIDS victims, more crowded living conditions, a poorer "general standard of mothering," and fewer visits to the physician or clinic. He emphasized that although these were statistically valid, they did not exclude cot death from families with excellent health care and high socioeconomic status. A new finding was reported, in contrast to the earlier presumption that these were totally normal children who died with no premonitory abnormalities: Carpenter found that SIDS victims had a generally unsatisfactory developmental pattern. Specifically, he reported they were (statistically) underweight at birth, developed slowly, and had a history of poor health. Again he emphasized that there were notable exceptions, suggesting another important concept: the infants who died suddenly and unexpectedly were not a truly homogeneous group. At this conference, Dawes asserted a general principle that is worthy of emphasis. For a cause of cot death that left no major anatomic derangement at autopsy, there would probably be a "near-miss" form, a less severe form of the phenomenon that did not cause death during the first episode. Such subjects then should be available for study once identified, to confirm or deny any proposed mechanism. (These comments were actually directed against the anaphylactic-reaction-to-milk hypothesis, but should be applied broadly.)

Although Froggatt had earlier speculated on an arrhythmia as the etiology of SIDS (Frasier and Froggatt, 1966), he was one of the first to document the history of prior cyanotic and apneic episodes in a few victims of SIDS (Froggatt et al, 1971). In retrospect, one of the papers published in 1970 (Harned et al) became important to the subject of SIDS, although the authors had not claimed that relationship. They showed in spontaneously breathing lambs shortly after birth that fluid introduced directly into the trachea produced apnea and very marked respiratory depression, sometimes of a lethal nature. In 1972, we reported (French et al) a study in infant monkeys of apnea induced by nasal occlusion, or by trigeminal stimulation with a cold, wet stimulus (dive reflex). Both methods were capable of producing struggle-free apnea, which was immediately associated with brady-cardia and vasoconstriction. The cardiovascular adjustments then were not disastrous, but were in fact beneficial in the sense of an oxygen-conserving reflex, which has been shown to preserve the available oxygen for the coronary and cere-bral circulations. The bradycardia and the occasional A-V junctional escape in the infant monkey were similar to those recorded by us in premature infants (Church et al, 1967), and in neither infant monkeys nor premature human infants was there any cardiovascular disintegration. Of considerable in-terest was the occurrence of prolonged apnea in two of the five infant monkeys, persisting after the removal of the stimulus and requiring active resuscitation. None of the five infant monkeys required resuscitation when re-tested at an older age. We speculated that the lack of arousal of the infant was a dangerous, if understandable, reversion to a fetal state when the absence of respiration was of no consequence. The particular event that initiated apnea, whether nasal occlu-sion or simply the cold, wet stimulus, seemed less crucial than the failure to interrupt the apnea. This failure seemed to be characteristic of the very young infant monkey. In that same year (French et al, 1972) we reported the radiographic, post-mortem examination of the upper airway of one hundred consecutive cases of infants dying suddenly and unexpectedly. Twenty-two of the subjects had an explana-tion for death found at autopsy, and seventy-eight remained unexplained after autopsy, and therefore examples of SIDS. The mean dimensions of the nasopharynx in the two groups were the same, and the prevalence in the SIDS group of airway obstruction, judged radiographically, was 2.6%, compared to the control group (explained death) of 4.5%. We concluded that, although obligatory nasal breathing is a definite phenomenon in the SIDS age group, nasopharyngeal obstruction did not appear to be a substantial cause of SIDS.

In 1972, Steinschneider published the first report of five infants studied during life, after an episode of prolonged apnea. All five infants were documented polygraphically as having episodes of prolonged sleep apnea with cyanosis, some requiring vigorous resuscitation, in addition to frequent brief respiratory pauses with REM sleep. The prolonged apnea episodes usually occurred in association with an upper respiratory tract infection. Two of the infants subsequently died and were judged to be SIDS on autopsy. Although the predictive value of the short episodes of "apnea" is questionable, the study nevertheless indicated that prolonged apnea could recur, and that apnea was associated with sleep, exaggerated by respiratory infection. Similar events were known to occur in the premature, and had led most centers to develop apnea monitors for that use. Daily et al (1969) described the association of bradycardia with apnea; they observed that most of the prematures could be stimulated to resume breathing by simple cutaneous stimulation, although 8% of the episodes required vigorous resuscitation.

In 1972, through the political efforts of some parent groups and a few physicians, congressional hearings were held on the subject of sudden infant death syndrome; accusations were made there, and in some editorials (Curran, 1972) that the subject was neglected medically and scientifically, leading eventually to the appropriation of increased, specified funds. The National Institute of Child Health and Human Development had actually increased their efforts on this problem in 1971; Eileen Hasselmeyer and Jehu Hunter (1975) organized meetings and encouraged basic and clinical research that might bear on SIDS. Actually, much of the basic research in this area had been done under the support of grants that were not especially marked for SIDS research by Congress, and it is not clear that earmarking large sums of money for specific disease research was or is capable of producing a cure or a prevention for disorders such as SIDS or cancer. It can reasonably be argued that narrowly dedicated appropriations are counterproductive in the long run, since they compete with more basic (as opposed to disease-oriented) research. Comroe and Dripps (1977) analyzed the origins of the most useful advances in recent cardiopulmonary medicine, tracing them back through a series of publications. In a very high percentage, the origins of these major medical advances were in basic research, based more on the scientist's curiosity than upon a likely application. Until those basic building blocks of information are available, it is not cost-effective to repetitively fund, at large cost, pedestrian research that is directly related to some socially significant disease. The situation in research is quite different from that of industrial development, where increased funding will predictably accelerate the development and application of new technology.

A case in point is the meticulous and highly original work done by Richard Naeye, originally supported by a grant from the National Heart Institute. He found increased musculature in pulmonary arteries of the victims of SIDS, in comparison to a control group of similar age (Naeye, 1973). The findings were quite similar to those of infants who live at an altitude with diminished alveolar oxygen pressure. He postulated that these victims of SIDS had prior hypoxic episodes of apnea before the fatal one. Naeye recognized two groups of SIDS victims, with and without evidence of pulmonary inflammation, and the distinction is important, relative to the homogeneity of the syndrome. The group with no pulmonary inflammation showed more evidence of pulmonary arterial abnormalities, whereas the SIDS victims who had evidence of respiratory infection had more normal pulmonary vasculature. The inference drawn is that the patients without inflammation may have had a more relent-less course of repeated episodes of apnea, whereas an acute infection might have precipitated a fatal episode without much prior apnea. It is instructive to recall that in 1965 Stevens reported four instances of infants two to three months of age who died under observation in hospital with rapidly progressing pneumonia, presumably viral. Each of these four infants had been admitted for an episode of pro-longed apnea with cyanosis and bradycardia, as the first clue of the respiratory infection. After resuscitation, each seemed only mildly ill for several hours before the respiratory dis-ease progressed to an irreversible state. Stevens speculated that the apnea response to a respiratory infection was capa-ble of producing SIDS before the full effects of the infection developed anatomically.

Support for Naeye's hypoxic theory was found in animal research on the formation of petechiae (Guntheroth, 1973). Although Handforth (1959) and Beckwith (1970) had de-duced that petechiae in victims of SIDS indicated airway obstruction, we could not produce petechiae in rats with airway obstruction, unless we repeatedly opened the airway again prior to death. Unremitting airway obstruction did not cause petechiae, whereas hypoxic death due to very low oxygen content of air breathed would regularly produce petechiae. Animals with ventricular fibrillation induced by injection of potassium into the coronary artery died without significant petechiae formation. (This and our earlier SIDS research were supported by National Heart Institute grants.)

In 1973 Guilleminault, Dement, and Monod speculated on sleep apnea as an important cause of SIDS. They showed on polygraph studies that adults with "insomnia" fre-quently had sleep apnea with subsequent arousal (Guilleminault, Eldridge, and Dement, 1973). The adult sub-jects were usually unaware of the apnea, but aware only of the interrupted sleep. That same year, Deuel (1973) reported polygraphic monitoring of five infants with severe apneic spells. He reported that intermediate length apneic spells were more common in quiet sleep, rather than REM sleep, and that these episodes were associated with striking brady-cardia. He emphasized that the origins of the apneic spells were not necessarily similar from patient to patient, and that at least one of the five patients had seizures as the precipitat-ing event. Although he did not speculate on SIDS, it is ob-vious that a seizure victim succumbing of prolonged apnea, unobserved, would have no lethal pathology and would be classed as a SIDS after autopsy.

In 1974 a conference on SIDS was held in Canada, and was easily the most eclectic and stimulating of all of the conferences on this subject (Robinson, 1974). Naeye added evidence from the autopsies of SIDS victims for the presence of hypoxia; he found increased retention of brown fat in the periadrenal area. Valdes-Dapena reported a drop in the in-cidence of SIDS. Steele reported some statistics that sug-gested, in at least some instances, an unwitting deprivation of the SIDS infant. He reported increased prevalence of smoking in mothers of the victims, generally younger mothers with poor spacing of births, a low prevalence of breast feeding, and a low utilization of health care. Car-penter and Emery presented a retrospective study of identi-fication of high-risk infants, and a preliminary report on a prospective application of these discriminators. As Houstek found in Czechoslovakia (1970), the high-risk infants were at risk for both explained *and* unexplained death. Predictors of cot death were an increased rejection of health care, the single most powerful criterion being the failure to keep the follow-up appointment after discharge from the maternity hospital (Carpenter and Emery, 1974). One of the problems for infants subsequently identified as having a disease was that the parents were unaware of the illness, or at least of its implications. Questions of the adequacy of mothering were raised by the presence of hypernatremic uremia in some children, which they attributed to the use of over-strength milk mixtures. In summarizing their findings, they specu-lated that prevention of "most unexpected deaths in infancy does not lie there (laboratory science) but in the field of social rather than laboratory pathology."

At the 1974 Canadian meeting, Steinschneider presented a predictive method for prolonged apnea based on measurements of respiratory activity, correlated with sleep state, which was probably the first attempt at prediction based on the behavior of the individual infant, as opposed to a population statistic. McGinty and Harper described an animal model for SIDS, sleep-deprived kittens. The frequency of prolonged apnea was substantially increased in the sleep-deprived state. They speculated that events such as respiratory infections in the infant might interfere with sleep to the point of sleep deprivation, and thereby increase the chances for prolonged apnea, as had been described earlier. These authors reported arrhythmias with the episodes of sleep apnea, although the published recording demonstrates an artifact interpolated between otherwise unaltered R-R intervals of the electrocardiogram. An additional presentation on developmental physiology concerned primary apnea, hypoxic apnea, and gasping (Guntheroth, 1974). In a study of more extreme cases of hypoxia, we had shown that there could be a variety of stimuli initiating primary apnea, including sleep apnea, seizures, laryngeal reflexes, nasal occlusion, and the dive reflex. The more specific problem, in relation to SIDS, was the failure to arouse from the primary apnea, presumably related to immaturity. Considering that the fetus is not required to breathe, apnea might not be alarming to the infant in the first few months of life. We suggested that one aspect of the fetal existence, the resistance to hypoxia, might be involved in the curious hiatus of the first month of life, during which SIDS is quite rare. The fetal capability for anaerobic metabolism, persisting after birth, could permit survival of the period of hypoxic apnea that follows the primary apnea, allowing adequate circulation to continue until gasping had occurred after a minute or two. Gasping could then autoresuscitate the infant, and this could provide the background necessary for Naeye's postulated hypoxic events, namely prior episodes of apnea with gasping and resuscitation.

In 1975, Guilleminault and co-workers showed that sleep apnea of the more serious form occurred with non-REM sleep, but that obstructive apnea could occur with REM sleep and that mixed obstructive and quiet apnea could be observed in the same subject. In the following year Guilleminault reported some preliminary studies on subjects that were "near-misses" and showed that they had increased episodes of prolonged apnea with bradycardia. The interest in prevention was stimulated by an increasing number of centers that began to monitor the infants who survived an episode of prolonged apnea (Steinschneider, 1972; Guntheroth, 1975; Shannon et al, 1975). An opposing philosophy surfaced, protesting that apnea monitors had not been shown to actually save lives, and that monitors would cause anxiety and interfere with the emotional well-being of the infant and family (Committee on Infant and Pre-school Child, 1975; Bergman et al, 1975). That debate continues, although the American Academy of Pediatrics has accepted monitoring as a reasonable choice (Task Force on Prolonged Apnea, 1978). To those of us who began using it in the first place, the value of a home monitor to a parent made anxious by an episode of profound apnea with cyanosis, seemed obvious. To blame the monitor for the anxiety is similar to executing the messenger with bad news. Part of the dispute seemed to stem from a strongly held position that SIDS "cannot be prevented" (Committee on Infant and Pre-school Child, 1972). Although a laudable motive, to reassure grieving parents, the continued insistence on this doctrine has interfered with scientific progress (Steinschneider, 1976); assuredly, the prevention of this disorder *should* be a proper goal of the medical profession, and for parent groups interested in SIDS.

Although cardiac instability in prematures (Church et al, 1967), and in the long Q-T syndrome, with and without deafness (Frasier and Froggatt, 1965), had been suggested earlier as relating to SIDS, no strong link had been found subsequently. Maron and co-workers (1976) investigated the Q-T interval in a group of parents of victims of SIDS, and reported a significantly high percentage of families with Q-T prolongation. They felt that they had demonstrated an autosomal dominant pattern of inheritance, which would be similar to that found for the Romano-Ward syndrome. Subsequently, many centers looked at that relationship and were unable to confirm it, either from the point of view of inheritance (Kukolich et al, 1977), or from the measurement of Q-T interval in survivors of near-miss episodes (Kelley et al, 1977; Haddad et al, 1979). Schwartz (1976) proposed a more general hypothesis, not involving the hereditary forms of prolonged Q-T, but one based on ordinary development of the sympathetic innervation of the heart. Earlier, he had presented evidence that the inherited syndrome killed by ventricular fibrillation, which in turn was provoked by an asymmetry of activity of cardiac nerves with a relative deficiency of the right stellate ganglion (Schwartz et al, 1975). Schwartz (1976) postulated that during early life, the human infant had an unequal development of the sympathetic nerves to the heart, which created a vulnerable period corresponding to that of SIDS. This theory is still vigorously proposed by Schwartz, and although it has not been disproven, substantial evidence for this as an explanation of any sizeable number of cases of SIDS has not been found.

Although the early descriptions of SIDS, almost by definition, assumed that the victim was a previously healthy infant with no disease other than a mild respiratory infection, evidence has gradually accumulated that the average SIDS victim is not entirely normal by history or by examination. Steele (1969) and Froggatt et al, (1971) both reported a history of previous respiratory difficulties, including episodes of apnea with cyanosis. Emery (1959) and Peterson et al, (1974) found that SIDS infants on the average have impaired post-natal growth, in addition to being smaller at birth. Naeye, Ladis, and Drage (1976) reported similar findings in a separate population of victims of sudden death, and in that same year (Naeye, Messmer et al, 1976) reported retrospective descriptions of behavior of the victims, based on parents' recollections. These infants were described as hypoacitve, hyporeactive, and having had abnormal cries. Physiological abnormalities in the survivors of near-miss episodes were reported by Shannon et al, (1977). They found that these infants had an abnormal ventilatory response to CO_2, suggesting a relationship between these patients and alveolar hypoventilation. It is possible that their medical center has attracted an unusual number of rare infantile cases of Ondine's curse, and it is also possible that neurological damage has occurred from repeated episodes of sleep apnea, which secondarily changed their ventilatory mechanism. Most individuals feel that the patients with primary hypoventilation are a distinctly different group, although without question, if they succumbed early in the course, SIDS would be diagnosed at autopsy. The more common forms of alveolar hypoventilation live to an older age than is typical for SIDS, and will frequently have cor pulmonale secondary to the chronic severe hypoxia, and will resemble more closely the adult Pickwickian syndrome, without obesity.

A meeting of Australian researchers in sudden infant death was held in 1976 (South Australia Committee). Turner suggested a totally new explanation for SIDS, an anaphylactic reaction to the house dust mite. Although not present, Tonkin's (1975) hypothesis of airway occlusion at the level of the oropharynx, from compression of the soft palate against the base of the skull was reviewed. Her theory was welcomed by Beckwith (1975) as confirmation of his earlier theory of airway occlusion, which he based on the presence of intrathoracic petechiae in SIDS autopsies. Additional suggestions of potential causes of SIDS in the past five years have included gastrointestinal reflux (Leape et al, 1977), thiamine deficiency (Read, 1978), botulism (Arnon et al, 1978), and hyperthyroidism (Chacon and Tildon, 1981).

In 1978, a task force of the American Academy of Pediatrics cautiously approached the subject of prolonged apnea, without taking sides in the somewhat emotional debate on whether patients with a near-miss are related to SIDS. The task force recommended that primary disorders should be ruled out, including such problems as anemia, esophageal reflux, and infection. They accepted the validity of home monitors as an aid in the management of the survivors, without recommending them. They also urged counseling of the family, including siblings, whether or not the families undertook to monitor the child at home. That same year (1978), Kelly et al reported a 93% success in keeping survivors alive, from episodes of prolonged apnea, using home monitors. Orlowski (1979) has reported a method of identifying patients at risk based on abnormal auditory evoked potentials (BAEP). Presumably, these abnormalities are the physiological correlates of post-mortem neuropathology found in the brainstem of SIDS victims (Naeye, 1976; Gadsdon and Emery, 1976). In 1980, an outstanding symposium was held on the control of breathing during sleep (Sullivan et al). Orlowski's work has not been confirmed.

Other efforts at prevention beyond the near-miss infant concern the prevention of child abuse, and the careful following of subsequent siblings of SIDS victims. The repetition rate for SIDS in a family is ten times higher than in the ordinary family (Peterson et al, 1980), although the actual rate is only 2%. Physiological studies of such subjects, labeled high-risk, have actually only a 1 or 2% chance of observing an untoward incident. Nevertheless, anxiety in such families is bound to be high, and in some instances the use of a home monitor may be a humane assistance to the family.

There seems to be little question but that some of the risk factors of SIDS could be prevented or reduced in impact by better maternal care. For example, placental infection (Naeye, 1977), maternal anemia, and prematurity itself, not to mention maternal addiction (Ragegowda et al, 1978) are amenable to treatment; success should reduce rates of SIDS, and probably *all* infant mortality.

Direct prevention of SIDS, focusing on the infant, may be less cost-effective. Although I agree with Valdes-Dapena (1980) that all of the methods of prospectively discriminating between victims of SIDS and age-matched controls are only moderately sensitive, and remarkably non-specific, this should not argue against applying some of the better methods of detection and prediction, since many practices in medicine are aimed at a relatively small percentage of the subjects. For example, relatively few women would have serious difficulties when delivering babies at home, but for the few that are at risk, the resources of a hospital, with all of the attendant expenses, are accepted as a worthwhile and cost-effective expenditure. Similarly, the ultimate prevention of eight thousand deaths a year from sudden infant death would easily warrant many efforts at detection and prevention in a much larger population of infants at risk.

In the chapters ahead, more detail will be provided for the various aspects of epidemiology and pathology, as well as various hypotheses of cause, detection, and prevention.

Chapter II

Pathology of SIDS

There is a paradox of post-mortem findings in the sudden infant death syndrome. To satisfy the requirements for the diagnosis of SIDS, no inherently lethal pathology should be present, either by gross autopsy or by microscopic study of the tissues. Thus, if the death can be explained, it is *not* SIDS. It is therefore surprising that physicians have looked to the post-mortem examination for answers to this tragic riddle. This is not to say that the post-mortem findings are without value in pursuit of the cause of SIDS, but it is essential for progress to admit that the findings only *permit* a diagnosis, rather than establish a causal relationship. For example, evidence of chronic hypoxia (Naeye, 1980) in post-mortem tissues from victims of SIDS is compatible with the hypothesis of recurrent apnea as the cause of SIDS, but cannot uniquely prove the hypothesis.

The limitation of autopsy studies in determining the cause of death in a unique and unambiguous manner is illustrated by reviewing some known lethal disorders and their non-specific post-mortem changes. It has been estimated that 10 to 15% of *all* deaths occur suddenly and unexpectedly (Moritz and Zamichek, 1946). Although sudden death occurs in two peaks—in infancy, and again at thirty-five to seventy years of age—it can occur at any age (Weiss, 1940; Adelson, 1953). In the older group, autopsy may reveal important abnormalities in the cardiovascular

27

system that may be inferred to have caused death, although even the role of coronary artery occlusion cannot always be demonstrated in patients that are thought to die of "a heart attack." Spain et al (1960) found only 51% of three hundred sixty-eight instances of unexpected death in adults, in whom the acute episode exceeded one hour, were associated with coronary arteriosclerosis, let alone thrombosis. In the younger adult population of apparently healthy soldiers under forty years of age, Moritz and Zamicheck (1946) were able to find one thousand cases of sudden death without trauma. Again, there frequently was absence of actual infarction or occlusion of coronary artery, even when a cardiac death seemed probable.

Abnormal function of reflexes has been proposed for the adult population of sudden deaths. Sir Thomas Lewis (1932) apparently coined the term "vasovagal" to describe syncope due to various forms of parasympathetic stimulation including gradual abdominal compression (Goetz reflex), compression of the eyeballs (Aschner-Dagnini reflex), forced extension of the neck (Ortner's reflex), and compression of the carotid sinus (Czermak's reflex). Soma Weiss (1940) listed twelve forms of syncope that, if not interrupted by the re-establishment of "normal equilibrium," could cause a lethal suppression of cardiovascular activity. More mysterious are cultural instances of sudden death such as Bangungut, a Tagalog word that literally means "to rise and moan." The malady affects young Filipino males in the twenty-five to forty-five year range during sleep. The victim becomes agitated, moves about fretfully, and moans or even yells. Violent coughing may occur, and a frothy fluid exudes from the mouth. The subject cannot be awakened and death shortly ensues. Necropsy findings are non-specific, although in some cases a mild to moderate pancreatitis is present. A similar disorder called pokkuri was reported in healthy young Japanese soldiers during World War II. These victims died during sleep, after a groan or some other indication of a distrubing dream, and autopsy failed to reveal any significant abnormalities that would explain death.

Some of the mysterious deaths that have been unexpected and sudden are undoubtedly explained by a more recently discovered syndrome, the long Q-T syndrome (LQTS). The syndrome was first described in its genetically recessive form, linked with congenital deafness (Jervell and Lange-Nielsen, 1957). Although James (1968) found abnormal histology in the conduction system in several victims of this disorder, most of these victims have no histological abnormalities observable at autopsy, and it seems likely that the findings of James were a coincidence. These victims, as well as those of the syndrome without deafness with Mendelian dominant inheritance (Romano-Ward syndrome) generally have no detectable abnormalities at autopsy that would explain the disorder. The syndrome has been studied thoroughly in many centers, and the subjects die of ventricular fibrillation. This arrhythmia occurs during marked exertion, or with strong emotions. Although Schwartz has made a convincing case that these subjects have asymmetrical sympathetic innervation of the heart that predisposes to ventricular fibrillation, the relevant point here is that at autopsy they have no observable changes in the vast majority of cases. There are many other disorders that can produce prolonged apnea or a major arrhythmia that may result in death without observable lethal pathology at postmortem. This is true even for intentional homicide, if suffocation is produced with a soft pillow. Even perinatal deaths occurring in hospital are unexplained by autopsy in 37 to 39% of the cases (Wright et al, 1964).

This leads to two important inferences that relate to the sudden infant death syndrome. First, autopsy findings may not reveal the cause of death in disorders that are definite, specific entities; and secondly, this allows the possibility, and even probability, that SIDS is not a single entity but may represent a heterogeneous group of causes of death. It follows that, to find an instance of sudden and unexpected death in a victim with a known disorder, such as the long Q-T syndrome, does not establish that this is a frequent cause of sudden death in that age group, whether infant or adult.

To return to the common post-mortem findings that are inherently non-lethal but characteristically found in SIDS victims, the most general finding was that the infant was reasonably well-nourished and not seriously ill. This meant that an infant in the first six months of life would usually have a fully developed thymus gland, in contrast to those infants who died of chronic illness, in whom the thymus was shrunken and therefore more typical of the involuted adult thymus. This led to the mistaken conclusion that the large infant thymus was abnormal, and further, that it was the cause of the sudden death through "thymic asthma" or "status thymico-lymphaticus." Although mistaken inferences from pathology led to mistaken inferences as to cause of death, the correction came from other pathologists. In a carefully constructed case, Lee in 1842 provided all of the evidence that any reasonable individual would require to understand that "thymic asthma" was not a disease entity, and that clinically observed, obstructed respiration was related to epiglottitis and bronchitis and similar problems of the respiratory tract, rather than obstruction produced by the thymus. Lee pointed out that the thymus was not enlarged in most instances of sudden death in infants, and that an enlarged thymus in the adult did not produce airway obstruction in any case. In spite of the impeccable refutation presented by Lee, this theory was subsequently resurrected by the application of a more "scientific" title of status thymico-lymphaticus. This theory did not die out until well into this century, perhaps due to the strong desire by physicians to have an explanation for untimely death. One of the more colorful denouements was written in 1927 by Greenwood and Woods. "The present use in certification and in evidence in coroners' courts of the phrases Status

Lymphaticus and Status Thymico-Lymphaticus is, we suggest, a good example of the growth of medical mythology. A nucleus of truth is buried beneath a pile of intellectual rubbish, conjecture, bad observations, and rash generalisation. This heap of rubbish is described in the current scientific jargon and treated as an orthodox shrine." They concluded that these deaths, ". . . apart from Status Lymphaticus would in more pious, but not more superstitious, days have been attributed to the visitation of God." The theory was still sufficiently prevalent when I was in medical school that the standard pathology texts usually listed this in the index, although in the text it was dismissed.

As mentioned in the first chapter, the early descriptions of the post-mortem findings of infants who died suddenly and unexpectedly were quite accurate, and are still a sufficient account of the gross changes at autopsy (Fearn, 1934). The report by Fearn also included a sensible bit of investigation into the events surrounding the death leading him to conclude that overlaying was difficult to invoke as a cause of death since the victim had been in bed alone.

Infection

Beginning at the turn of the century, pathologists began to examine the victims more carefully and found evidence of infection (Brouardel, 1895; Farber, 1934; Goldbloom and Wigglesworth, 1938). In these studies, the pathologists observed only the tissue changes due to infection, with increased leukocytes and other mild changes of inflammation, predominantly in the respiratory tract. However, there is the peculiar paradox that if major signs of infection were uncovered, such as lobar pneumonia, or as in the cases reported by Farber, generalized sepsis was proven, the case would *not* be considered by modern standards to fit into the category of sudden infant death syndrome. By 1950, it was abundantly clear that overwhelming bacterial sepsis, which killed so swiftly that post-mortem inflammatory findings were insignificant, had been ruled out as a frequent cause of SIDS by post-mortem cultures from many laboratories. The possibility of viral infections as the cause of SIDS remained.

Werne and Garrow (1953) reported thirty-one consecutive autopsies during 1950 from the Borough of Queens on infants dying suddenly in apparent good health, excluding those with gross necropsy findings to explain death. They found microscopic inflammatory lesions in the the upper and lower respiratory tract in all thrity-one, and concluded that death was caused by "fulminating respiratory disease."

Adelson and Kenny (1956) reported a survey of a geographical area, and found evidence of microscopic inflammation in the respiratory tract of 84% of the infants who died suddenly. However, they were unable to isolate any viruses, perhaps due to the inefficient and limited means of viral isolation at that time.

The frequent finding of mild inflammatory changes suggesting infection in dead infants led to speculation about other disorders that might reconcile the divergence between the mildness of post-mortem changes and death. Spain et al (1954) speculated that an ordinary upper respiratory infection was lethal because of the occurrence at an age when the immune globulins were at a nadir. Although the decline of the gamma globulins occurs during early infancy, Valdes-Dapena et al (1963) found that the victims of SIDS had no greater diminution in gamma globulin than the normal population of the same age, and in fact had somewhat higher levels, suggesting early exposure to other infectious agents.

Other investigators offered alternative hypotheses. Stowens (1957) went so far as to deny any role for infection, and postulated laryngospasm or bronchospasm as the basis of the disorder, to account for the post-mortem findings of localized pulmonary hemorrhages, emphysema, and edema. These same post-mortem findings led other pathologists such as Handforth (1959) to postulate laryngospasm, based in part upon his inability to isolate any organisms, although he thought that an early phase of a respiratory infection might be a trigger for the airway obstruction. Gold and his co-workers published the first report of successful viral isolation from victims of SIDS in 1961, but in only twelve of forty-eight infants dying of SIDS. All of their isolates were enterovirus. Valdes-Dapena and Hummeler (1963) isolated only a single virus from one hundred nine infants dying suddenly and unexpectedly. With improved techniques, both in terms of sites of collection and the rapidity of collection after death, Ray (1970) recovered non-polio isolates from 37.5% of SIDS victims, compared to only 16% in a control group of infants of comparable age. Brandt (1970) reported 44% isolation of viruses, and 15% pathogenic bacteria, out of a population of seventy cases of SIDS. Ray and Hebestreit (1971) showed on post-mortem studies of one hundred nineteen victims of SIDS that none of twenty had viremia, and only four of one hundred nineteen had detectable levels of serum interferon, both methods confirming that viremia was not a major part of the lethal disorder.

To summarize the post-mortem studies, a high percentage of SIDS victims have evidence of mild infection, based on history, histology, and virology, but approximately 25 to 30% of the victims had no evidence at all of infection. Even those that have infections have mild enough autopsy changes to preclude them as the immediate cause of death. The viruses for the most part are the same that are endemic in the communities involved, producing mild diseases not requiring hospitalization, and frequently not even the attention of a physician. Accordingly, most investigators would conclude that the infection may act as a trigger for apnea, or some other lethal disorder of cardiopulmonary function, such as diminished capacity for arousal from sleep apnea.

Before leaving the subject of infection, two studies by Naeye (1977 and 1979) found an association between maternal bacterial infections and a higher rate of SIDS in the resulting infant. In the first report, comparing seventy-nine victims of SIDS with over thirty thousand control infants,

Naeye found a significant increase in evidence of infection in the umbilical cord and the placental membrane of SIDS victims compared to the control. Although the differences were highly significant, it is important to note that the actual prevalence was not great; neutrophils were found in 11% of the SIDS victims, compared to 4% for controls. As has been the case for other post-mortem findings recorded by Naeye, there were two sub-groups; those SIDS victims who had a respiratory infection, and those who did not. The former group had less evidence of placental abnormalities, compared to the non-infected group. We will return to this dichotomy later, but a reasonable inference can be made that some of the SIDS victims may have had no prior problems, but died due to the effect of an acute respiratory infection, whereas the majority of SIDS victims have evidence of prior health problems. One of the common relationships between Naeye's 1977 paper and the 1979 one is prematurity. The placental infections noted in the victims of SIDS are of the type generally thought to cause premature delivery. The 1979 study of maternal urinary tract and amniotic fluid infections in the fifteen days prior to delivery showed a much increased frequency of pre-term deliveries (Naeye, 1979).

Pre-Existing Abnormalities

There is increasing evidence that a majority of SIDS victims were not entirely normal. Prematures were reported to be at higher risk for SIDS in 1963 by Valdes-Dapena. Both Emery (1959) and Peterson et al (1974) reported that the post-natal growth, on the average, for SIDS victims was at a lower rate than for controls. Thus, SIDS victims as a group appear to have both prenatal and post-natal failure to thrive (Naeye et al, 1976), although there are many exceptions. Naeye described retardation of the same degree in growth of bone, brain, and other organs of SIDS victims and thought it unlikely that simple under-nutrition was responsible (1965).

Sinclair-Smith and co-workers (1976) examined the thymus, rib, and liver from two hundred children with SIDS, and in 90% of these children the costochondral junction indicated a retardation in growth prior to death. A similar proportion had fatty changes in the liver and thymic changes compatible with a normal reaction to infection in one-half of the children. These reports provide evidence of a subtle handicap for the victims of SIDS, both before and after birth, and as we will see in a review of epidemiologic data, that evidence also reveals social and maternal handicaps, on the average. Before any inference is drawn however, these same findings may well be a non-specific indication of vulnerability for an infant, whether from SIDS or any other disorder of infancy.

In the remainder of this discussion on the pathology of SIDS, we will address specific organ systems, particularly the cardiovascular, respiratory, and neurological.

Much of the recent advances in autopsy information of SIDS came through the work of Richard Naeye and his co-workers, relating to subtle changes that are also found in conditions commonly associated with chronic hypoxia. The first report, in 1973, found that victims of SIDS had 1.6 times as much muscle in their small pulmonary arteries as did control subjects. This was compared to infants living at high altitude at the time of death who had 2.3 times as much muscle in their arteries. There were two groups in his patients with SIDS, those who had no pulmonary inflammation and those who had mild but definite inflammatory changes in the lungs. The group with pulmonary inflammation had statistically less muscular hypertrophy in the pulmonary arteries than the group with no inflammation, but also had significantly more hypertrophy than the non-hypoxic controls. Approximately 60% of all the victims of SIDS had muscle mass in the pulmonary artery that exceeded the range of normal (Naeye, 1980). If the hypertrophy was caused by hypoxia, the pulmonary vascular resistance would have been increased, as well as the pulmonary artery pressures, postulating a normal cardiac output. If that were the case, persistence of the right ventricular muscle mass characteristic of the fetal state might be expected, and Naeye reported in 1976 that many of the victims of SIDS had abnormally heavy right ventricles, and that the weight was directly proportional to the mass of muscle in the small pulmonary arteries, and to the presence of an abnormal retention of brown fat around the adrenal glands (Naeye, 1974). There was also a direct proportion between the weight of the right ventricle and the presence of hepatic erythropoiesis. Comparing the two groups of SIDS victims, the infected ones died at an older age and had somewhat smaller thymus glands and larger spleens, and there was a greater proportion of males in that group. Naeye concluded that these findings were suggestive of increased exposure to hypoxia, more marked in the children who died without the evidence of infection, at a somewhat earlier age. These abnormalities of lung arteries were supported by Mason et al (1975), disputed by Kendeel and Ferris (1977), and again confirmed (Williams et al, 1979; Valdes-Dapena et al, 1980). The finding of increased periadrenal brown fat cells in SIDS was confirmed by Emery and Dinsdale (1978), and Valdes-Dapena et al (1976). Naeye's report of increased extramedullary hematopoiesis in SIDS victims (1974) was confirmed by Valdes-Dapena et al (1970). Naeye and his colleagues reported an additional subtle indicator of hypoxia prior to death; they studied the volume of the carotid glomus cells, corrected for body weight, and found that two-thirds of the SIDS victims had a subnormal volume, and 23% had an enlarged volume (1976). Although there was not an exclusive relationship between the two groups and hypoxia, Naeye concluded that the more severe history of hypoxia and hypoxemia occurred in the victims with enlarged glomic tissue. These findings were disputed (Dinsdale et al, 1977), but a 1979 ultrastructural study (Cole et al) found a reduction or absence of granules of the carotid chemoreceptor cells, as well as a reduction in cell number and size, in SIDS victims.

Although there are conflicting data, the overall post-mortem evidence of prior hypoxia leads to a reasonable inference that Naeye was correct, that many of the SIDS victims had prior experience with hypoxia, either prolonged alveolar hypoventilation, or perhaps repeated episodes of acute but severe hypoxia, or both. It is also clear that the post-mortem findings in SIDS victims are not unique, or uniform, and that the population includes at least two groups: infected and non-infected, and possibly an hypoxic and a non-hypoxic group.

The pulmonary changes in infants dying suddenly and unexpectedly were the first to be recognized at post-mortem, over a century ago. The petechiae on the surface of the lungs, right ventricle, and intrathoracic thymus were noted by inspection and microscopic study. Acute hemorrhagic pulmonary edema and/or petechiae are present in a very high percentage of cases of SIDS (Werne and Garrow, 1953; Adelson and Kinney, 1956). Neither group regarded the petechiae as specific for a particular mechanism of SIDS; Werne and Garrow thought that petechiae were characteristic of SIDS, *in contrast* to known cases of airway obstruction by strangulation. Swan (1960) thought petechiae were caused by asphyxia, including strangulation, but listed a wide range of causes of asphyxia in his series, including drowning, brain injury, carbon monoxide poisoning, hypoxic suffocation, barbiturates, etc. However, the desire to infer a specific cause of death, namely airway obstruction, was an early trend, seen in historical conclusions of overlaying and "thymic asthma." Handforth, in 1959, concluded that these post-mortem findings were suggestive of airway obstruction in the infant, produced by laryngospasm, and he produced similar petechiae in anesthetized rats by sudden occlusion of an intratracheal cannula. Several years later I examined the model used by Handforth, looking for additional causes of petechiae, to examine the hypothesis that they were specific for airway obstruction. Much to my surprise (Guntheroth, 1973), we were unable to produce intrathoracic

petechiae with airway obstruction, although we could produce them by hypoxic asphyxiation with 100% nitrogen; we
could not produce them by respiratory paralysis, nor by
cardiac arrest. When we re-examined carefully the method
used by Handforth, it was clear that when the animal ceased
breathing, after one minute of vigorous attempts at breathing, Handforth re-opened the airway, and if necessary, gave
artificial respiration to the animal. It was not stated how
many times the rat was subjected to this treatment, but with
the additional information that Handforth did not kill the
rats with an unremitting airway obstruction, there was no
conflict between our findings and his. It must be emphasized that for airway obstruction to cause SIDS *and*
petechiae, the infant would have to have airway obstruction
for a prolonged period, producing severe hypoxia, followed
by partial recovery, and then death before complete recovery. The proponents of airway obstruction as the cause of
petechiae and therefore as the cause of death in SIDS are a
persistent group, led by Beckwith (1970, 1975), although in
the second international conference on SIDS in Seattle,
Marshall (1970) argued that in known instances of suffocation with a plastic bag, the majority did not have petechiae,
nor when the airway was obstructed with a foreign body. In
1981, Beckwith in a televised condemnation of monitoring of
infants with apnea, as related to SIDS, asserted that it was
likely that a true SIDS victim could *not* be resuscitated even
if it were detected, because of unremitting active airway
obstruction.

The assumption of airway obstruction led Shaw to a
highly original hypothesis of nasopharyngeal obstruction
(1968). He correctly pointed out that infants were obligate
nose breathers, who gradually converted to oral *or* nasopharyngeal airways after a few months; he postulated that
the period of obligate nose breathing coincided with the
vulnerability to SIDS. He suggested that the respiratory infection which SIDS victims were known to have was the
source of obstruction of the nasopharynx at a time when the

infant was still dependent upon the nasal airway. However, French et al (1972) using lateral x-rays of SIDS victims and a control population of comparable age, found no significant difference in the mean dimensions of the nasopharynx in the two groups, and no significant frequency of nasopharyngeal obstruction in either group (2.6% in the SIDS group, and 4% in the control group). We pointed out that the greatest dependence of the infant on a nasal airway was at birth, gradually decreasing over the next few weeks, whereas the first month of life is generally spared in SIDS, a discrepancy that could not be accounted for by Shaw's theory. Also, adenoids (pharyngeal lymph tissue) are virtually absent in the first few months of life, which also would lower the tendency toward nasopharnygeal obstruction with respiratory infection. We concluded that, although nasopharyngeal obstruction in an infant still dependent upon a nasal airway would be lethal, it seemed unlikely that this was a common cause of SIDS.

In the British symposium on sudden and unexpected death in infants, Cross (1972) offered additional speculation that nasal obstruction was indeed involved in SIDS. However, Camps pointed out that, in his very considerable post-mortem experience, abrupt death due to sudden and continuing airway obstruction did not produce petechiae, in contrast to slower forms of hypoxic death. Spector (1972) agreed, and reminded everyone that petechiae are very non-specific. Still, the proponents continued to infer airway obstruction, including Tonkin (1974) who argued that the tongue, when the head was acutely flexed, would occlude against the palate. Thach and Stark (1979) recently proposed that apneic spells in pre-term infants produced spontaneous neck flexion and the possibility of airway obstruction during these apneic episodes. It is important to recall that there was an entire generation or two of non-medical coroners who regularly concluded that SIDS was due to inadvertent suffocation by improper positioning of the infant, causing occlusion of the airways by bedclothes, or simply posture. The possibility of this type of accidental airway occlusion in otherwise healthy infants was denied by Wooley back in 1945, who demonstrated that it was extraordinarily difficult to cause airway obstruction in a healthy infant by posture, or bedclothes. (We will discuss obstructive sleep apnea in a later chapter, but it is fair to say that these episodes are not unremitting, and the subjects can be resuscitated, if necessary).

The evidence of respiratory tract infection led various individuals such as Handforth to conclude that these might be involved as a trigger mechanism that resulted in laryngo-spasm, and thereby sudden infant death. Some have found evidence of ulceration and even necrosis of vocal cords in victims of SIDS, but as Cullity and Emery (1975) point out, these lesions are quite non-specific, and occur in infants dying in hospital, and in children dying of miscellaneous disorders.

The two most common findings in SIDS at post-mortem, intrathoracic petechiae, and microscopic evidence of re-spiratory infection, appear to have a link. In 1980, we reported our attempts to reproduce our earlier experiments of producing petechiae in rats (Guntheroth et al, 1980). We were interested in the site of vascular leak, and chose to produce the petechiae by exposure to 100% nitrogen, result-ing in an hypoxic death, which had earlier been capable of producing petechiae in more than 80% of the animals (Guntheroth, 1973). We were chagrined to find that none of our dozen rats killed in this manner had intrathoracic pete-chiae in our new series. After some detective work, we learned that rats who age in animal colonies almost invaria-bly have a chronic respiratory infection of mycoplasma. By coincidence, all of the original experimental rats that devel-oped petechiae had been retired breeder rats. We found that deliberately infecting young, mature rats who had arrived fresh from the breeder, produced petechiae quite regularly when the rats were then exposed to hypoxic asphyxia. The virus used was a parainfluenza virus that is enzootic for rats, the Sendai virus. We repeated the airway obstruction experiment, and again, intrathoracic petechiae were not produced by airway obstruction, with or without infection. We conclude that intrathoracic petechiae are produced by hypoxia, and usually require the presence of infection, or some other toxic agent that affects the endothelium. During these experiments we also examined some possible mechanism that might explain the *absence* of petechiae in airway obstruction. Beckwith (1975) assumed that a forceful inspiratory effort against a closed airway would generate a very negative intrathoracic pressure, thereby greatly increasing the transmural pressure for the pulmonary vessels. We measured pulmonary artery pressures in the presence of airway occlusion, and found that the transpulmonary pressure did not change; the intrathoracic pressure was directly transmitted to the lumen of the vessel (Fig. II:1). In short, Beckwith's assumption was based on a further assumption that the intrathoracic pressure would not be transmitted to the blood vessels themselves. Still, the absence of petechiae in airway obstruction was somewhat surprising, since the animals died of hypoxia, and petechiae did not occur even when the animals were infected. We compared the lung volume from five rats who were killed with airway obstruction to five who were killed with nitrogen. The lungs of the obstructed airway group were 25% smaller, a significant difference (Guntheroth, unpublished data). The absorption of oxygen from the lungs after obstruction is relatively complete, and is an adequate explanation for the diminished lung volume with complete airway obstruction. We postulate that the smaller lung volume, with airway obstruction, causes a reduction in the shearing forces (friction) of the surface of the lung against the rib cage, thymus, and heart. The friction between a fully expanded lung and the other intrathoracic structures, could account for the observed distribution of petechiae on those organs. Again, we conclude that airway obstruction is very difficult to reconcile with the observed facts, as an explanation for SIDS.

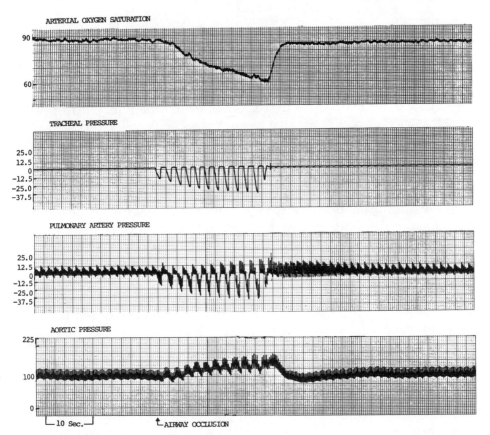

Figure II:1 A record of the effects of airway occlusion in an anesthetized rabbit, to demonstrate that the transmural pressure (pulmonary artery pressure minus intrathoracic pressure) does not increase, since the compliant pulmonary vessels transmit the tracheal pressure faithfully. Note the marked and prompt fall in arterial oxygen saturation (in percent). Pressures are in mmHg.

Naeye et al (1980) correlated the presence of petechiae in intrathoracic organs to a higher level of cortisol on post-mortem exam in subjects with sudden infant death syndrome. These authors concluded that the stressful events causing an increase in cortisol were of somewhat longer duration in the group with petechiae. Although they inferred a relationship between that and the duration of hypoxic episodes, cortisol production could respond to any stress.

A French post-mortem study of the central adrenergic neurons found decreased enzyme activity in the respiratory and cardiac nuclei (Denoroy et al, 1980). Although these findings would seem to conflict with reports from the Columbia group of evidence of increased peripheral activity of the sympathoadrenal system in near-miss SIDS (discussed later), it is important to note the general lack of correlation between central and peripheral activity of this system. In fact, there is evidence of a negative feedback from peripheral to central parts of the sympathetic system (Gale, 1973).

Completing the evidence of a subtle but chronic disorder in the victims of SIDS are the histologic changes in the central nervous system at autopsy. Naeye (1976) found approximately one-half of SIDS victims had abnormal proliferation of astroglial fibers in their brainstems. Generally, this type of proliferation follows destruction of nearby neurons during an hypoxic episode. In this report, an enlarged mass of chromaffin cells in the adrenal medulla was found in the same subjects, which Naeye concluded was further evidence of chronic hypoxia. These findings are significant, although by no means universal. Lesions in the white matter of the brain of victims of SIDS are also statistically greater in prevalence than in infants who die of known causes (Takashima et al, 1978b); 21.6% of SIDS infants had areas of leukomalacia, 24.8% of infants with congenital heart disease, but only 4.4% of infants with other acute causes of death had leukomalacia. The authors, in a second paper (1978a) concluded that hypoperfusion might be the crucial defect, rather than generalized hypoxia, because of the association with congenital heart disease. However, generalized hypoxia would produce a similar pattern, depending upon the critical nature of diffusion pathways; neural cell hypoxia could be produced by either hypoperfusion or hypoxia. Gadsen and Emery (1976) found fatty changes in the brain in one-half of the forty-one infants who died suddenly and unexpectedly, and in relation to their experience with other disease states, concluded that chronic hypoxia was a likely cause of these changes. A possible link between neuronal abnormalities and apnea has been reported by Quattrochi et al (1980). They examined the dendritic spines of the reticular substance of the pons and medulla with Golgi staining. This work is based on normal maturation in which the spines are present early, and with maturation, disappear in this area of the brain thought to be intimately related to respiratory control. They found persistence of these spines on reticular dendrites in seventeen out of nineteen of the SIDS victims (89%), but in only two of the control infants (22%). They speculated that delay in normal maturation of these crucial cells could be the basis for malfunction of the neural control of respiration. Similar reasoning linked the discovery of defective maturation of the vagus nerve in SIDS victims with astrogliosis of the vagal nuclei in the medulla (Sachis et al, 1981); however, these authors questioned whether the pathology was the result or the cause of hypoxia.

In summary, the post-mortem findings of victims of sudden infant death are multiple, and characteristic. However, no single finding is universally present in these infants. Medvedev (1978) summarized the status of pathology: "SIDS is an abstract notion including various pathological conditions which are thus far difficult to interpret from nosological positions." The post-mortem findings, by definition, are not capable of explaining death, but are compatible with a malfunction of some system, most likely respiratory control. There is substantial evidence that these infants did not die of uninterrupted airway obstruction, but there are many post-mortem findings strongly suggesting that hypoxia has been present prior to the terminal event, either as repeated severe episodes, or a more chronic form of hypoxia. Infection, although not universally present, and not involving lethal pathogens, is nevertheless present in the majority of the victims, approximately one-half by viral iso-

lation, and in 80% by histologic evidence of mild inflammation. The evidence of chronic disorder involves a wide range
of systems and raises the hope that eventually the infants at
risk can be discovered prior to the fatal event, and their
sudden death prevented.

Table II:1
The Five Most Significant Post-Mortem Findings in SIDS

---

1. *No* inherently lethal pathology
2. Evidence of mild respiratory infections, usually viral
3. Intrathoracic petechiae; patchy pulmonary edema and emphysema
4. Histopathology suggesting pre-existing hypoxia: increased muscle mass in pulmonary arteries and right ventricle; smaller thymus, extramedullary erythropoiesis, increased periadrenal brown fat cells, enlarged adrenal chromaffin cells
5. Neuropathology:astroglial proliferation in brainstem, leukomalacia, delayed loss of dendritic spines in reticular substance

---

Chapter III

Epidemiology of SIDS

More has probably been written about the factors presumed to determine the frequency and distribution of SIDS than on any other aspect of this disorder. As was the case with the post-mortem findings, the characteristics of the population of infants dying suddenly and unexpectedly are non-specific; although epidemiologists have claimed that any theory as to the cause of SIDS must conform to the known observations, none of the characteristics of the population are universal, except for the age distribution of one to six months. Even that is somewhat arbitrary, because a child of one or two years who dies without known cause, whose autopsy reveals no lethal changes, was formerly acceptable to authorities writing on the subject. Similarly, neonates are usually excluded from SIDS, although a satisfactory cause of perinatal death may not be found after a thorough examination (Wright et al, 1964).

Much has been made of the state of ignorance about the subject of infants dying unexpectedly, with implicit and sometimes explicit claims that all progress began when a group of parents became politically active and sought funds for research on the subject. There is no question about the beneficial effects of support from lay groups, but history should not be "revised" too glibly, even for a noble cause. The description of the two hundred fifty-eight infants dying in Dundee, Scotland, by Templeman in 1892 includes most of the important currently accepted factors for SIDS. Templeman described the remarkably poor conditions in this industrialized community before the turn of the century, with obvious over-crowding, frequently requiring many individuals in the same bed, if for no other reason than to keep warm. The bed was frequently nothing more than a pile of burlap sacks. He found that three-fourths of all of the cases of infant death occurred in families living in only a single room. Although that degree of crowding seems extraordinary, he pointed out that two-thirds of the entire population of Dundee, Scotland, lived in only one or two rooms at most. In other words, the social conditions found in SIDS were only quantitatively different. Thirty-two percent of all of the cases investigated were illegitimate, but the illegitimacy rate in the overall population was 10.3% at that time. For age distribution he found a high rate in the first three months that rapidly diminished thereafter, and there were no cases at all after the age of nine months. Sixty-two percent of the deaths occurred during winter. A finding which is no longer characteristic of SIDS was that 46% of all of the patients were discovered on Sunday morning. He observed that these families worked long and hard during the week, including Saturday, and that frequently the mother also worked in the mill; Saturday night was the only night that the parents stayed up late, and they slept late on Sunday. He postulated that they also drank heavily on Saturday night, further contributing to sleeping soundly and increasing the probability of accidental overlaying. Alternatively, there is good reason to believe that sleep deprivation for infants may increase the likelihood of deep sleep and apnea when sleep finally comes. Thus, the epidemiology that Templeman described led him to diagnose overlaying, but is compatible with SIDS. Similarly, his autopsy findings were completely characteristic for SIDS. Given the single bed for an entire family, his inference of overlaying in 1892 seems quite reasonable.

Templeman's description of the social problems related

to SIDS includes a mixture of compassion and punitiveness. He was convinced that liquor was behind the problem of overlaying, and considered these deaths due to negligence but free of criminal intent. He advocated the "German law" which prohibited infants from occupying the same bed as any other individual, and urged punishment for offenders. On the other hand, he clearly valued these infants, and cried out against the loss. He recognized the deplorable status of many of the subjects, and seemed sympathetic, other than for the "needless deaths." He reported that many thought these unfortunate infants were victims of infanticide, attributable to life insurance as a financial incentive. He analyzed the amount of money available, and concluded that it would not even pay for interment, and that in any case, the insurance in England at that time would not pay anything in the first three months, when "overlaying" was most common.

The second significant report of the epidemiology of SIDS did not occur until 1956. Adelson and Kinney analyzed one hundred twenty-six cases in Cuyahoga County, Ohio. This project was begun twelve years prior to the first Seattle conference on SIDS. Again, a thorough investigation, plus an astute perspective, allowed Adelson and Kinney to provide numerical descriptions of the population of SIDS that left out very little. They also included sixteen control cases to permit comparison with the population at large, a necessary feature that was not always followed subsequently. They found that there were slightly more males than females, 55% of the total being male, a difference that was not statistically significant. They found almost twice as many black infants in their population of unexpected deaths as was present in the general population. Their age distribution was similar to Templeman's subjects, 85% of the cases occurring before seven months of age. They explicitly excluded deaths in the first ten days, to avoid possible confusion with perinatal deaths. They found that 14% of the infants were premature, a significantly greater proportion than could be found in that urban population, with an overall rate of prematurity of 8%. They found three victims who were one of a set of twins, and although they lacked general population statistics of twinning, this clearly was a greater occurrence rate than for twins in the general population.

Adelson and Kinney described certain features of the pregnancy and of the individual patient which have proved to be important leads, confirmed repeatedly in subsequent studies. They found a high percentage of maternal illnesses during pregnancies that produced the SIDS victims, although in this case they had no control data for the general population. They felt that 60% of the victims came from "good homes," and 40% came from poor homes, and made no pretense as to quantification, except that these gradings were done by individuals who were acquainted with the community at the time, and had a reasonable, qualitative grasp of the prevailing socioeconomic state. These trained health personnel also gave a qualitative assessment of the quality of the care provided for the infant, or "mothering." The quality of care was found to be poor in 67% of the poor homes, but in only 12% of the good homes (60% of the total) was the care perceived to be poor. One of the most important clues with etiologic implications was that 54% of the dead infants had been exposed to a respiratory infection in the ten days prior to death. Fifty-three percent of these infants had a history of mild symptoms. Although most of these infants were found dead and presumably died in their sleep, twenty-seven of one hundred twenty-six were "seen to die." They carefully point out that some of those instances were probably misperceptions, but there were several that were observed to be alive at the time they arrived in the emergency rooms at the hospitals, providing evidence that sleep is not a universal requirement for sudden and unexplained death in infants.

Emery (1959) studied sudden and unexpected deaths in Sheffield, a community of half a million, served by a single pediatric hospital. He found, on follow-up visits, that there was a history of symptoms at least forty-eight hours before death in over 90% of SIDS victims. He confirmed Templeman's findings of increased frequency of deaths during winter months, but found no significant difference in the frequency by day of the week, if deaths in hospital were included. However, the greatest frequency of home deaths occurred on Sunday and Monday.

At the 1963 conference on SIDS held in Seattle, Landing estimated the national mortality rate due to this disorder on the basis of Los Angeles County, at 10–15,000 deaths per year. In 1965, Carpenter and Shaddick, based on a study of one hundred ten cot deaths, estimated that there were probably eleven hundred similar deaths in England and Wales annually. They found that, at least statistically, there was a greater use of a soft pillow, that the SIDS victims were more likely to be bottle-fed, particularly early in life, and apt to have symptoms of respiratory disease prior to death. It is not clear to this day what the significance of the first of these findings was, although it may have been influenced by a general conviction that some of these infants may have died by suffocation.

The role of bottle-feeding, or the lack of breastfeeding, has had a different significance to different investigators. At one time, it appears that English mothers were convinced that if they strengthened the formula, prepared from dried solids, the infant would gain weight more rapidly, a presumably desirable end. There were well-documented instances of hypernatremia, which still may be the case in some areas, but this assuredly is not presently a common cause of sudden infant death. Secondly, the higher rate of SIDS in bottle-fed infants strengthened a conviction that SIDS was a death of hypersensitivity to cow's milk (Parrish et al, 1960) that became almost an obsession with some British scientists; that argument occupied a surprising proportion of the first SIDS conference in Seattle. The fact was that the dead infants had titers against cow's milk no different from control populations (Gold and Godek, 1961), and there were increasing numbers of infants reported dead of SIDS who had *never* been given cow's milk. The meaning of bottle-feeding as a population average may relate to mothering, and perhaps to some extent whether the mother had to work and therefore was unable to breast feed, and could simply be a sociologic feature of the population at risk. But many of the victims of SIDS are breast fed, and have excellent mothering, in spite of the population statistics.

In 1966, Steele and Langworth in Ontario reported more characteristics of the mothers of infants dying with SIDS. They found that SIDS mothers were usually of a lower age at the time of marriage and at the time of their first pregnancy, as well as being relatively young at the time of the SIDS pregnancy. They tended to have delayed prenatal care, and they were more likely to smoke cigarettes than matched controls. (There were also significant differences for blood groups, found in other studies in other areas, although not consistent from one area to another). Steele and Langworth thought that the link between maternal smoking and SIDS might be the higher rate of prematurity related to both.

In 1966, Peterson reported that in King County, Washington, there were 2.87 cases of SIDS for one thousand live births, with almost double that rate for the non-white population. Although no day in the week was worse than another, there were at least twice as many infants discovered in the morning than at any other time of day.

In 1969 at the second conference on SIDS in Seattle, seven separate reports of the incidence of SIDS ranged from a low of 1.2 to a high of 3 per thousand live births. Froggatt emphasized that the sparing of the first month of life was probably real, and not simply a result of an arbitrary definition. He presented evidence that many of the SIDS victims were small, not only at birth, but when corrected for age. He also, for the first time, noted the higher frequency of SIDS in subsequent siblings of SIDS victims: 2% versus 0.2%. This finding should not be surprising, considering the several reports of significant differences in maternal behavior and health, and does not suggest a genetic factor. Houstek made a crucial observation, not much considered at the time. He pointed out the parallel between the incidence of SIDS and general infant mortality. This has subsequently been confirmed in other studies, and calls for caution in inferring specific cause-and-effect relationships. Steele, reviewing his earlier epidemiologic data, added an important observation of etiologic significance. In twenty-six cases of SIDS, seven had a history of "serious" pulmonary disease or difficulty in breathing, including a history of apnea.

Froggatt and his colleagues (1971) confirmed Houstek's general observation and found a greater prevalence of SIDS in males than in females, but they observed that this was true for infant mortality in general. They also confirmed the observation of Steele and his colleagues of relatively younger mothers of SIDS victims, and in addition noted that the dead infant represented a relatively high birth order, considering the age of the mother.

In 1972, Pierson et al reported a surprisingly frequent occurrence of SIDS in mothers who were on methadone maintenance, who had previously been addicted to heroin. (This was confirmed in a more formal epidemiologic survey in 1978 by Rajegowda et al.)

In 1973 the group at Sheffield, England, (Protestos et al) described significant differences between a group of infants who died of cot death and survivors born in the same hospital. For the first time, they began to apply this list to identify infants at high risk, with the obvious intent of some form of intervention, or at least surveillance. The single best discriminator between an average and a high-risk infant was whether the mother brought the infant back to the follow-up clinic after discharge from the maternity hospitalization. There were other differences between the mothers, both in their health and in their attitude. The mothers of the SIDS victims had a greater chance of having had influenza during pregnancy, and antepartum hemorrhages. These mothers were also younger, and had been pregnant more often. Their social class tended to be lower. As had been noted, breast feeding—both the mother's stated intention and in the fact—was less common in the SIDS group. Certain characteristics of the infant were also observed to predict difficulty in the first few months of life. They found that sex was not a useful predictor, but that symptoms of the infant, particularly dyspnea, were important. They postulated that that related to prematurity, as did tachypnea and other respiratory disturbances. They found no significance for the requirement of oxygen by the infant in the neonatal period.

Froggatt's report of underdevelopment in 1970 was confirmed in 1974 by Peterson et al who found, in addition to lower weight in the victims of SIDS compared to age-matched controls, that their length and head circumferences were also less than for controls. The evidence argues that SIDS victims are *not* without problems, both chronic and acute. Steele, in reviewing his 1966 study, commented at the Canadian SIDS meeting (1974) that there was evidence in the SIDS victims of an "unwitting maternal deprivation." Carpenter and Emery similarly reviewed their earlier maternal risk factors and reported on a prospective application; indeed, the high-risk group did quite poorly compared to the control group. One of their inferences, based on observations during home visits by nurses was that serious disease symptoms were sometimes not recognized by the mothers. They emphasized that the risk of SIDS seemed to parallel the general risk of the infant, which included the skills of mothering, or the lack of those skills. (The importance of skilled observers in detection of abnormalities was recently reported by Mandell (1981); he found that 37% of nurse mothers noted apnea, cyanotic episodes, wheezing, or unusual breathing in their infants who subsequently succumbed to crib death, compared to 6% of non-nurse mothers.)

At the 1974 Canadian meeting, Valdes-Dapena reported an apparent drop in the rate of SIDS deaths in Philadelphia between 1960 and 1972. This dropped from 1.22 to 0.60 for white infants, and from 4.41 to 3.64 for non-whites. Overall, the incidence fell from 2.29 to 1.92 per one thousand live births.

Although twins individually seemed more susceptible to SIDS than the average infant, genetics does not appear to be involved. Using pairs of twins, both of whom died, and comparing like-sexed with unlike-sexed twins for concordance, Spiers (1974) found no difference, and concluded that any excess risk of a second twin dying of SIDS could be explained by a common environment, rather than a Mendelian characteristic.

In 1976 the collaborative perinatal project, following up on nearly sixty thousand pregnancies between 1959 and 1966 in several communities, confirmed many of the risk factors already reported (Naeye et al, 1976). The differences between the SIDS victims and matched controls from the larger group were highly significant, but the ratios do not supply any uniqueness to their interpretation. For example, 59% of the mothers of SIDS victims smoked, compared to 48% of the matched control; separating out the heavier smokers, 46% of SIDS victims' mothers smoked more than six cigarettes per day, compared to 25% of the controls. Although that is significant at the .001 level, it is obvious that more than half of the mothers of SIDS victims did *not* smoke heavily. Maternal anemia and proteinuria were other risk factors that had not previously been identified. The SIDS infants also presented significant differences from the control group, but none of them of a marked frequency. Nevertheless, a pattern was evident: the SIDS victims were not as "normal" as their matched controls; they required resuscitation more often, they had delays in beginning their feedings, they were jittery, etc.

Some of the maternal factors for SIDS were attributed to a common feature, short inter-pregnancy interval (Spiers and Wang, 1976). This could account for the maternal anemia found by Naeye and his colleagues, and for the relatively low birth weight of the infant. These authors emphasized that the depletion of maternal reserves would place the product of the pregnancy at risk, and this was true for all infant mortality, not for SIDS alone. In that same year, Naeye and his co-workers reported a retrospective study of the behavior of SIDS victims, and found further evidence that the SIDS victim, on the average, was not quite normal. Although they cautioned that recollections of the temperament of an infant after a tragedy such as SIDS might not be entirely objective, there was nevertheless an interesting and probably significant pattern (Naeye, Messmer et al, 1976). The victims of SIDS generally had less intense reactions to emotional stimuli, they were less active physically, became more breathless during feeding, and their cry was "different" or even abnormal. They found positive correlation between this type of behavior and behavior they attributed to chronic hypoxia, although this inference of cause was not well-documented.

The identification system for infants at risk of sudden death was applied by Carpenter and Emery (1977), and the "treatment" consisted largely of non-specific observation, including home visits. Fifteen percent of their population of eleven thousand babies were scored as high risks. Out of this group, nine hundred twenty-two infants were treated as a control high-risk group, with no intervention, and had a substantially greater rate of sudden death, 0.98% compared to 0.32% of the "observed" high-risk group. The subjects originally selected for observation, but who refused to participate, had an even higher percentage of unexpected death, 14.3 per one thousand live births. The low-risk group had only 1.6 per thousand (.16%). This success is striking, although others have criticized it on the basis of its poor specificity. Nevertheless, the intervention was effective, and the prediction was relatively sensitive for identifying the group at risk.

Another British group, who subsequently found that the Sheffield system did not work when applied to other communities (Oakley et al, 1978), did find confirmation of one of the important conclusions reached by the Sheffield group. Stanton et al (1978) investigated the terminal symptoms in one hundred forty-five children who died at home unexpectedly, and found that 59% of these infants had definite symptoms, and even more startling, 48% appeared to have had major symptoms of disease which were missed, or at least misinterpreted. They found that the symptoms were present sometimes for several days before death, but only twelve of the sixty-nine children with major symptoms had been seen by a physician within twenty-four hours of death. Although they concede that the symptoms were not always dramatic, or did not appear to be life threatening, they nevertheless concluded that many of the patients should have been seen by physicians and admitted to hospital. This lack of information about the seriousness of health problems may be the basis for improved mortality produced by the surveillance instituted in the Sheffield community.

One epidemiologic report, by Kukull and Peterson (1977) deserves mention, and criticism. In examining a hypothesis of Asch (1968) that many of the SIDS cases were infanticide under the effects of a post-partum psychosis, they compared the number of known infant homicides for the ages of one to four months, and found a relatively constant rate for the years from 1950 to 1974. They contended that the SIDS rates are one hundred times larger than the published figures for homicides and that, in addition, SIDS became a certifiable classification only in 1963. They implied that the slope would have changed at that point, if there was a difference in the actual cause of death that had been used for reporting. Their inferences on that data seem impeccable, but they extended the argument to include the assertion that a post-mortem examination could distinguish infanticide from SIDS. Specifically, they asserted that the presence or absence of intrathoracic petechiae would distinguish between the two. There are, in fact, specific examples of homicide having been misdiagnosed as SIDS (Adelson, 1961), and no less an authority than Valdes-Dapena has stated that there is no way to reliably distinguish between these two. That is not to say that any sensible investigator believes that infanticide accounts for more than a rare instance of sudden infant death, but it is important to distinguish theory from epidemiology.

Almost every analysis of the victims of SIDS has concluded that low birth weight and prematurity are definite, if not independent risk factors for SIDS; however, only one study has reported the outcome of premature infants who "graduated" from a neonatal intensive care unit (Kulkarni et al, 1978). For those infants who survived to age twenty-eight days, forty-four out of one thousand infants subsequently died. Ten percent of the deaths were attributed to sudden infant death syndrome. SIDS and infection constituted the largest contributors to mortality out of the population of infants who were truly viable, with no major problems such as congenital malformations or hypoxic brain damage. They found the same risk factors that contributed to prematurity were risk factors for the infants on "graduation" to home.

Recently, a useful negative study was published, which ruled out atmospheric pressure variations as having any link to sudden infant death syndrome (Heaney and McIntyre, 1979). Such studies are frequently never remembered, and yet, they are essential to an open-minded consideration of folk wisdom, which occasionally contains useful information.

In 1979, an episode in the United States and one in Naples illustrated some of the not-so-scientific aspects of certain health problems. In Naples, "il male oscuro" was blamed for killing almost sixty infants in late 1978. On investigation (Marshall, 1979) there were probably two "epidemics." One of these appeared to be a respiratory viral infection, but in at least one quarter of the cases, the dead children had received a diphtheria-tetanus immunization one or two days before the day of death. (There was no apparent link between the two types of illnesses.) It seems obvious that the "whitewash" of the vaccinations was done thoughtfully, on the grounds that a wholesale abandonment of the immunization program would be far more disastrous to the general population than the rare sudden and unexpected death of an infant following immunization. However, there appeared to be no discussion of the risk/benefit ratio of delaying the start of immunizations to five months of age, rather than beginning at two or three months, which is the current custom. It is a fact that beginning immunizations at two or three months of age coincides with the time of maximal risk for SIDS. Just as we suspect that a respiratory infection is not directly lethal, it is unlikely that the immunization is directly lethal. However, the rates of occurrence of mild fever (31.5%), pain (51%), fretfulness (53%), and drowsiness (31.5%) found with diphtheria-tetanus-pertussis (DTP) immunization (Cody et al, 1981) should be considered in the context of sleep deprivation in an infant otherwise susceptible to SIDS. The possibility of the immunization acting as a trigger for SIDS is a very real one, for which there is at least some evidence. There can be little escaping the inference of cause and effect to parents whose infant dies shortly after an immunization shot, no matter how many denials or reassurances are issued by health authorities.

In an excellent, broad review of the epidemiology of sudden infant death, Peterson et al (1979) reminded us that the risk factors for SIDS are also associated with other causes of death, the one exception being that of the rather unique age distribution of SIDS. The other somewhat unique attribute of SIDS is its seasonal variation, in common only with respiratory infections. In 1980, Peterson reviewed the current rates for much of the world. The rates varied from a low of 0.6 per thousand; the United States average is approximately 2.3. The frequency is similar in both Northern and Southern hemispheres and it is not particularly affected by urban versus rural communities. In contrast to Valdes-Dapena's report of a declining rate in Philadelphia,

Peterson found no overall change in King County, Washington, except for a general trend following the birth rate (higher rate of SIDS for higher rates of birth). In a separate article, Peterson et al (1980) confirmed Froggatt's repetition rate for SIDS in subsequent siblings—nearly ten times as high as for the average population, but only 2%. They also found that the incidence of SIDS among first cousins of the victims of SIDS was the same as for the population at large. These data, along with Spiers' data on monozygous and dizygous twin pairs, rule out an inherited disorder, such as the long Q-T syndrome as a significant cause of SIDS.

The risk factors identified in several countries have included maternal attributes such as health during pregnancy, willingness to seek medical care, illegitimacy, cigarette smoking, and short intervals between pregnancies. A similarity between some of these characteristics, particularly young maternal age, premature delivery, and some aspects of neonatal morbidity, are common to SIDS and infant abuse (Roberts et al, 1980). In fact, in following up subsequent infants in one hundred sixty families that were ascertained to be involved in the abuse of an infant, there were three times as many unexpected sudden deaths as in a comparable population. These authors pointed out that infants in families that are abusive do not thrive, and that perhaps this non-specific factor may account for an overall increased mortality of these infants, as well as an increased incidence of SIDS. They reviewed the background of parents who abuse and even kill their infants, and found—not surprisingly—a failure to form a normal bond between the infant and the mother. These mothers are understandably out of touch with the infant, and may well fail to react to symptoms of illness in an infant. Such links between SIDS and child abuse are important to consider, even though the mere juxtaposition will cause resentment, and perhaps hurt for the parent who has provided the best in love and care for an infant who developed a respiratory infection and died. Nevertheless, child abuse is very frequent, many times more prevalent than SIDS, and must be dealt with for the sake of those infants. We must simply repeat that the risk factors described, some of them so unflattering, are found only in a minority of the parents of SIDS infants.

Table III:1
The Ten Most Significant Facts in the Epidemiology of SIDS

---

1. AGE: SIDS spares first month, rare after six months
2. SEASON: more common in winter
3. SOCIOECONOMICS: more common in poor and non-white population
4. ILLNESS: most victims had mild symptoms prior to SIDS
5. MATERNAL FACTORS: SIDS more common in unwed mothers, younger mothers, multiparous mothers with shorter interpregnancy intervals, cigarette-smoking mothers, and mothers who utilize health care facilities less and later
6. INFANT FACTORS: SIDS more common in prematures and small-for-gestational-age infants; their growth after birth is slower than average
7. SLEEP: most deaths unobserved; sleep common, although not universal
8. FEEDING: bottle-feeding more prevalent in SIDS, but breast-fed infants not immune
9. FAMILIAL RECURRENCE: greater than normal population, but only 1 to 2% risk. No evidence of genetic link
10. SPECIFICITY: occurrence rate of SIDS parallels the rate for general infant mortality.

Chapter IV

The Near-Miss SIDS

Sudden infant death syndrome is clearly capable of provoking strong emotion, not only in the bereaved, but in the physicians and scientists involved in the care and research of this disorder. Osler's plea for aequanimitas seems infrequently answered when the problem at hand is SIDS. The failure for rational dialogue has been even more prominent, if possible, concerning the patients referred to as aborted or near-miss SIDS. The problem began at the 1963 Seattle International Conference on SIDS. I had suggested that there logically should be a less than lethal form of a disorder that characteristically left no lethal pathology in the victims that died of the disorder, having personally observed infants in emergency rooms and on the wards who had apnea and cyanosis, with bradycardia, who were successfully resuscitated and survived normally. Francis Camps objected on the grounds that the lethal form of the disorder had not been successfully defined or characterized, and that to proceed to characterize a non-lethal form was premature. My reasoning, in introducing the near-miss in the very early part of the conference, was that the *final* definition of SIDS should be compatible with such a near-miss form, since ultimately, the overriding concern of physicians should be the preservation of life, and not simply the understanding of an aspect of death.

The emotional aspect of the sometimes acrimonious

debate stems from a thoroughly laudable desire to diminish or prevent guilt in the parents of SIDS victims. The parents who had lost infants and who accused themselves of some imagined neglect were sometimes accused of negligence or even homicide by relatives, neighbors, and occasionally the police. The response by well-meaning individuals such as Bergman and Beckwith was to declare that SIDS was a clear-cut, circumscribed entity that was well understood, and that it was not preventable. Neither of these two statements are sufficiently true, since the post-mortem results are by definition inadequate to explain death, and as we have reviewed, a number of etiologies of sudden death have been proven, although no single one of them seems likely to account for all of the sudden infant deaths. If there is a non-lethal form of SIDS, such as prolonged apnea, it immediately contradicts the second dogma, that SIDS cannot be prevented. It is abundantly clear that we cannot prevent all of the cases of SIDS, or even more than a few, but the physiology and epidemiology of the group of survivors of near-miss episodes constitute a far more productive source of information that might lead to a more widespread prevention of SIDS. The logic is simple: if the post-mortem examinations cannot explain death, and the post-mortem findings that are present are not lethal, it follows that a disorder of function is the probable mechanism of death, and function is rarely the province of the pathologist. This chapter will review the data, and particularly the studies of function in near-miss SIDS, which now amount to a very substantial number of subjects, some of whom have subsequently died, and who were found at post-mortem to be characteristic of SIDS (they had no lethal pathology or any recognizable disorder other than SIDS).

Adelson (1953) wrote in a forensic journal about sudden and unexpected death in adults. In the experience of almost every pathologist, a certain number of men and women dying abruptly are found at post-mortem to have no lethal changes. This led Adelson to speculate that these subjects have had a sudden disorder that resulted in a lethal arrhythmia, which he termed "vago-cardiac." His reasoning was simply that, absent an occluded coronary artery or other irreversible lesion, the disorder was some reflex mechanism that was ordinarily reversible in the normal, but not in the subject of his discussion. We will review in a subsequent chapter the evidence for and against death by arrhythmias in children, but assuredly, a cardiovascular death is *one* of the two rational choices for the etiology of sudden death, whether for an adult or for an infant. The only other possible pathway to death is cessation of air exchange, whether by apnea, airway occlusion, or by an inadequate oxygen source in inhaled air. For any conceivable mechanism that would produce death by either cardiac or respiratory arrest that would leave no lethal changes at post-mortem, there are non-lethal forms, and the study of these survivors, when identified, must greatly enhance our knowledge of SIDS, and improve our chances for preventing it.

In 1963, the evidence we introduced on the nature of a near-miss episode was drawn from clinical experience. Some of these infants could be resuscitated, like the premature infant with prolonged apnea, by vigorous stimulation, but some required mechanical ventilation and oxygen supplement. Thus, at least some infants who almost died had apnea as the primary disorder, and the cardiovascular system remained functional. (Bradycardia is an essential part of the oxygen-conserving reflex, and should not be considered failure [French et al, 1972; Guntheroth, 1979]). In the Second Conference on SIDS in Seattle I suggested that sleep apnea was a probable cause of both near-miss and SIDS (Guntheroth, 1970). The original suggestion of sleep apnea, however, had been made by Dr. John Scott in a planning meeting organized by the Neurological Sensory Disease Program of the Public Health Service in 1967. The neurologists had observed apnea in some adults with sleep, which could be lethal if not treated. This syndrome was called Ondine's curse by Severinghaus and Mitchell (1962). The importance of sleep apnea was that it could be detected by apnea monitors which were being introduced into premature centers, and at least allowed for the possibility of resuscitation. There was an attractive presumption that the disorder might be a maturational problem, and that the victim, once resuscitated and surviving the first six months of life, might be normal thereafter. At that 1969 meeting, Bergman reported that two of approximately twenty infants who had come into Children's Orthopedic Hospital in Seattle with apnea had subsequently returned dead on arrival, and at autopsy had findings consistent with SIDS. It was also in 1969 that Daily and his colleagues described sleep apnea in premature infants, and the relative ease of resuscitation if the infant was in the hospital. The epidemiologists had already shown that prematures were in fact at a substantially increased risk of dying of SIDS at home.

In the British Conference on SIDS in 1970, Dawes challenged individuals who championed obscure etiologies as the cause of SIDS to come forth with a near-miss that could be tested for that hypothesis. He was focusing at the time on a proposal by some of his British colleagues that an anaphylactic reaction to cow's milk was the cause of cot death. He suggested that failing to find a less than lethal form constituted an argument against that hypothesis at a time when there were approximately ten thousand cases a year of the lethal form in the United States, and over one thousand in Great Britain. SIDS is not rare, and consequently, a reasonably alert team of physicians should, on occasion, see a near-miss of any common form of SIDS (Dawes, 1972).

In 1972 Steinschneider reported five infants with recurrent apnea, two of whom subsequently died of SIDS (the autopsy findings were consistent with that diagnosis). These five crucial observations alone provided more subjects with a disorder hypothesized to cause SIDS than have been found for any other etiology. As we will see, these observations of apnea have been repeated many times, in many centers throughout the country. The infants reported by

Steinschneider had onset of cyanotic episodes at one month of age. They were observed in hospitals to have a number of prolonged apneic and cyanotic episodes, "some requiring vigorous resuscitative efforts." Consistent with the known epidemiology of SIDS, the infants under study had the most severe and prolonged episodes of apnea in conjunction with an upper respiratory infection, and during sleep.

Later that same year, in a well-meaning contretemps, the American Academy of Pediatrics Committee on Infant and the Pre-School Child reasserted in strong terms that "sudden infant death syndrome is a definite entity that cannot be predicted and therefore cannot be prevented" (1972). They argued that child abuse should not be seriously considered in the death of an infant, and the general tenor of the report revealed a preoccupation with psychiatric aspects of surviving parents, rather than a strong advocacy for the infant and child characteristic of pediatricians.

A report of twins, both of whom had a viral respiratory infection, was made by a letter in the JAMA in 1973 (Speer). The first twin was observed to stop breathing by the mother at home, and she rushed the entire family to the hospital, where continued vigorous resuscitative efforts were finally successful. During the resuscitation, the other twin stopped breathing in his grandmother's arms in the waiting room of the hospital. Fortunately, that one responded to relatively simple stimulation. Both twins survived the episode, and Dr. Speer suggested that the sequence of infection and apnea during sleep was instructive as to the etiology of sudden and unexpected death in infancy.

In 1973 Guilleminault and colleagues reported their syndrome of insomnia with sleep apnea in adults. The adult usually did not die of these episodes, but complained of insomnia, and when studied polygraphically in a sleep laboratory was found to have prolonged sleep apnea, which aroused the subject when he became sufficiently hypercarbic and hypoxic. In the Canadian conference on SIDS in 1974, I suggested that the *ability* to arouse from sleep apnea was literally the difference between life and death in infants. We had shown in 1972 (French et al) that quite young infant monkeys failed to commence breathing again after removal of a stimulus that caused primary apnea, such as gentle occlusion of their nares or stimulating a dive reflex with cold water on the face. Of the five infant monkeys originally tested, two failed to resume breathing, whereas they all promptly commenced breathing again when tested at an older age. It seemed to us that the infant might not be alarmed by apnea, since many months of fetal life had been associated with apnea, without disastrous effects. The first six months after birth was seen as the vulnerable period during which the infant, if primary apnea occurred for some reason, might not be alarmed enough to arouse and interrupt the apnea. We found in subsequent studies in monkeys and other species (Guntheroth and Kawabori, 1975) that when apnea persisted sufficiently long for the oxygen content of the blood to reach a low level, the hypoxia would *maintain* the apnea, even though the primary stimulus had been removed. Hypoxic apnea occurs at a PaO_2 of approximately 10 to 15 mmHg. Once this state is reached, associated with marked cyanosis, apnea persists until death, or resuscitation. The situation can be likened to removing a child or an adult who is not breathing from a swimming pool. If they still have circulation, then they are in a state of hypoxic apnea, and the subject must be ventilated for recovery to occur. If drowning, and the implication of resuscitation, were as emotional as SIDS, we might find some centers arguing that, since the subject was resuscitated successfully, and didn't die, that the patient therefore wasn't a near drowning, and that we could learn nothing about drowning from the subject who is successfully revived. In clinical practice, and by common sense, a cyanotic, apneic infant should reasonably be considered at extreme risk of death, and if resuscitated, should be considered a near-miss of SIDS.

At the Canadian meeting I reported our additional findings that the infant monkey was capable of resuscitating himself by gasping. The gasping mechanism is almost universally associated with birth, but its effectiveness in autoresuscitation seems to disappear after only a few weeks in the human, although it may persist in some animals such as rats (Guntheroth and Kawabori, 1975). We proposed that this period of effective gasping in the first month of life accounted for the absence of SIDS in that period, whereas an infant who had previously had such episodes and recovered during the night, might die subsequently when the remarkable anaerobic capability of the neonate had been lost. It seems likely that cardiac glycogen, abundant in the newborn, permits persistence of cardiovascular function during apnea and hypoxia. If the infant died subsequently, the post-mortem findings suggesting prior hypoxia, reported by Naeye, would be expected. We concluded that the evidence in 1974 favored persistent apnea as the cause of crib death, and that this provided "encouragement for the development of apnea monitors and predictors of the infant at risk for crib death" (Guntheroth, 1974). I had personally begun to manage a few near-misses in this manner, more out of sympathy for the parents than from a conviction that we could alter the course in these infants. As a pediatric cardiologist, I occasionally received a referral of an infant having possible cyanotic heart disease, but after a careful work-up, concluded that they had no heart disease, were not cyanotic at rest, and that the event which precipitated the referral was actually an episode of prolonged apnea with cyanosis. Having told the mother and father of our conclusions, the question of recurrence invariably was raised. The answer was unfortunately that there was a substantial risk of it occurring again, judging from Steinschneider's small series. Some parents reacted by not wishing to take their child home but leaving him at the hospital until he was six months old, and at least one family decided to take turns staying up all night with the infant, in the event that apnea recurred. It seemed only humane to provide the families with some kind of assistance at home that would allow them to continue some semblance of normal life, and we began monitoring simply as a means of *reducing* anxiety for the parents. I recommended this as a reasonable principle of management of the near-miss SIDS in 1974. Later we recommended a simple bradycardia alarm system as adequate, with fewer false alarms, and much simpler to operate (Guntheroth, 1977). The emotional subject of monitoring, however, had only begun to heat up. Lewak (1975) reported an infant who had been admitted as a near-miss to the hospital and placed on a monitor. Several apneic episodes did indeed occur, but during the sixth episode the nurse decided that the patient was not blue, and instead responded to an apnea alarm on another baby. When she returned she was unable to resuscitate the subject of the report. At autopsy SIDS was diagnosed. Lewak quoted the American Academy of Pediatrics Committee who stated that same year that "there is no evidence to date that electronic monitoring prevents the sudden infant death syndrome." Lewak concluded that their experience with a single case, with an admittedly delayed response by the nurse, was evidence in favor of the Academy's position. The monitor had prevented death on his infant on five occasions, and a death which appeared preventable by the description published, makes a strong case that SIDS *could* be prevented if diagnosed in time. Similarly, for the Academy (1975) to blame a monitor for anxiety in the management of an infant who very nearly died of apnea, seems so illogical that one must presume that emotion, rather than reason, prevailed in that recommendation against monitoring.

Perhaps the most misleading single collection of information was published as an editorial in *Pediatrics* in 1975 by Bergman, Beckwith, and Ray. They cited their own work as having helped establish SIDS as a "distinct disease entity," and claimed that as the most fruitful dividend from a decade of research. Although three of the characteristics of SIDS they listed are not controversial, neither were they new in the decade preceding their editorial. For the fourth "characteristic" of SIDS, they asserted as a fact that sudden respiratory obstruction was the "mode of death," based on Beckwith's continued assertion that intrathoracic petechiae are uniquely related to respiratory obstruction. They clearly rejected the idea that a near-miss was related to SIDS, and insisted that near-miss SIDS could not be defined, whereas they felt that the post-mortem clearly defined the true SIDS. The fact that the "true SIDS" is defined by the *absence* of lethal pathology did not seem to matter. They attacked home monitoring for prevention of SIDS, and even suggested that monitors might adversely affect apneic episodes. They reported only one case of SIDS out of forty near-misses, a figure at variance with Bergman's earlier report of two out of twenty in the same hospital. They insinuated that the interest in home monitors was a plot for "boundless profits," and attacked "armchair investigators" for press coverage of new theories of the cause of crib death. It is ironic that they frequently had resorted to television to publicize the "unrecognized" problem of SIDS.

Fortunately, one year later, Steinschneider replied point by point in a restrained and factual manner. In his refutation of their assertions he also managed to present a concise summary of the "state of the art" (Steinschneider, 1976).

In 1975 Guilleminault and his co-workers applied their sleep laboratory techniques to infants. They studied fifteen prematures and eight full-term babies who had been brought to the emergency room for apneic episodes. In these latter infants, a thorough examination by the pediatric team failed to discover any major abnormalities, nor an explanation for the apnea. Five of the eight presented with respiratory infection at the time of hospitalization, but these appeared to be minor. They defined apnea as cessation of air exchange lasting ten seconds or longer, as opposed to brief respiratory pauses, with or without periodic breathing. Among the premature infants, apneic episodes were frequently recorded, the longest episodes with quiet sleep, and the apnea was of the central (non-obstructive) type. Frequent brief respiratory pauses were recorded in the prematures, but with rapid eye movement sleep (REM). Of these, two-thirds were central apnea, but 9% occurred with breathing against a closed upper airway, and 23% with "mixed apnea," involving both types. They found that severe bradycardia occurred more quickly with upper airway apnea, but would occur in all forms. They also reported that the oxygen saturation measured by ear oximetry fell more rapidly with the upper airway apnea, presumably reflecting the increased muscular effort of breathing against a closed airway. (They borrowed from their experience with adult sleep apnea to speculate on serious arrhythmias, but there were no instances of ventricular tachycardia in their infant population.)

In 1976, the first of several meticulous studies was published by the group at the Massachusetts General Hospital (Fagenholz et al, 1976). Ten infants with near-miss sudden infant death were compared to normal controls; they found no significant differences in ventilatory responses to 100% oxygen (peripheral chemoreceptor response), nor to 5% carbon dioxide (central chemoreceptor). They concluded that prolonged apnea could occur in infants who had normal central and peripheral chemoreceptor activity. In a more selected group of near-miss SIDS, the same group reported one year later (Shannon et al, 1977) on eleven infants who had at least two episodes requiring resuscitation because of prolonged apnea. This group included three infants who died subsequently at home, and whose autopsy revealed no apparent cause of death, and therefore were diagnosed as sudden infant death syndrome. This group of eleven infants had significant differences from normal controls in their ventilatory behavior, in particular, hypoventilation, defined as a resting alveolar PCO_2 greater than normal, and with a lower ventilatory response to inhaled carbon dioxide. Although they noted that three of the infants had abnormal EEGs following resuscitation, they concluded that the abnormal ventilatory responses were not due to sustained hypoxia from earlier spells of apnea. However, they recognized this as a valid alternate hypothesis to the conclusion that they had reached, that the SIDS victims have an intrinsic defect in ventilation control. Certainly, this defect had *not* been found in their 1976 study.

The Columbia group compared aborted SIDS infants with age-matched controls during various sleep states, studied serially. They found similar minute ventilation in the two groups, but the tidal volume was smaller in the aborted SIDS group, and the rate faster, in both quiet and REM sleep. When 2% CO_2 was given, the near-miss subjects had a somewhat greater increase in tidal volume than controls. They concluded that the aborted SIDS group were not hypoventilating, but actually were in a chronic state of increased sympathoadrenal activity (Haddad et al, 1981).

These studies clearly establish that the near-miss group are heterogeneous, just as the autopsied SIDS appear to be. Even though the averages for certain functions may be statistically different from a normal control group, these functions are not universally abnormal in near-miss SIDS.

Thoman et al (1977) emphasized that *all* babies have sleep apnea in early life, based on a study of twenty-three normal, full-term infants. Unfortunately, they defined apnea as a period of two seconds or longer which will assure frequent occurrences of "apnea" during REM sleep, which is characteristically associated with irregular respirations. One of their infants subsequently died unexpectedly and at autopsy was diagnosed as an instance of SIDS. On review of his sleep recordings, they found the only difference was that this infant had actually fewer episodes of apnea during the recording, and his overall respiratory rates during sleep were significantly more rapid than other normal infants. A second infant with similar findings was placed on an apnea monitor at home, because of the earlier SIDS experience, and at five months of age developed a series of prolonged apneic episodes of greater than twenty seconds during quiet sleep. The infant survived these episodes and is reported as normal. They speculated that brief apneic episodes are normal, and that their absence in a maturing infant deprives them of maturation of respiratory control mechanisms. In any case, their data shows a lack of direct correlation between brief respiratory pauses of two to four seconds and prolonged apnea.

Stein and colleagues (1979) found direct correlations between apnea duration and frequency of apneic episodes, in one hundred twenty-nine long-term recordings of forty-six full-term infants at home. They found no normal infants experienced apnea greater than fifteen seconds duration at forty weeks post-conception, or eleven seconds at fifty-two weeks post-conception. These definitions of "normal" sleep apnea seem more consistent with findings of other laboratories than the relatively unique findings of Thoman et al (1977).

In a review article, I criticized the stand of the American Academy of Pediatrics on monitoring, reasoning that anxiety in parents was intense after an episode of near-miss, and that an apnea monitor at home was a reasonable compromise between keeping an infant in the hospital until six months of age, or sending the infant home with only prayer for protection (Guntheroth, 1977). The Academy magnanimously invited me to serve on a committee to discuss the situation. The Task Force on Prolonged Apnea (1978), in a careful concensus, addressed the subject of prolonged apnea, without agreeing to call it near-miss SIDS, but did clearly indicate that some of the infants with prolonged apnea had subsequently succumbed to SIDS. The Task Force defined prolonged apnea as twenty seconds or longer, associated with bradycardia, cyanosis, or pallor. We urged the consideration by the physician of underlying disorders such as "seizures, severe infection, significant anemia (especially in premature infants), gastroesophageal reflux, hypoglycemia, and other metabolic disorders, and impaired regulation of breathing." Although not discussed in the report, this list of disorders is instructive in relation to SIDS, diagnosed at autopsy. Except for a bacterial infection, none of these disorders could be diagnosed at autopsy if the initial episode had occurred without observation, and the child had died. In other words, these clear-cut disorders would simply have produced no lethal post-mortem changes, in spite of producing lethal functional disorders. This leads to the inevitable conclusion that post-mortem SIDS includes a broader range of disorders than does near-miss of SIDS, when these specific disorders may be investigated in a surviving infant. I have no doubt that both SIDS and near-miss SIDS are heterogenous, but it seems disingenuous to pretend that the autopsy SIDS is a simple, single entity, and that the near-miss syndrome is less defined. The opportunity to examine the near-miss patient immediately offers the opportunity to diagnose these functional disorders, and to learn more about the pathophysiology. The concensus of the AAP group, without endorsing monitors, was a major advance in accepting the home monitor as a reasonable form of medical management. The panel also agreed that a family confronted with an infant with prolonged apnea would be subjected to significant stress, "whether or not monitors are included in the management plan."

Gastroesophageal reflux (GER) is a particularly interesting and hopeful subset of patients who have prolonged apnea with bradycardia. Herbst et al (1978) reported fourteen infants with apnea and cyanosis, requiring resuscitation. Only five of the infants had a history of vomiting, although several more had a history of "wet burps." Eleven of the infants had mild x-ray changes suggesting aspiration pneumonitis. The GER was documented by barium eosphagogram, and thirteen were documented by studying the motility and pH of the esophagus. (The last patient was not studied because of very severe and frequent apneic episodes.) One of the patients, treated successfully for some time with positional therapy (head up), was subsequently found dead and diagnosed as SIDS at autopsy, after the parents discontinued the therapy against medical advice. The GER patients with prolonged apnea may have a better chance of surviving the episodes of apnea by virtue of being awake, at the time, and are therefore more likely to be observed by a parent, and therefore of being resuscitated and being brought to medical attention.

Additional centers, with different populations of patients, have reported respiratory abnormalities in patients with prolonged apnea. Brady et al (1978) found that five patients with aborted SIDS, when exposed to 17% inhaled oxygen, developed an increase in periodic breathing and an increase in the number and the duration of respiratory pauses. They concluded that these babies had a unique respiratory response to mild hypoxia. In the discussion, they commented on a previous infant studied in their laboratory who subsequently had died of SIDS, who had been studied repeatedly with carbon dioxide stimulus. On three occasions they found the infant unresponsive to carbon dioxide stimulation, but on five occasions the response was quite normal, indicating that the lack of sensitivity was intermittent. This suggestion is borne out also by the report by Guilleminault and Ariagno (1978) who found only 7% of infants referred to them for aborted crib death had second episodes requiring resuscitation. On the other extreme, one of the infants on whom they performed a twenty-four-hour sleep study died within twenty-four hours of the monitoring. The experience of the Massachusetts General group (Kelly et al, 1978) appears to be with infants with substantially more grave conditions. Out of eighty-four infants that had been monitored to that time (mid-1977), 27 infants had subsequent episodes of apnea that required resuscitation, using bag and mask. Seventeen infants required more than one resuscitation at home, and although the resuscitation had been successful in all at least one time, four of them subsequently died, diagnosed as SIDS at autopsy. Of particular interest in terms of our subsequent discussion of cardiovascular versus respiratory theories of the cause of death, Kelley et al reported that *none* of the successfully resuscitated infants required cardiac massage or defibrillation.

Another center reported sleep studies on near-miss SIDS (Cornwell et al, 1978). Although they did not report the numbers involved, they found many episodes of sleep apnea in their near-miss babies of ten seconds or longer, and found that the duration of these episodes was longer than in controls of the same age. The controls had frequent respiratory pauses of less than ten seconds, particularly during rapid eye movement sleep. In addition, they observed the same phenomenon reported by Steinschneider—that a respiratory infection substantially increased the chances of a near-miss event.

Guilleminault et al (1979) reported on twenty-nine full-term infants who had experienced a near-miss for SIDS, compared to thirty normal infants. The only significant difference in the two groups was the number of mixed and obstructive apneas of greater than three seconds duration. Obstructive apnea was defined in their polygraphic studies by continued respiratory effort, without air exchange, judged either by independent airflow transducers, or by an esophageal pressure transducer. Mixed apnea is a combination of central apnea, with no respiratory movement, and obstructive apnea, in sequence. In contrast to other studies, they did not find a significantly increased frequency of longer lasting sleep apnea, of ten seconds or greater. The difference in these studies may reflect the fact that Guilleminault's patients included many infants who did not have repeated attacks, whereas Kelly and Shannon selected patients who had two or more episodes of severe apnea. Guilleminault found no increase in periodic breathing, but Kelly and Shannon (1979) found excessive amounts of periodic breathing in infants with near-miss of SIDS.

Guilleminault and Korobkin (1979) reported the concensus of a group of investigators who were involved in studying the near-miss group. We agreed that for full-term infants, the limit of normal duration for apnea was fifteen seconds between one and six months of age, but for premature infants, up to twenty seconds was not exceptional. The group agreed upon key items of history, including maternal health, and developed a minimal work-up for the near-miss infant. We will return to those recommendations in a later chapter.

A new approach to the study of near-miss SIDS was the recording of brainstem auditory evoked potentials (BAEP) by Orlowski et al (1979). They found abnormal responses in the near-miss infant, compared to normal controls. This report was of particular interest because the recordings include potentials generated by the eighth nerve, which is in the vicinity of the brainstem thought to be responsible for ventilatory control. This also is the area of astroglial proliferation found by Naeye (1976), and the area found to have abnormal dendritic spines in the victims of SIDS (Quattrochi et al, 1980). However, in July of 1981, *Science* reported that two other centers have been unable to reproduce the results of Orlowski (Marx, 1981). Stockard at San Diego found no significant irregularities in the BAEPs in any of seven near-miss SIDS infants; one of these infants subsequently died of SIDS. Other investigators at the New York Academy meeting also reported that they were unable to find abnormal BAEPs in a total of nine near-miss SIDS babies (Dorfman and Guilleminault). In rebuttal, Orlowski reported that they have studied a total of eighty near-miss SIDS infants and one hundred normal infants and asserted that they can distinguish between the normal and abnormal in 80 to 85% of the cases. One of the obvious possibilities, suggested by Stockard, was that the BAEP changes are simply secondary to oxygen deprivation following a long apneic episode, rather than a primary brainstem disorder. This possibility has been discussed earlier, and seems to be a very reasonable possibility—and in my opinion, a probability, along with some of the abnormal ventilatory responses. The differences between centers could reflect differences in severity of injury in their population of near-misses.

Other types of studies of the population of near-miss SIDS include heart rate, and heart rate variability during sleep (Leistner et al, 1980). They found that the Q-T interval was actually smaller in the aborted SIDS group than in normal infants, and that they had a faster heart rate than the control, and a smaller overall heart rate variability. They suggested that these changes in cardiovascular parameters reflected an increased sympathetic activity, or perhaps circulating catecholamines. In the light of that hypothesis, it is useful to reconsider the results of respiratory studies (Hoppenbrouwers et al, 1980) and of heart rate (Harper et al, 1978). They studied a group of patients which they labeled as "at risk for sudden infant death syndrome" that are in fact subsequent siblings of the victims of SIDS. There are adequate studies showing that SIDS has no convincing pattern of inheritance, and therefore, any increase in risk in subsequent siblings represents an environmental factor rather than a genetic one. Although the risk of SIDS in this group of subsequent siblings is four to six times that of the normal population, it is important to bear in mind that the rate would be only eight to eighteen per thousand of normal births, which is approximately 1 to 2% chance of finding a single subject who was truly at risk for SIDS in a study of these subsequent sibs of SIDS. It seems an exaggeration to call this population a group "at risk for SIDS." In any event, this group of subsequent sibs were found to have a higher heart rate than the control group in the first few months, and the heart rate variability was less than with the normals for the same age group. These results suggest the very real possibility that these infants also have increased sympathetic activity, perhaps reflecting maternal anxiety, or other subtle influences of the environment or the mothering.

Southall et al (1980) provided some useful normative data on heart rate and respiration and their interaction, with home recordings, in an attempt to obtain rates in conditions less disrupted, and presumably less stressful than in hospitals. In fifty normal term infants, they found that 58% had apneic episodes of ten seconds or more, and that the 95th percentile for the maximum duration of apnea was eighteen seconds. They observed episodes of bradycardia (less than one hundred per min) in 17% of episodes of apnea of ten to fourteen seconds, but they found bradycardia in all four episodes of fifteen to nineteen seconds, and in both episodes greater than twenty seconds duration. The arrhythmias observed during these recordings were junctional (nodal) escape rhythms (28%), and 10% had supraventricular beats and 4% had ventricular premature beats. These authors also studied, with the same technique, five near-miss cot death infants, in hospital, and found that three of them showed prolonged apnea (greater than forty seconds) or extreme bradycardia of less than fifty per minute, or both. They also studied eleven infants who were selected because of arrhythmias on standard electrocardiograms. Two of these eleven demonstrated bradycardia with associated apnea of ten to fourteen seconds duration, which is within the limits of normal apnea for that age. Of the eleven infants, nine did not demonstrate apnea during the arrhythmias, suggesting that arrhythmias are not the initial disorder leading to prolonged apnea and SIDS. There are of course many physiological phenomena that are present in the normal infant that will produce transient bradycardia, such as bowel movements, burping, and as has been discussed, gastroesophageal reflux. Southall et al speculated that hypoxic brain damage may be associated with subsequent attacks of apnea and bradycardia, in both infants and adults (Theorell, 1974; North and Jennett, 1972).

Very recently, additional abnormalities have been confirmed in at least some of the near-miss SIDS infants (Hunt et al, 1981). They studied thirty-six near-miss infants and twenty-three control infants, and found that the near-miss group as a whole had a significantly smaller increase in ventilation in response to hypoxia, as well as to hypercarbia. They emphasized that the overlap between normal and the near-miss SIDS was substantial and that this would prevent prediction based on their ventilatory responses, in spite of the statistically significant differences between the means.

An additional observation of potentially great significance is that they were unable to achieve comparably low alveolar oxygen levels in control infants, as could be obtained in the near-miss SIDS infants because the normal infants would awaken at PAO_2 levels of 80 Torr. They found that their near-miss SIDS group demonstrated decreased frequency of arousal from both hypercarbia and hypoxia, compared to control infants (Hunt, 1981). They cited other studies in adults showing a positive correlation between changes in hypercarbic and hypoxic ventilatory drive (Hirshman et al, 1975). We also have been impressed with the difficulties of arousal, leading to uninterrupted apnea in newborn monkeys (French et al, 1972; Guntheroth, 1974). In the infant monkey, it did not appear to matter whether the dive reflex, or simply occlusion of the nares, initiated the apnea, in terms of the persistence of the apnea, once begun. Several types of reflexes that can produce apnea have been described. Whether the primary apnea is induced by gastro-esophageal reflux, central apnea, or obstructive apnea seems less crucial than the maturing of the central nervous system, manifested by arousal, avoiding hypoxic deterioration into hypoxic apnea and possible death.

By simply counting all of the near-miss SIDS that have been recorded in major journals up through 1981, there have been over four hundred instances. All of these have involved prolonged apnea, frequently with cyanosis, and invariably with bradycardia, and to the observer appeared to be irreversible unless intervention was undertaken. There are no comparable reports of infants in the age group of one to six months that were resuscitated from a serious arrhythmia. Although, as we have just discussed, there is no necessarily unique form of the primary apnea leading to these prolonged and life-threatening apneas, the evidence seems overwhelming that the final common pathway in SIDS or near-miss SIDS is apnea. Of the patients counted in these four hundred near-misses, at least thirteen of them subsequently died and were shown at autopsy to have SIDS. The percentage is only 3.2%, or 32 per thousand, but this number should be compared with the rate in the normal population of only two per thousand for SIDS. This sixteenfold increase is even more significant if one recalls that many of these near-misses have been managed intensively with apnea monitors in hospital and at home, and as is evident in the reports from Shannon and Kelly, many of them had repeated episodes requiring resuscitation which otherwise would have resulted in a much higher mortality rate. Our work with hypoxic apnea (Guntheroth and Kawabori, 1975) demonstrated that profound hypoxia with prolonged apnea was a lethal situation in the older child or adult, reversible by external resuscitation, or by gasping in the first three or four weeks of life. The four hundred near-misses then could reasonably be expected to have died without the resuscitation, providing overwhelming evidence of a link between near-miss and SIDS. To deny that apnea monitoring in the presence of personnel trained for pulmonary resuscitation does not prevent death is as foolish as denying that there is any point in artificial respiration in a drowning. Since there are only two lethal pathways, apnea or a lethal arrhythmia, there appears to be only one degree of freedom in assigning these lethal pathways. Assuredly, an occasional failure of resuscitation for apnea detected by a monitor, whether in hospital or at home, cannot be seriously suggested as a reason for not monitoring or not resuscitating these infants. Only a controlled study for near-miss infants, with random assignments into "no monitoring" and "monitoring" would finally settle the issue, but I suspect that very few parents would agree to such management at this time, and considering the pathophysiology of hypoxic depression of ventilation, the experiment would probably be unethical. To assert that there is no absolute proof of the relationship between SIDS and prolonged apnea is one thing, but to use that as a basis for arguing against reasonable medical management of prolonged apnea is quite another. Fortunately, the parent groups for SIDS, the National Foundation for Sudden Infant

Death Syndrome, and the Guild for Infant Survival are involved at present in home monitors and assisting in the management of these children. It seems hypocritical to continue to contend that SIDS is not preventable, in those instances where the near-miss episode allows the parents and physician a "second chance."

Although we would concur that admission of ignorance is necessary before progress can be made, this admission should start with the admission of the limitations of autopsy in explaining disease processes that leave no lethal post-mortem changes. The post-mortem group of SIDS is actually more of a waste basket than the near-miss group since the function of a live infant can be measured in many respects, and not at all after death.

Chapter V

Theories of Cardiovascular Causes of SIDS

Biological death requires the cessation of circulation by definition. The prior cessation of breathing is, even in adults, a frequent occurrence, and with the use of relatively simple mechanical ventilators, a patient can be maintained in a state of biological life without spontaneous respiration. (We are not involved here with the question of meaningful life, for which most medical authorities would require cerebral activity, documented by the electroencephalogram). For the purposes of assigning a mechanism of death to the syndrome of sudden infant death, it is important to consider the two vital functions, respiration and circulation, separately, and with particular emphasis on the initiating or primary event. If apnea occurs intially, after a period of increasing cyanosis and hypoxia, the cardiovascular system will also cease to function after only a minute or two, with the terminal event being cardiac arrest (or ventricular fibrillation followed by arrest). In this chapter, our concern will be whether arrhythmias are a *primary* disorder in SIDS, and terminal arrhythmias will not be further considered.

Some other general considerations relative to primary disorders of rhythm as a cause of sudden infant death, include the admission that a lethal disorder of heart rhythm, without unobserved pathology, in the age range of one to six months, would be classified at autopsy as sudden infant death. Straight-forward genetic disorders such as the Romano-Ward syndrome (the long Q-T syndrome) would be diagnosed at autopsy as SIDS, if the victim died in the first six months of life, and had not previously had an electro-cardiographic diagnosis of long Q-T syndrome. The more important question at this point is, how often does this syndrome explain sudden infant death, either as the genetic disorder, or as a vulnerability produced by asymmetric development of the sympathetic nerves to the heart of the infant?

A second question that must be asked of reports of pathology in the conduction system of the heart suggested as possible causes of sudden infant death: Were the pathologic changes coincidental, agonal, or truly significant? Were the same findings present in the control population, at the same frequency? Did the pathologist who reviewed the cases know in advance of the diagnosis? And, paradoxically, if there was significant pathology present in the victim, it is axiomatic that the final diagnosis could not then be sudden infant death.

It is also worth recalling that the cardiovascular system is remarkably robust in infants, even when disease is present. In the first three or four weeks of life, and particularly in the fetus and in the newborn, the ability of the cardio-vascular system to perform in an hypoxic state is astounding. The arterial PO_2 for the coronary artery in the fetus is necessarily the same as in the ascending aorta, which averages 25 to 28 mmHg. Presumably because of this hypoxemia, glycogen stores are very well developed in the fetal heart, and permit an optimal chance for autoresuscitation of the newborn. The ability of the newborn animal, including the human infant, to withstand prolonged periods of hypoxia are legendary. In our study of fetal monkeys delivered by Caesarian section (Guntheroth and Kawabori, 1975), an effective cardiac output and blood pressure were maintained for over thirty minutes of breathing 100% nitrogen, whereas adult animals lost effective circulation and blood pressure after only one to five minutes. At that point, the adult animal could not be resuscitated even if oxygen and mechanical ventilation were supplied. The ability to tolerate tachyrhythmias can also be found in the cardiology literature in children. It has been known for many years that paroxysmal atrial tachycardia in children will not usually produce congestive failure unless the tachycardia has been present for twelve to twenty-four hours. Even then death is rare, and the presence of congestive failure is abundantly clear, clinically, and at autopsy. Ventricular tachycardia, an emergent problem in the adult because of rapid deterioration into ventricular fibrillation, is not nearly so emergent a problem in the pediatric age group. We have reported our experience with five pediatric cases of ventricular tachycardia who were successfully treated over the years with quinidine, without abolishing the arrhythmia, but simply slowing it to a rate that could be tolerated without congestive failure (Bergdahl et al, 1980). Again, as with paroxysmal atrial tachycardia, ventricular tachycardia in infants does not behave in a catastrophic, sudden manner that is required by the definition of SIDS, an infant with no serious illness. Assuredly, congestive failure with tachypnea, in addition to the tachycardia, grunting respirations, pallor, and cold perspiration are obvious to most mothers. At the other extreme of rate, complete heart block (third degree A-V block) with a heart rate of less than one-half of the normal commonly permits normal growth and activity during infancy and childhood, and neither syncope nor congestive failure are likely, without some additional cardiovascular lesion. The ability of the heart to improve its stroke volume, thereby maintaining a relatively normal resting cardiac output in the face of a slow rate, has been well-documented for many years. The excellent compliance of the young blood vessels assist in absorbing the large stroke volume, releasing it gradually in diastole permitting remarkably normal activities in healthy children with heart block. This ability of infants to tolerate bradycardia cannot be ignored by proponents of bradycardia as an explanation of disaster in infants or children.

For the sake of completeness and order, we will consider

in this chapter some conditions which have been implicated in sudden death of adults, and in some cases in infants, that are cardiovascular in origin, and then discuss in detail the evidence for and against their role in SIDS.

Cardiovascular Disorders

Adelson (1953) described the frustration of the pathologist over an occasional adult or younger person who had no anatomic explanation for death, who nevertheless had suffered "instantaneous physiologic death" (Weiss, 1940). Adelson concluded that this form of instantaneous death was almost always cardiac in origin, and speculated that it was "reflex vago-cardiac, or reflex systemic dilatation with a profound fall in blood pressure, or a combination of these two mechanisms." In point of fact, systemic vasodilatation with bradycardia is characteristic of ordinary fainting, and it is a common and non-lethal problem in an otherwise healthy subject. On the other hand, any individual with borderline cerebral or coronary perfusion secondary to atherosclerosis might well suffer a fatal outcome of simple fainting, since the hypotension is quite real, even though physiologically induced. As Soma Weiss emphasized, "the essential difference . . . lies in the ability of the patient to reestablish normal equilibrium."

Pulmonary embolism is a vascular disorder that is quite capable of producing sudden death in the adult, through marked increases in pulmonary vascular resistances, and acute right heart failure. It also seems likely that there are some reflex mechanisms involved, since some sudden deaths with this disorder have disproportionately mild abnormalities at autopsy. Since this disorder can easily be diagnosed at autopsy, it will not be considered further here, except to rule it out as even a rare cause of SIDS.

In contrast to the vasovagal disorders, shock is produced by inadequate cardiac output causing hypotension, in spite of tachycardia and some degree of vasoconstriction. In relation to SIDS, most causes of shock are obvious at autopsy, such as occult blood loss into the gastrointestinal tract; overwhelming bacteremia with shock is diagnosed by post-mortem culture.

Cor pulmonale can be either acute or chronic. We have presented the post-mortem evidence by Naeye of increased musculature of the pulmonary arterioles, and increased weight of the right ventricle in many of the victims of SIDS. However, these changes indicate moderate increase in pulmonary vascular resistance, with secondary increase in right ventricular pressure and are not the same as cor pulmonale, which would require dilatation of the right heart, hepatic congestion, and edema (in short, right heart failure). Cor pulmonale is not a feature of SIDS. The absence of cor pulmonale is partly attributable to the fact that the infant is born with very high pulmonary vascular resistance. In fetal life, the resistance to blood flow through the pulmonary circuit is actually greater than systemic vascular resistance, permitting bypass of most of the output of the right heart into the patent ductus and down the descending aorta. With the first breath containing oxygen, the neonate lowers the pulmonary vascular resistance markedly, but it is still quite high, relative to the adult standard, and requires several weeks to fall to normal levels. During that period, the anatomic markers are still present, increased muscle mass in the pulmonary arteriole. When moderate hypoxia occurs, the increase in pulmonary vascular resistance then is only relative, and there is not usually a marked change in the right ventricular pressure load.

A vague term, "cardiopulmonary failure" was introduced by Baker and McGinty (1977) in describing kittens during sleep, in their animal model of sudden infant death. The cardiac component of "failure" was: (1) a "depressed heart rate," and (2) "cardiac arrhythmia with ectopic beats." Accordingly, the problem is an arrhythmia, and will be discussed under those headings. Briefly, however, a depressed heart rate is bradycardia, which, with vasoconstriction, is part of the dive reflex or oxygen-conserving reflex. The "arrhythmia" presented in their illustration was an artifact (Guntheroth, 1979).

Bradycardia and Arrhythmias

In an experimental animal, stimulation of the vagus nerve produces an immediate slowing of the sinus node, and frequently, a partial block in the conduction between atrium and ventricle. If the stimulus is maintained, and the stimulus is strong enough, it is possible to produce permanent cardiac arrest (Adelson, 1953). Usually, however, vagal escape occurs, with establishment of a pacemaker in the lower part of the A-V node, now fashionably called A-V junctional rhythm. The lower pacemaker has an intrinsically lower rate than the sinus node ordinarily would have; the existence of this pacemaker in the His bundle greatly reduces the possibility of a lethal outcome from an otherwise benign reflex. Although bradycardia has been suggested as a precursor of death, even a primary event (Allen et al, 1954), a careful review of that report suggests that their patients had what is more recently considered gastroesophageal reflux (GER) producing apnea, with *secondary* bradycardia. They reported success with the use of atropine, and assuredly, atropine will block the bradycardia (French et al, 1972), but the survival of this patient had more to do with the improvement of his GER and apnea than from the blockade of the bradycardia; the presenting complaints of the infants were apnea and cyanosis. The secondary nature of bradycardia following apnea was documented in prematures by Daily et al in 1969. They found that if apnea persisted for thirty seconds or more that bradycardia was inevitably present. Earlier, we had reported in two papers (Morgan et al, 1965; Church et al, 1967) a high prevalence of bradycardia in prematures, compared to full-term infants. In the second

paper we speculated that the bradycardia seen in the premature infant, shown to have a greater susceptibility to sudden
infant death, might indicate some form of instability of cardiovascular control. At the time, our recordings were solely
of the electrocardiogram, and lacked any means of recording
respiration, which would have provided the missing data
that was documented by Daily. In our observations of the
premature, we found sudden-onset sinus bradycardia in
twenty-seven of thirty infants. The bradycardia resulted in
nodal escape in eighteen of the twenty-seven. At various
times, we also noted the presence in four infants of atrial or
ventricular premature contractions, or both, and in one,
varying A-V block. All of the thirty infants survived the first
six months of life, and their arrhythmias proved to be of no
prognostic significance, and the frequency of the arrhythmias diminished as the infants became older. Although
these infants all survived, the overall prevalence of SIDS in
the graduates of the premature nursery at that time was four
in two hundred prematures of birth weight or less than 1500
grams, or 2%. That was approximately ten times the rate of
SIDS in the King County area at that time. A point worth
emphasizing was the observation in our prematures that
other physiological stimuli were capable of producing the
bradycardia, in addition to apnea. In particular, we noted
that events relating to the gastrointestinal tract seemed to
produce these vagal episodes, so that apnea was not always
present when bradycardia was present.

In 1970, Ingman et al confirmed that apnea of over ten
seconds duration, or even hypoventilation without apnea,
preceded bradycardia in the premature infant 80% of the
time. In four infants they used atropine, which simply
delayed the bradycardia but did nothing for the apnea, except to make it more difficult to detect with cardiotachometer
monitoring. We had shown in our study of infant monkeys
in 1972 (French et al) that the oxygen-conserving reflex was
comprised of both bradycardia and vasoconstriction; the effect of the latter on the blood pressure was disguised by the

former, and only when atropine was administered did the hypertension develop, since the bradycardia was blocked; the combination of a normal heart rate with vasoconstriction produced increased blood pressure. After a disappointing experience at home with respiratory monitors, and a very satisfactory experience with bradycardia monitors, we proposed that a cardiac monitor was actually superior for apnea monitoring (Guntheroth, 1977) because both upper airway apnea and central apnea would produce bradycardia, and the cardiac monitor was substantially cheaper, simpler and more portable.

The presence of bradycardia in infants and the histology of the conduction system of the heart suggested to some that slowed conduction and bradycardia might be involved as a primary mechanism in sudden infant death. Thomas James reviewed the conduction system of a number of victims of SIDS (1968) and found that "an unusual histologic process involved the A-V node and His bundle" although the same changes were found in control infants who died of other causes rather than SIDS, in the same age group. He suggested that the remodeling process might create a vulnerability to lethal cardiac arrhythmias, triggered by more or less innocuous occurrences such as premature contractions. Valdes-Dapena et al (1973) reviewed the conduction system in forty-seven infants, without knowledge of the cause of death. Their interpretation of the histology was somewhat different, although both groups found no significant differences between the SIDS victims and their control subjects. However, Valdes-Dapena and her co-workers disagreed that there was any ground for suspecting a fatal function on the basis of their inspection of the conduction system.

Ferris, a British pathologist, has persisted in his implication of the conduction system in SIDS. In 1973 he serially sectioned fifty hearts from SIDS, and in eleven cases found petechial hemorrhages in the region of the sinus node and some of the inter-nodal connecting tracts. Unfortunately, there were no controls, and in any case, the essential role of inter-nodal tracts is debatable. In the families with sick sinus syndrome, a condition that may have a familial distribution (Guntheroth and Motulsky, 1981), death in infancy is rare, and in fact has not been reported. The symptomatic children with sick sinus syndrome are usually the ones with the "tachy-brady" syndrome, in whom an ectopic atrial tachycardia will cause suppression of lower centers, so that on termination of the tachycardia, no nodal escape occurs, and syncope or death may result. Simple bradycardia, seen in most of the children with sick sinus syndrome, is rarely symptomatic, does not require therapy, and is not life-threatening.

A second study (Kendeel and Ferris, 1975) found fibrosis in the conducting tissue of the heart in both SIDS and in a control group in "almost every case." They reported an increase in the fibrous tissue with age in both groups, but "more fibrosis" in the SIDS group than in the controls. The increase with age does not correlate with the age distribution of SIDS, and the findings have not been substantiated by other groups (Anderson et al, 1974; Lie et al, 1976). Froggatt, with James (1973), defended the arrhythmia theory of the cause of SIDS, but admitted that the remodeling process was orderly, and "there is no associated inflammation, hemorrhage, or massive necrosis. Such orderly cell death is not unusual in morphogenesis: it accompanies digit formation and without it, for example, all babies would have imperforate ani." In spite of these negative studies, James (1976) argued that there still could be functional disturbances in the A-V conduction that could cause SIDS even if the histologic studies showed no significant differences between SIDS and a control group. This is an argument difficult to refute, and will emerge again later related to the subject of the long Q-T syndrome. It can be said without contradiction that *if* an arrhythmia occurred during sleep, and it was immediately fatal, that the infant might indeed be diagnosed as SIDS at autopsy. The question is whether this occurs as a frequent problem and is a major cause of SIDS.

Considering the number of near-miss infants who have been studied by this time, and the rarity of arrhythmias of any sort except for those associated with the oxygen-conserving reflex, there seems little chance that conduction abnormalities play an important role in SIDS.

The British group at Brompton Hospital equipped with a two-channel recorder similar to the Holter, have issued a series of papers (Southall et al, 1976, 1977; Keeton et al, 1977; Southall et al, 1980) suggesting that there are many more occult arrhythmias in this age group than are diagnosed with conventional electrocardiography, and that they may well play a major role in SIDS. The first point agrees with our own recordings ten years earlier (Morgan et al, 1965; Church et al, 1967). As to the second point, they found fifty-seven babies out of eight hundred eighteen newborns who had records that fell outside of the "accepted normal range." Two of the infants died suddenly, one of whom had an abnormal conduction system at post-mortem, and had abnormal conduction on the electrocardiogram. They concluded that this may indicate a link between "conducting tissue abnormalities and the sudden infant death syndrome." In the second paper (Southall et al, 1977), they reported on two thousand newborn infants studied, and found thirty-five with arrhythmias or conduction abnormalities. From 24-hour ECG monitoring they asserted that serious tachyrhythmias such as ventricular tachycardia and slow heart rates could be present without clinical disturbance. They again asserted, "the alarming ECG appearance of some of the arrhythmias suggested a possible etiological link with some unexpected sudden infant deaths." An alternate conclusion would be that the arrhythmias were benign since they had caused no clinical disturbance. This group extended their argument for ECG screening of infants (Keeton et al, 1977) in a report of six infants with cardiac conduction disorders "that *might* have been fatal if diagnosis and treatment had been delayed" (emphasis added). The most serious case was an infant with retardation after an episode of cerebral hypoxia that was "associated" with an arrhythmia related to Wolff-Parkinson-White syndrome. In general, W-P-W is ordinarily benign unless it produces paroxysmal atrial tachycardia, which rarely produces symptoms except after several hours. In 1980, Southall and his colleagues reported 24-hour tape recordings of ECG and respiration, with some useful normative data. In fifty healthy term infants they found 28% had junctional escape rhythms, five had supraventricular, and two ventricular premature beats. Sixty-eight percent had apneic episodes equal to or greater than ten seconds duration with the 95th percentile for duration of apnea at eighteen seconds in this group of normal youngsters. Episodes of bradycardia were associated with fifty of two hundred eighty-eight episodes of apnea of ten to fourteen seconds duration, and with all episodes greater than fifteen seconds duration. They also studied five near-miss cot death infants, three of whom had prolonged apneic episodes of greater than forty seconds, and extreme bradycardia (less than fifty beats per minute). Of particular interest was a final group of eleven infants with arrhythmias studied on the basis of a screening ECG revealing an arrhythmia. Most of them had no episodes of apnea with their arrhythmias, although two of the five babies had bradycardia following apnea, but the apnea was well within the duration of normal, defined by this group. If one reviews their statements carefully, they did not really claim an important role for arrhythmias in SIDS, and in the final paper, warned that the bradycardia and apnea in near-miss infants could indicate prior hypoxic brain injury.

Two additional studies of arrhythmias failed to show any substantial role for arrhythmias as the cause of SIDS. Montague (1980) used 24- and 48-hour continuous monitoring of the electrocardiogram in nine near-miss SIDS. All of these subjects required actual resuscitation from episodes that otherwise were judged would have caused SIDS. None of them had excessive bradycardia without apnea, and all had normal Q-T intervals. One extraordinary infant in their series had been treated with a demand pacemaker because of an earlier episode of marked sinus bradycardia at four weeks of age. This infant had a second near-miss episode at six weeks, and at eight weeks was found dead; an autopsy diagnosis of SIDS was made, and the electronic pacemaker was functioning normally.

Another survey of one thousand normal neonates consecutively born was reported by Jones and his co-workers in 1979. From the conventional electrocardiogram, approximately 5% had a disturbance of cardiac rhythm or conduction. Twenty-five babies were screened with continuous 24-hour monitoring, who had abnormalities on the screening ECG, and twenty-five additional babies without such abnormalities. They concluded that the Holter monitoring did not produce substantial additional information and questioned the cost-effectiveness of the recommendation by the Brompton group of this type of screening. They also raised the question of the clinical significance of many of these neonatal arrhythmias and conduction disorders, and questioned their relationship to SIDS.

Arrhythmias Associated with Sleep Apnea

The brilliant work by Guilleminault and Dement, with the Stanford Sleep group, will be discussed in further detail under apnea. However, their experience with adults led to speculation that arrhythmias evoked by sleep apnea might produce a fatal outcome, prior to arousal. Some of these arrhythmias were indeed spectacular, including sinus bradycardia of less than thirty beats per minute, asystole of up to six seconds, second degree A-V block, and ventricular tachycardia in two patients (Tilkian et al, 1977). While awake, these adults had only occasional ventricular premature contractions in six of the fifteen subjects. They noted that "atropine was partially effective, and tracheostomy was highly effective in preventing the majority of these arrhythmias during sleep." They speculated that these arrhythmias also might be present in infants and cause SIDS, but they presented no data to substantiate that prediction. As we mentioned earlier in this chapter, Baker and McGinty (1977) asserted that they found serious arrhythmias in their kittens during sleep apnea, but in the published figure in *Science* in 1977, as well as in the Canadian publication *SIDS 1974*, the "arrhythmias" are artifacts (Guntheroth, 1979).

One study comparing near-miss and control infants for heart rate and rhythm found that near-miss infants actually had less variability of heart rate in both REM and non-REM sleep (Leistner et al, 1980). Also, their overall heart rates were faster, and their Q-T intervals, corrected for rate, were shorter than the normal infant. They speculated that this might result from increased sympathetic activity, in some way reflecting the stress of the original near-miss episode, or a behavioral adjustment induced by maternal anxiety, etc. These findings may explain the study by Harper et al (1978) of subsequent siblings of SIDS. This group also showed a higher heart rate at three months of age, compared to normal controls. It is easy to imagine that the mothers of these subsequent sibs would have a high level of anxiety concerning these infants, just as the mothers of survivors of a near-miss episode would have.

The Long Q-T Syndrome

It is understandable that a disorder capable of causing sudden death in adults and children and that leaves no consistent lethal autopsy findings would be suspected of causing sudden infant death. In the adult world, this syndrome was initially regarded as an example of voodoo-like death secondary to extreme emotional stress acting on a normal heart. Jervell and Lange-Nielsen (1957) reported a syndrome of profound deafness and syncopal attacks in families with a recessive pattern of inheritance. The only cardiovascular abnormality was a prolongation of the Q-T interval on ECG. The Q-T interval represents the duration of depolarization of the average population of myocardial cells. Although this interval can be prolonged in many disorders of the heart, the finding of a prolonged Q-T interval in a subject who has an otherwise normal heart is unusual, when compared with standards of normal, corrected for heart rate (Park and Guntheroth, 1981). Correction for rate can be performed by dividing the Q-T interval by the square root of the interval between heart beats, the R-R interval. This value, the QTc, should be less than .425 in older children and adults, but for the infant, the values may be substantially higher. Walsh (1963) found a mean of .40, but a maximum of .49 in a population of otherwise normal infants during the first week. The value had dropped to .38 average by three months, with a maximum of .45, and in the age range of six months to one year, the average was .40, with a maximum of .44. Zeigler (1951) found, for the age group of one to three months, an average Q-T index of .397, and a maximum of .50. From three to six months, the values respectively were .39 and .46. Välimäki (1969) reported newborns with an average QTc of .43, with a maximum of .48 for otherwise normal children. Schwartz (1981), following a large number of newborns, found an average QTc on the fourth day of life to be .40, but the 95th percentile would include up to .45. At the second month he found an average of .41, with the same upper limit. Although there were subsequent differences with age, the QTc remained somewhat greater than the value of .425. As Schwartz (1981) points out, "clinically important changes in the Q-T interval are, in fact, rather large, and within the normal limits, a few milliseconds difference in either direction may be statistically significant and clinically irrelevant." We will return to the Q-T hypothesis of sudden infant death, but should warn here about measuring the Q-T interval. Since the end of the T-wave is a curve, exponentially approaching the baseline, the decision as to precisely where that curve intersects the baseline can be somewhat arbitrary. An unconscious bias must be guarded against, and any useful conclusions about the Q-T in relation to any disease process, including SIDS, must be based on determinations done without knowledge of the clinical findings and diagnosis. An additional consideration is the non-specific nature of the Q-T interval, and its association with a variety of diseases and drugs. As Abildskov pointed out in a recent review (1979), the "Q-T may be prolonged in virtually all varieties of organic heart disease." It may be prolonged with electrolyte disorders, particularly hypocalcemia and hypokalemia, and of particular potential significance in infants who have had birth injury or hypoxic injury, the Q-T interval may be prolonged with a variety of central nervous system disorders. Therefore, the finding of a long QTc by no means establishes that the subject involved has either a primary genetic or developmental form of the long Q-T syndrome.

Only a few years after the report of the surdo-cardiac syndrome (Jervell and Lange-Neilsen, 1957), a similar problem, without deafness, was reported independently in Italy and Ireland, with a dominant inheritance (Romano et al, 1963; Ward, 1964). These patients also had a long Q-T interval, syncopal attacks, and many of them eventually died during these syncopal episodes. Schwartz and his colleagues (1975) made a brilliant and convincing case that the long Q-T syndrome represents an imbalance of sympathetic innervation of the heart, between the right and left stellate ganglia. The different innervation of the myocardium of the two ventricles permits uneven recovery periods, and this inhomogeneity favors the initiation of ventricular fibrillation following a random extrasystole. In examining the epidemiology of the genetic forms of long Q-T syndrome, the majority of the cases are discovered in childhood after an asymptomatic infancy. In the families that we have followed with this syndrome, there were *no* instances of sudden death in infants for several generations (Park and Guntheroth, 1978), and no onset of symptoms prior to five years of age.

However, the original report by Romano et al (1963) cites three infants with onset of syncope or death. Still, of all two hundred three reported cases (Schwartz et al, 1957) only eight had syncope in the first year, and only two (1%) died in infancy. As Schwartz points out, ventricular fibrillation in these patients is often self-terminating, and it is rare for a patient to die during their first episode.

The first speculation that the long Q-T syndrome might be involved in sudden infant death was in a letter to *Lancet* in 1966 (Fraser and Froggatt). They correctly pointed out that no gross cardiac lesion is demonstrable in the syndrome, and that if an infant *should* die without medical observation, such a case would be "classified as cot death." Their original letter is worth reviewing since they speculated that the syncopal attack would be most likely to occur when the infant began to walk; they assumed that cot death included children up to two years of age, whose death was "unexplained by necropsy findings and irrespective of where and how the death occurred." We would disagree with this on two grounds: most authorities would not accept a death as SIDS past six months of age, nor if the death did not occur in the crib; even though these restrictions are somewhat arbitrary, they are based on epidemiology and consensus. Fortunately Fraser and Froggatt concluded their letter with the modest claim that only a small proportion of SIDS would be likely to have been caused by genetically determined disorders of cardiac rhythm. In a later examination of the role of long Q-T syndrome, Froggatt and James (1973) calculated that if this syndrome were to account for a majority of cot deaths, "we would have to accept a mutation rate . . . many hundreds of times greater than any yet postulated for man—an unrealistic assumption." In 1978, Froggatt added more arguments against his own hypothesis, in the best—if uncommon— tradition of science. His infant with the "cardio-auditory syndrome, during the typical age for cot death, had only "self-terminating nodal bradycardia and sporadic late cycle ventricular ectopics such as previously reported in immature infants and which did not lead to syncope" (Froggatt and Adgey, 1978).

In 1976 the group at the National Heart Institute announced publicly as well as in journals that they found a very significant number of parents of SIDS victims with prolonged Q-T intervals (26%), and in 39% of sibs of SIDS cases (Maron et al, 1976). They concluded that there was an autosomal dominant pattern of inheritance. They also found one near-miss of SIDS with prolongation of the Q-T interval. They speculated that a considerable proportion of SIDS might be explained by the long Q-T syndrome. Three years later, Smith and colleagues (1979) reported a single infant who had an electrocardiogram taken at one day of age who died at twenty days of age and was diagnosed at autopsy as having SIDS. They asserted that the Q-T was prolonged and that furthermore there was alternation of T-waves, a finding characteristic of some patients with long Q-T syndromes (Schwartz et al, 1975). Although the child had not been observed since birth, and was not observed to die, they claimed that their patient confirmed the long Q-T syndrome as a cause of SIDS. In a letter to the *American Heart Journal* (Guntheroth, 1979) I objected that the great majority of complexes in the published electrocardiogram showed a Q-T interval that was within the normal limits for age, using the conventional table; by calculating the QTc, the majority of beats had a value of only .44, the mean value according to Välimäki (1969), and substantially less than the upper range of .49 (McCammon, 1961; Alimurung et al, 1950). Close inspection of the published electrocardiogram showed no alternation, but a wandering baseline. In short, this patient had a casual electrocardiogram at one day of age, which was in fact within the limits of normal.

A report of two infants with prolonged Q-T intervals and cardiac arrhythmias and sudden infant death in one was reported by Southall and colleagues (1979). Interestingly, these infants had arrhythmias diagnosed prior to birth. After birth, the first infant had bradycardia and died at home at thirteen days of age. Autopsy failed to reveal the cause of his death, which they therefore placed in the SIDS category, although his age and the history of a cardiac arrhythmia would cause him to be excluded in most centers. His electrocardiogram was analyzed retrospectively, to reveal a junctional rhythm, with a 2:1 conduction to the ventricle. The fact that the Q-T was prolonged has approximately the same significance as the junctional rhythm, indicating a substantial myocardial disturbance, and establishes nothing relative to the idiopathic long Q-T syndrome. The second patient had a long Q-T interval and ventricular premature beats, and was treated with propranolol and remains well. Although the long Q-T in this patient is undeniable, according to the theory, the ventricular premature beats should have led to ventricular fibrillation, prior to the treatment with propranolol.

A recent series of papers from various centers have refuted the role of disorders of the long Q-T syndrome in SIDS. Kukolich et al (1977) studied the Q-T interval in one hundred eight first-degree relatives of victims of SIDS, and compared these records with ninety-nine subjects from twenty-two control families. There was no significant difference in the Q-T interval in these two groups, and considering the expected rates for a dominant disorder such as the Romano-Ward syndrome, this effectively rules out that entity as playing a significant role in SIDS. If either the Jervell and Lange-Neilsen syndrome or the Romano-Ward syndrome played a major role in SIDS, the expected recurrence rate would be as high as 25 to 50%, whereas the known recurrence rate in families is only 2%, a level inconsistent with Mendelian forms of inheritance. They attributed the earlier findings of Maron et al (1976) to the failure of that study to include control observations; they did not comment on the fact that that group also failed to use "blind" reading. Schwartz (1981) has criticized the study by Kukolich and colleagues because they used a computer-based statistical method of correcting for the heart rate in comparing the Q-T intervals. Although the method is complicated, it was applied to both populations and is as valid as the standard formula which is ultimately justified on the basis of population statistics. Schwartz also objected that they sometimes used leads other than Lead II; the other leads had a shorter Q-T. This is a surprising statement, since careful biophysical studies have shown many years ago that there are no capacitive or inductive components of the electrocardiogram that would be distorted from one lead to another. However, Schwartz finally agreed with Kukolich's conclusion that the long Q-T syndrome is unlikely to play a major role in SIDS. (He argued that it did not affect his special Q-T hypothesis, involving a maturational equivalent of this syndrome, to which we will return.)

Several major centers reported their studies of the Q-T interval in near-miss SIDS. Kelly et al (1977), Steinschneider (1978), Haddad and his colleagues (1979), and Montague (1980) all reported that the QTc for near-misses were no different from the control groups; in fact, the QTc for near-miss SIDS was actually shorter than for the control infants. Schwartz (1981) correctly states that his Q-T hypothesis of the cause of SIDS should not be confused with the discredited proposal by Maron of a relationship between SIDS and the Romano-Ward syndrome. Schwartz proposed in 1976 that the cardiac sympathetic innervation wasn't complete at birth in the human. He cites evidence by Hirsch, which unfortunately is anecdotal and unconvincing. Hirsch (1970) studied fixed hearts from one premature, a one-day old, a twenty-one-day old, a thirty-five-day old, and from subjects two months and four months, and three subjects at five months. Only qualitative observations were made and the entire description occupies only a single page, from one day to three months. The changes with age are only quantitatively different and Hirsch reported *no* absence of innervation early but simply a general increase of number and size with increasing age. In fact, Hirsch comments, "the endocardial plexus of fibers and fibrils and the epicardial plexus are established in the early stages of embryonal growth. The initial nerve elements laid down, expanded rapidly in dimensions and in the extent of distribution in the myocardium as the cardiac tissues develop. Nerves and their ganglia appear in the epicardium as definitive structures during fetal life." Although Hirsch's descriptions do not invalidate a quantitative argument of innervation, they are not much help for Schwartz' Q-T hypothesis that the right or left stellate distribution are under-represented at an earlier age.

In his 1976 paper, Schwartz argued that since REM sleep "is known to be accompanied by bursts of autonomic discharges," and since REM sleep was more frequent in younger infants, that death in SIDS might occur during REM sleep. In contradistinction, Haddad et al (1979) found that the Q-T index was significantly smaller in REM than in quiet sleep in patients who were near-misses of SIDS, as well as in the normal controls.

The Q-T hypothesis, based on developmental asymmetry, predicts a "time limited imbalance," and if the infant survived the critical period, would be expected to have a normal electrocardiogram and life expectancy. This explanation would account for the tapering off of SIDS after five months, and its disappearance for all purposes after six months, but it would not account for the first month of life, which is usually spared in SIDS. On the contrary, if the imbalance is developmental, the younger the infant, the more vulnerable he should be. Although the first month hiatus is not addressed specifically, Schwartz does comment in the 1976 paper that adults with ventricular fibrillation associated with the long Q-T syndrome frequently survive episodes of ventricular fibrillation by spontaneously reverting to sinus rhythm. He then speculates that it would not be surprising to have infants at risk have several episodes of self-terminating fibrillation, escaping attention of the parent. In his 1981 publication, however, he ignores his own earlier comment, and suggests that there are no near-misses of a cardiac form, because ventricular fibrillation is "fast and silent. There are simply more statistical chances that a mother will find her baby dying a respiratory than a cardiac death, and this will allow her to interrupt the deadly process and the end result will be a new near-miss." In spite of Schwartz' attempt to explain the absence of cardiac near-misses as being clinically improbable, the patient reported by Froggatt and Adgey (1978) diagnosed as a long Q-T syndrome in the perinatal period survived until two years of age; his first attack of fibrillation was recorded at five months of age.

The greatest weakness for Schwartz' contention that a developmental form of the long Q-T syndrome is involved in a substantial part of sudden infant death lies in the numerous studies of the near-miss infants from many centers who do not exhibit a long Q-T. Schwartz attacks the concept that the near-miss is closely related to SIDS, and although some of his points are valid, the effect is that of a brilliant polemic without substance. He does correctly point out that the evidence that sleep is an essential part of sudden infant death is based on an interesting metamorphosis of an observation of Bergman et al (1972), beginning with "the time of discovery however coincided with hours of sleep," through "the finding that all cases of SIDS *apparently* died during their sleep," to a conclusion, "the fact that all babies died during sleep." Schwartz (1981) and Dawes (1974) contend that the relationship of sleep and SIDS is largely an inference, based on circumstantial evidence. Schwartz proceeds to state that "no SIDS death has yet been reported while the victim was being monitored for sleep state." There are two problems with that statement. For one thing, some patients monitored by Shannon and Kelly had indeed succumbed of prolonged apnea, during sleep. It is also unreasonable to assume that a patient on a monitor who triggered the alarm would be allowed to die to establish the argument. To place this in a reasonable perspective, suppose a victim is found in a swimming pool, brought to the surface, and is found of course to be apneic but with a slow heart beat. Would any ethical individual simply observe the subject? On the contrary, resuscitation attempts would be made, and in most instances, the victim would be revived. Would it be logical then to deny that the subject was a "near drowning" victim?

The fact is that most of the near-misses of SIDS that have been monitored have been observed to have repeated attacks of apnea, followed by bradycardia, but rarely, and only terminally developed any ventricular tachyrhythmia of the type postulated by Schwartz. Although Schwartz argues for his prospective study, measuring the Q-T in normal births, as the only way to rule out a role for arrhythmias in sudden infant death syndrome, he ignores the thousands of hours of monitoring experience in prematures in hospital, who are usually on both an electrocardiographic and a pneumograph monitor. If the developmental theory were valid, the premature would be even more likely to have asymmetry of cardiac innervation, and would be more at risk for ventricular fibrillation. This is not the case. The prematures have bradycardia and junctional rhythms, and although a rare premature ventricular contraction may be observed, this does not precipitate ventricular fibrillation as is inherent in Schwartz' long Q-T hypothesis. As we have reported (Bergdahl et al, 1978), we have observed ventricular tachycardia in infants, and as in the older child, it is remarkably stable, leading more often to congestive failure, if it persists, than to ventricular fibrillation.

Finally, there is a danger inherent in Schwartz' suggestion that a major portion of SIDS might result from a developmental form of long Q-T syndrome. He suggests that "beta-adrenergic blocking agents would be the drug of choice" for an infant "at risk." This drug recommendation is based on the dramatic effectiveness of this therapy on subjects with the inherited forms of the long Q-T syndrome. From our experience in five adult volunteers, and in animal experiments, beta-adrenergic blockers also reduce the hypoxic ventilatory drive, which could be disastrous considering the substantial evidence that many of the near-miss infants have a reduced ventilatory drive, either primarily, or perhaps secondary to several episodes of prolonged apnea with hypoxic injury. The same hypoxic injury could also produce a prolonged Q-T interval, secondarily, and the identification of that electrocardiographic finding as a primary problem, followed by beta-blockade, might lead to a disaster of irreversible apnea.

In short, the long Q-T syndrome either in genetic form or in a hypothesized developmental form *could* lead to death in the infant age group, and at autopsy would be classified as SIDS, since there would be no lethal pathological findings at post-mortem. There is no evidence that this occurs except on rare occasions, and the substantial number of prematures and near-misses that have now been monitored without finding either a prolonged QTc, or ventricular fibrillation as an early arrhythmia, provide convincing evidence that this is *not* a likely cause of most cases of SIDS. Froggatt, an early proponent of the "cardiac hypothesis," summarizes sagely: "a cardiac hypothesis is somewhere between 'unproven' and 'discredited'" (1977).

Chapter VI

Possible Respiratory Causes of SIDS

Having stated that there are only two final pathways for death, cardiac or respiratory arrest, and having concluded that cardiovascular causes are infrequent or improbable, it should be no surprise that this chapter contains the most crucial considerations as to the cause of SIDS. Although the guilty party has already been implicated, the mechanism is subtle, and there are many contributing factors that require consideration. Compatible with the definition of SIDS, the mechanism of death in any specific infant cannot be known with certainty. If we knew the mechanism in advance, it is obvious that the infant would have been treated and/or resuscitated, and a live, functioning infant could be argued to be unrelated to SIDS. It has been seriously proposed that the infant need not even be monitored, since this relationship is unproven, and that a true SIDS could not be resuscitated in any event. Such fatalism may be appropriate for an undertaker, but for me that is unacceptable sophistry. To place a higher priority on the prevention of grief or guilt than on saving infant lives is inappropriate for physicians.

We will begin with the beginning, airway obstruction.

109

Airway Obstruction

The presumption for over two thousand years was that an infant found dead was a victim of airway obstruction. The infant of the harlot in First Kings was presumed to have been overlain; the subsequent history of "overlaying" was reviewed in the introduction. The dilemma, which remains even today in rare circumstances, was that intentional smothering of the infant could not be distinguished by post-mortem inspection from an accidental asphyxiation. The response of some well-meaning physicians in the last century, and part of this century, was to invent a remarkable fiction, status thymicolymphaticus. The good effects of that theory was to relieve the bereaved parents, and an occasional wet-nurse from accusations of neglect or even infanticide, but its bad effects were an unknown number of malignancies produced by irradiating the thymus in an attempt to prevent SIDS. The overlaying theory became increasingly untenable as cribs or cots became more widely used in our civilization, and for those who did not believe in status thymicolymphaticus, accidental suffocation by bedclothes became the standard explanation for sudden and unexpected death in the infant. When I arrived in Seattle in 1957, most of the deaths that were unexpected in infants were recorded by the non-physician coroner in King County as "due to suffocation by bedclothes." Armed with the work of Adelson and Kinney (1956) and Stowens (1957), I wrote to our coroner, with an excellent response. (At the time, I could not find any reference by Woolley showing that it was nearly impossible to suffocate a well infant, asleep or not, with bedclothes.)

Although the first accusations of infanticide appeared several centuries earlier, Templeman (1892) rejected the accusation of his day that infanticide was motivated by life insurance. He rationally pointed out that the proceeds of the insurance policies then sold in Great Britain would not even equal the cost of burying the infant, and even more crucial, the policies did not pay off for the first three months of life. Although Templeman is frequently regarded as insensitive, he saw no more reason to suspect the poor of Dundee, Scotland, than the more fortunate.

The dilemma of protecting children from child abuse, and remaining sensitive to the grief of innocent parents who have lost an infant to SIDS, is illustrated in the contributions of Lester Adelson. His 1956 report on SIDS remains a hallmark in the field, but in 1961 he warned of the "slaughter of the innocents." This was a study of forty-six homicides in which the victims were children, from Cuyahoga County, Ohio. Ten of the victims were under one year of age, and five were in the age group of less than six months. Most of these victims were killed either by parents, or by someone acting in that capacity. Frank psychosis was the most important factor in his study, and when mental illness was involved, asphyxia was the common method of destruction. Asphyxia in general accounted for 35% of all of these deaths in children. Three of the victims were starved to death, and five were drowned! Adelson warns that the children were sometimes pronounced dead on arrival at a hospital, and were labeled crib deaths initially, and the correct diagnosis was made later after investigation of the events, and a thorough autopsy.

Another well-known expert in this field, Valdes-Dapena has also warned of the difficulty of ruling out intentional suffocation and warned that this could not be excluded at autopsy with certainty (1967). One family in Philadelphia reported in the lay press to have lost seven infants to SIDS was suspected by the chief medical examiner in Philadelphia of homicide. The family had insured the children for sizeable amounts, outside of the area, with false statements that no other children had died. The evidence was never sufficient to prosecute. In Seattle, I am aware of a similar situation, with even more bizarre behavior that escaped punishment. The mother was married, but twice deliberately became pregnant by another male, insured the infant, and both infants died, under similar conditions. The second one occurred when the mother had been provided with a monitor because of fears expressed; she continued the monitoring for five months. She informed her primary physician that she wanted to take the child camping and would therefore need to take him off the monitor, in spite of the fact that her first infant had died on a camping trip. Needless to say, she was strongly advised against this. Although she did not take the child camping, she claimed that the monitor had stopped working the day after she had called, but she did not call for assistance and the child died that night.

It is a tragic fact that physical child abuse is far more common than SIDS, with an incidence that is calculated to be at least twenty times that of SIDS (Light, 1973), and if criminal neglect and sexual abuse are included, one hundred times that of SIDS. Some of these deaths are particularly obvious; abuse should always be suspected when there are external bruises, burns, abdominal hemorrhages, or long-bone fractures (Kempe et al, 1962). The forensic pathologist is charged with discovering and prosecuting such crimes, not only to uphold "law and order," but because of the terrifying regularity of recurrences. The early activists in the SIDS movement, including both physicians and parents, were relentless in their persecution of coroners or pathologists who did not follow their "party line." One recorded example is an exchange between Bergman (1972) and Helpern (1972) in letters to the *New England Journal of Medicine*. Bergman's accusations were amplified by the medical-legal editor of that journal, without consulting Helpern (Curran, 1972). Milton Helpern probably had done more to establish the science of forensic pathology than anyone in this country. At that time, there were over one hundred SIDS deaths per year in his jurisdiction, and he pointed out that the death scene was routinely visited, a report was prepared, and the body was autopsied before death was certified. The police were not involved unless there were suspicious circumstances, including autopsy evidence of physical abuse or neglect. The most celebrated case was a family that was charged with homicide, after indictment by a grand jury. The father had initially told the police that the child had not been fed for several days, and at autopsy the gastrointestinal tract was in fact empty. The police had not contacted the office of Helpern, because of the earlier statement by the father (subsequently retracted at his hearing).

The second, publicly televised accusation was by Mrs. Choate, the then Executive Director of the National Foundation for Sudden Infant Death, who had accused Helpern's office of some remarkably ugly behavior, including an extreme delay in informing anyone of the diagnosis. Helpern responded in the *New England Journal of Medicine* that the death was certified as SIDS the day following the death, and denied any basis for the accusations "that Mrs. Choate has insisted on making on many occasions and has embellished during the past seven years as part of her advertising campaign for NFSID. There is nothing in the report of the medical investigator, Dr. Kurt Lauer, to indicate that he asked such absurd questions as 'How many times did you hit the baby?' or 'Did your other child choke or in any way abuse the infant?' or 'Did you let the dog bite the baby?' Furthermore, Dr. Lauer completed his investigation at the Choate home before noon. He did not arrive late in the afternoon as she states. The death was not reported to the police and was never considered suspicious." Helpern added that his office had done research on the subject of SIDS, supported by the bereaved parents of an infant who died of SIDS. He concluded that "a death cannot be called a crib death until a complete investigation at the scene and post-mortem examination and autopsy have been performed. The NFSID has been willing to accept certification of such deaths without autopsy as having resulted from a natural syndrome. I dread to think how many of these would prove to have had a demonstrable cause such as an unsuspected infectious disease, congenital malformation, traumatic injury or neglect."

Berger (1979) reported two cases of child abuse which

simulated "near-miss sudden infant death." He warned that the social factors that were risk factors for child abuse were also common to SIDS, and that investigation of both problems is difficult, capable of causing anxiety and guilt. He warned, although the SIDS family deserved a prompt resolution of the case so that they could return to a normal pattern, that it was equally important to recognize and obtain help for the family in which child abuse is a problem, thereby giving the infant a 'second chance.'

Few believe that infanticide is a major part of SIDS, and generally have not seriously regarded the report by Asch in 1968. Asch suggested that a large proportion of crib death "in the United States are covert infanticides, manifestations of a post-partum depression in the mother." Kukull and Peterson (1977) analyzed vital statistics, and made a convincing case that homicides had a different epidemiology from SIDS. Unfortunately, they speculated incorrectly that a post-mortem examination could successfully distinguish infanticide from SIDS on the basis of intrathoracic petechiae. The evidence as to the non-specificity of petechiae has been presented; at this point I would simply reiterate that SIDS cannot be established with certainty without a careful autopsy and any suggestions of neglect or abuse must be carefully investigated (Adelson, 1961). We are learning how to cope with child abuse in a less punitive fashion but still retaining a primary goal of preservation of the life and health of the child. Even when the victim is dead, there is a strong probability that there will be additional pregnancies and additional victims, if an abuser of children is treated as the "victim."

Another example of an excessive swing of the pendulum reflecting socio-political pressures is that of accidental suffocation. Although bedclothes are not likely as a cause of SIDS, strangulation due to catching the head or neck between crib slats, the accidental entrapment by a drop rail, or hanging by a pacifier cord continue to extract a substantial toll. Bass (1977) emphasizes the irony of two of fifteen cases where accidental strangulation occurred; information was withheld by the parent because of concern about accusations of neglect. In one case the parent actually rearranged the child in the crib. A total of three cases of crib asphyxia had been signed out by emergency room physicians as sudden infant death syndrome, even though information indicating accidental asphyxia was available. Smialek et al (1977) warned that Federal regulations governing new cribs, which have improved their safety significantly, do not affect existing unsafe cribs, which are more apt to be used in less affluent neighborhoods. Feldman and Sims (1980) published a thorough review of two hundred twenty-three cases of childhood strangulation, in an attempt to alert pediatricians and other health professionals to potentially hazardous play equipment and other dangers in an infant and child's milieu.

Anatomic airway obstruction, exclusive of laryngospasm, could occur in the nasopharynx or lower. Beinfield (1954) reminded the medical profession that the neonate was an obligatory nose breather. Consequently, choanal atresia, particularly if it was bilateral, could be fatal in early life. Similarly, unilateral choanal atresia would increase the vulnerability, requiring less additional acute pathology to close off the nasopharynx. Shaw (1968, 1970) proposed a similar mechanism leading to SIDS—nasal obstruction from upper respiratory infection. This theory was compatible with the high prevalence of respiratory infections in the victims of SIDS, and the presence of obligate nose breathing in the infant. Cross and Lewis (1971) indeed found a single case of cot death with mucopus obstructing the posterior nares at autopsy. In a study of infant monkeys, we found that obligate nasal breathing was present in the very young monkey, and that it disappeared later (French, Morgan et al, 1972). Later that year, we (French, Beckwith et al, 1972) reported a series of one hundred consecutive cases of unexpected death in infants with x-rays of the nasopharynx at post-mortem. In seventy-eight SIDS victims, an open nasopharyngeal passage was identified in all but two (2.6%), and in a control group of twenty-two infants of unexpected but explained death, there was one (4.5%) case of inadequate definition of the air passage. There were no significant differences in the mean dimensions of the nasopharynx in the two groups. We emphasized that the prevalence of obligate nasal breathing is highest at birth, diminishing rapidly by three to five weeks (Ardran and Kemp, 1970), a relationship that is almost the reciprocal of the one for SIDS, which spares the first month. The infant's nasopharynx is also favored by a resistance that is proportionately less than in adults (Polgar and Kong, 1965), and by the absence of adenoids or pharnygeal tonsils in the infant, for the first few months of life (Ardran and Kemp, 1970).

Beckwith, on the basis of the intrathoracic distribution of petechiae, concluded early in his work that airway obstruction was the final pathway leading to SIDS (Bergman et al, 1970). He remarked during a commentary (1975) that his initial suspicion was that the airway obstruction was positional, but later proposed that the obstruction was due to laryngospasm. This 1975 commentary was in support of Tonkin's hypothesis that the infant has an anatomic vulnerability at the oropharyngeal level between the soft palate and the base of the skull. Although Beckwith in the accompanying commentary asserted that Tonkin "succeeds where we fail, in developing a concept that is based on the anatomical vulnerability of the infantile upper airway. . . ," both of them overlooked the earlier studies of Woolley (1945). Beckwith asserted then, and subsequently, that the presence of intrathoracic petechiae are evidence for airway obstruction as the cause of death. The petechiae are viewed by other pathologists as non-specific, including Werne and Garrow (1953), Swann (1960), Marshall (1970), Camps (1972), and Spector (1972). Marshall, at the second Seattle conference on SIDS (1970), made the point vigorously in a session chaired by Beckwith: "Whether or not visceral petechial hemorrhages have any significance, one thing is certain: they cannot be accepted as indicating an 'asphyxial' termination, if by the use of the term 'asphyxia' we infer mechanical obstruction to the entry of air into the alveoli. This was an erroneous view held by our forebears, and it has persisted longer than most other medicolegal myths. But it has now been discarded." Spector, in the British conference on sudden and unexpected death in infancy (1972), argued that petechiae were not directly related to respiration, but to the hydrostatic pressure in the microcirculation in the presence of asphyxia. In a strong comment, he stated "We note from daily experience how non-specific these changes are and I cannot think of a more non-specific change than petechiae on the thoracic viscera. I beg of you to accept that once and for all." Our own experimental studies failed to produce petechiae with airway obstruction without infection (Guntheroth, 1973) or with infection (Guntheroth et al, 1980). Even Beckwith was unable to produce petechiae in two primates with airway clamping (1970, p. 122). Handforth (1959) produced petechiae in rats with airway obstruction, but not with unremitting clamping, but by repeatedly allowing the animal to recover, prior to death. The requirement of repeated episodes of obstruction to produce petechiae was confirmed recently by Campbell and Reid (1980). Beckwith argued that the petechiae within the thorax are evidence of increased negative pressure from the violent respiratory effort under obstruction, submitting as evidence the fact that the cervical portion of the thymus was spared the petechiae, but not the intrathoracic portion. The assumption is that the negative intrathoracic pressure would effectively increase the transmural pressure for the pulmonary vessels, leading to rupture. In point of fact, we have measured the pressure in the pulmonary artery during airway obstruction in a rabbit, and have demonstrated that the pressure in the pulmonary vessels follows quite faithfully the intratracheal pressure. The structures within the lung are, in the normal state, highly compliant, and the negative intrathoracic pressure is transmitting faithfully to the blood vessels, so that the transmural pressure (intravascular minus intrathoracic pressures) will not be affected. Because we were surprised at the lack of petechiae with unremitting airway obstruction (Guntheroth, 1973; Guntheroth et al, 1980) we recently studied ten rats of the same age and weight when anesthetized. Five were killed by breathing 100% nitrogen atmosphere, and the other five by tying off the trachea. The trachea of the rats dying after breathing nitrogen were also tied and the lungs from all ten animals removed en bloc, and the lung volumes determined by displacement of normal saline. The lung volumes for the rats killed by occlusion were 24% smaller than the volumes of the lungs from animals breathing nitrogen. The difference is a significant one at the 5% level using the Mann-Whitney nonparametric rank-order test. The oxygen contained in the lungs at the time of occlusion is absorbed by continued circulation, favored by the gradient for oxygen between the alveoli and blood. However, the gradient for CO_2 will change relatively little at the end of ventilation, and the net result will be a substantial drop in volume of the occluded lung. The diminished lung volume will reduce the shear or friction between the lung surface and the rib cage. These shearing forces are the probable explanation for the distribution of petechiae, with movement of the lobes of the lungs with vigorous respiration such as gasping, in the presence of increased fragility of the blood vessels secondary to hypoxia and infection (Guntheroth et al, 1980).

There are some real and dangerous consequences to Beckwith's continued assertions that airway obstruction is *the* cause of death in SIDS. He asserts publicly that sleep apnea is a different disorder, unrelated to SIDS, and even argues that monitoring will be to no avail in true SIDS, and cites anecdotal experience to prove this point (Beckwith, 1979). He has been less than charitable to theories relating to the cause of SIDS, describing many of the theories as "productions of misguided zealots who attach their pet biases like so many leeches to new or poorly understood afflictions of mankind." Although he remains the "guru" of what is thinkable about SIDS in the Seattle area, fortunately, the National Sudden Infant Death Syndrome Foundation has advanced under the remarkable leadership of Caroline Szybist, herself a mother of a SIDS victim. Her positive translation of her own loss into active programs of prevention, while continuing the thoughtful support of the bereaved parents, is truly inspirational. Evidence of that positive—and forgiving—nature may be found in the appointment of a former critic, myself, to their medical program board, under the leadership of Fred Mandell.

Apnea

Apnea was suggested at the 1963 meeting on SIDS as the initial problem in infants occasionally seen in emergency rooms or on hospital wards, since the infants still had a heart beat (Guntheroth, 1963). The experience led to the concept of near-miss or aborted SIDS, because these infants could be resuscitated with mouth-to-mouth resuscitation or external thoracic compression. We proposed that these infants should be considered as a part of the spectrum of SIDS, since, had they not been resuscitated, and died, they would necessarily have had non-lethal pathology, since they clearly did *not* have a lethal, irreversible problem. The belief that the infant would have died without resuscitation relates to hypoxic apnea, which will be discussed later in this segment. At very low oxygen tensions in the blood, respirations cease and remain absent until death, or until gasping or resuscitation occur prior to cardiac arrest.

Considering that sleep was thought to be a common accompaniment of SIDS, the coincidence of apnea with sleep, producing sleep apnea, is an obvious possibility. In the second conference on SIDS, I introduced this concept, and for support, cited evidence that there was an immediate depression of ventilatory drive with sleep, even in the normal (Guntheroth, 1970). We had become interested in the relationship of sleep to arterial blood gases during a study of patients with tetrad of Fallot who have "blue spells" (Guntheroth et al, 1965). These infants and children with cyanotic congenital heart disease will begin to breathe with increased depth and frequency after waking, and the harder they breathe the more cyanotic they become, until they lapse into unconsciousness. The conclusion we reached was that hyperpnea in a patient with markedly limited pulmonary blood flow caused an even greater degree of cyanosis with a positive feedback, in contrast to the normal individual in whom voluntary hyperventilation will increase the arterial PO_2. Of particular importance to the subject of sleep apnea is the finding that our children with the tetrad of Fallot had an increased oxygen content in their arterial blood while sleeping, in contrast to normal subjects who drop their arterial PO_2 and increase their CO_2 with sleep (Robin et al, 1958; Sieker et al, 1960). The rise in arterial PCO_2 and the fall in arterial PO_2 in normal sleep are clear evidence that the ventilatory drive diminishes during sleep, on a central basis. Given a decrease in ventilatory drive with sleep, it follows that sleep would be a state of increased vulnerability for individuals with respiratory diseases, or those with abnormal ventilatory drive. Severinghaus and Mitchell (1962) described the danger of sleep to patients who had undergone cervical cordotomy for intractable pain, and applied the imaginative term, "Ondine's Curse." In the play by Jean Giraudoux, the water-nymph Ondine placed a curse on her unfaithful Hans. The curse required him to consciously will all of his bodily functions, and as Hans described it, "a single moment of inattention and I forget to breathe." (There is an earlier form of the legend in German, but Undine didn't bother with subtleties; she killed her lover with a kiss.)

In the 1969 SIDS meeting I drew a parallel between the sleep apnea leading to SIDS and the sleep apnea of the premature infant (Guntheroth, 1970). The parallel was therapeutically important since that same year, Daily and his co-workers (1969) reported on the clinical feasibility of continuous monitoring of respiration in the premature. They also reported the relative ease of resuscitation, frequently requiring only stimulation, although if the apnea was prolonged, resuscitation by bag and mask was required. The possibility of hypoxic apnea was suggested (Guntheroth, 1970) as a secondary and more ominous phase of apnea, since hypoxia could further increase the respiratory depression, resulting in death. We suggested then that an apnea monitor might prevent death in an infant known to be at risk, and asked for improved descriptions of risk factors.

In 1972, Steinschneider made a crucial contribution, reporting five infants studied in the sleep laboratory who had been referred at one month of age because of cyanotic episodes. These infants were found to have prolonged sleep apnea, specified as more than fifteen seconds. Of particular significance was the discovery that the apneic episodes increased in frequency during upper respiratory infections. Two of the infants subsequently died, and were diagnosed at post-mortem as having sudden infant death syndrome. Although Steinschneider reported that apnea occurred most often during REM sleep, he referred to relatively short episodes of apnea, as little as two seconds in duration, and considering the frequent association of REM sleep with irregular respiration, the relevance of the short episodes of apnea is uncertain. In any case, this appeared to be the first encouraging observation in human infants that SIDS might be predicted, and prevented.

In the same year, we reported a study in infant monkeys, designed to test the presence of the dive reflex, and obligatory nasal breathing (French et al, 1972). The subject of reflexes in relation to SIDS will be reviewed shortly, but relevant to apnea, we were impressed that two of the five infant monkeys failed to spontaneously resume respiration when the original stimulus had been removed. When these same animals were re-tested several months later, all of them promptly resumed respiration when the stimulus was removed. This evidence led us to speculate that the vulnerability of the infant monkey, and by inference the human in the first six months of life, might be the "acceptance" by the infant of apnea. Since the fetus does not regularly breathe for nine months in spite of blood gases that would be remarkably stimulating to a mature animal, apnea in an infant might not be alarming to the infant. The failure to arouse could then be lethal.

It is interesting that sleep apnea in the adult population escaped medical attention for so long. The central hypoventilation syndromes, particularly the Pickwickian syndrome, were known to produce polycythemia and somnolence, but the sleep disorder of apnea does not appear in the English literature until the review by Guilleminault, Eldridge, and Dement in 1973. (Gastaut and his colleagues described "somnolence avec apnee obstructive" in 1965.) In adult sleep apnea, the patient did not usually die, but presented with complaints of insomnia, accompanied by daytime somnolence; when polygraphs were recorded, the sequence was discovered of prolonged apnea, followed by arousal, with resulting disturbed sleep. Longer apneic episodes were more commonly associated with non-REM sleep than with rapid eye movement sleep. In the initial patients, Guilleminault et al found that the apneas were mostly central, with airway obstruction playing a negligible role. Deuel (1973) observed five infants with severe apneic spells with polygraphic recordings, and found that the more prolonged apneic episodes were associated with quiet sleep rather than REM sleep. He felt that the mechanism of apnea varied from one infant to another and identified seizure disorders as a specific cause. Guilleminault and colleagues (1975) studied a group of premature infants with apnea and some infants who were near-miss for SIDS. They made a useful distinction between apnea, defined as ten seconds or longer, and more brief episodes, which they termed respiratory pauses. They distinguished central from upper airway apnea, by recording respiratory movements without air exchange in the latter. A third class was termed mixed apnea, which was initially central apnea followed by obstructive (upper airway) apnea. In the premature infant, the longest apneic episodes were always associated with quiet or indeterminant sleep, and the apneic episodes were of the central type. However, respiratory pauses frequently occurred during REM sleep, a distinction which seems to resolve the conflict between Steinschneider's earlier report of apnea occurring during REM sleep since he included as apnea pauses as brief as two seconds. The near-miss infant (Guilleminault et al, 1975) had many apneic episodes of ten to thirty-five seconds duration, and their apneas tended to be more obstructive than central, if one grouped the mixed with the obstructive. They found that respiratory infections increased the frequency and severity of apnea and increased the tendency toward obstructive apnea. Although they remarked on ventricular tachycardia occurring with obstructive apnea, the only documented recording is from an adult. Bradycardia, however, with junctional escape was common. In short, there is no documentation that arrhythmias are a lethal consequence of sleep apnea in infants. However, Guilleminault and his group provided a sound argument for heart rate monitors; they warned that relying on chest displacement may not produce an alarm in obstructive apnea, whereas bradycardia occurred early in that type of apnea.

The Canadian symposium on SIDS (Robinson, 1974) provided an important opportunity for discussion of the newer work, including a thorough review by Dr. Steinschneider of his studies of sleep apnea, and a presentation of data on a group of infants who had apnea only with feeding, and a third group who had apnea with both feeding and when asleep. There was a fourth, heterogeneous group including infants with breath-holding spells, and some with seizures. He also reported that they had initiated home apnea monitoring in managing some of these infants.

A study in kittens by McGinty and Harper was presented at the 1974 meeting. They found a significant increase in the frequency of apnea in kittens subjected to sleep deprivation, although the mean duration of apnea was not changed appreciably. A possible connection between these experiments on sleep deprivation and SIDS may be in the sleep disturbance produced by respiratory infection in infants, considering the epidemiology of frequent mild infections in SIDS. In those infections, there is also a probability of increased resistance to airflow in the nasopharanyx. However, the persistent reports of deaths from SIDS the night following DPT innoculations would not involve the respiratory tract, but the systemic reactions such as fever could cause interference with normal sleep patterns. It also is interesting to recall the epidemiology in Templeman's studies at the turn of the century when a remarkably high percentage of the victims of "overlaying" were found on Sunday morning. He speculated that the parents stayed up late on the night preceding their one day of rest; that would obviously interfere with the sleep patterns of the infant in a one-room dwelling.

Our own animal experiments were reviewed at this meeting (Guntheroth, 1974) and I emphasized that the stimulus for primary apnea, such as sleep apnea, or the laryngeal reflexes presented by Johnson, as well as the older dive reflex, were less specific to SIDS than the *continuation* of apnea once begun. I reviewed the work of Guilleminault on adults with insomnia in the sleep apnea syndrome, emphasizing the ability of the adults to arouse themselves after a period of apnea, and survive. In contrast, the infant was suggested as lacking the development or integration of an alarm mechanism. Failure to arouse with primary apnea would permit progression into hypoxic apnea. The hypoxic apnea continues until either gasping occurs in the very young infant, or external resuscitation, or death ensues. We urged apnea monitors for those few infants that could then be identified as at risk for crib death.

In the years following the early reports by Stein-schneider, and Guilleminault and his colleagues, there has been a rapid expansion of sleep studies, including the studies in the home by Shannon and Kelly and their co-workers, that have clearly demonstrated apnea, predomi-nantly sleep apnea, as the mechanism of near-miss episodes, reviewed in an earlier chapter. The culmination of this ex-plosion of information on sleep apnea can be reviewed in a recent volume of *Sleep* (Vol. 3, 1980). This excellent volume represents the proceedings of a symposium in Australia. Guilleminault reviewed the pathophysiology of obstructive sleep apnea. Normal upper airway patency is protected by activity of the pharyngeal muscles, which must increase their tone during inspiration to prevent collapse. He sug-gested that the airway obstruction occurs as a failure of these pharyngeal muscles. (Weitzman disagreed, arguing for ac-tive obstruction.) Guilleminault also reported on sleep deprivation in adult patients, which caused a significant increase in the mean number of apneic episodes during non-REM and REM sleep. However, there was no significant effect on the duration of apnea in non-REM, although there was a trend toward longer events. Apneas were significantly prolonged with sleep deprivation during REM sleep. Using alcohol as a depressant for the central nervous system, an increased number of apneic episodes was measured. This suggested to Guilleminault that phenothiazines used in cough medicines in Europe might have increased the incidence of SIDS due to this sleep depressant effect (Guilleminault, 1980).

Sullivan and Issa (1980) at the Australian symposium on sleep emphasized arousal as the crucial event terminating obstruction in patients with severe sleep apnea. Their data indicated that the arousal was directly related to the degree of hypoxemia. They found that longer apneas were asso-ciated with REM sleep, and that, understandably, longer apnea was associated with lower oxygen saturation. The implication is that REM sleep "attempts" to maintain the sleep state, permitting a lower degree of oxygen desaturation before arousal occurs.

In another chapter, Phillipson and colleagues (1980) expanded the concept of sleep deprivation to include sleep fragmentation by multiple arousals of the sleeping subject. They found that with sleep fragmentation there was a diminution of the arousal response to various respiratory stimuli including hypercapnia and hypoxia, although the ventilatory responses were not changed. In addition, arousal response to laryngeal stimulation was impaired. They proposed that a respiratory infection in an infant could lead to sleep fragmentation, resulting in a critical impairment of arousability.

Hunt (1981) found arousal abnormalities from sleep in a group of twenty-five near-miss infants when stimulated with either CO_2 or hypoxia. Although the mean values were not significantly different from a control group, the number of near-miss infants that aroused from hypoxia was only 29%, compared to 76% of the control group ($p < .01$).

The interaction between fever and sleep apnea has not been examined fully. At least three groups have reported increased occurrences of prolonged apnea in near-miss infants when they have respiratory infections, and it seems likely that an elevation of temperature might well have been an associated factor. There are some physiological and clinical observations that suggest to me a possible role of fever in increasing apnea. Similarly, a febrile response to DTP immunization occurs in one-third of infants (Cody et al, 1981), along with pain and fretfulness in over one-half. The vulnerability to increased sleep apnea for both infection and immunization may be through sleep deprivation, but the interaction of thermal regulation and ventilation should be considered. In premature infants, a neutral ambient temperature where there is neither heat loss nor heat gain by the infant, produced an increased number of apneic episodes (Perlstein et al, 1970). At the other extreme, cold is one of the stimuli for the onset of respiration after birth, and in general, cold ambient temperatures will arouse an infant, interrupting his sleep, resulting in shivering. The interaction between the room temperature, the infant's temperature, sleep state, and finally apnea, seems established for some states at least, and the interaction may prove eventually to be an important contributing factor for sudden infant death.

In full-term infants, several experienced neonatologists reported anecdotes of rapid warming that caused apnea (Oliver, 1963). Recently, Stanton and colleagues (1980) found subtle post-mortem changes in the small intestine of SIDS victims that were similar to those found in overheating. They cited the susceptibility to apnea of the premature and the newborn to ambient temperature as a possible mechanism of death. Sunderland and Emery (1981) found that many SIDS victims have higher rectal temperatures on arrival at the hospital morgue, suggesting to them a febrile state prior to death. They postulated "thermolabile syncope," involving an exceptionally strong vagal reaction causing cerebral anoxia. They called attention to the rarity of febrile convulsions before six months of life, and the rarity of SIDS *after* six months. They speculated that the two disorders were equivalent responses to fever, the expression depending on the maturity of the infant. They cited Stephenson (1978) who found that children with febrile seizures frequently had abnormally long asystole with ocular compression; this abnormal "oculocardiac reflex" was suggested by Sunderland and Emery as the common pathologic mechanism for both SIDS and febrile seizures depending on the age of the child. Of course, it is one thing to produce asystole by vagal stimulation, and another to document the occurrence during a near-miss episode; prolonged asystole has not been observed in the many infants monitored for aborted SIDS, as an early event.

Reflex Apnea

In sleep apnea, the airway obstruction is a passive collapse due to a lack of pharyngeal muscle activity that normally maintains the airway in inspiration. In this section we will discuss active reflexes such as laryngospasm and those involving active inhibition of respiration.

Stowens (1957) suggested a massive autonomic discharge as the cause of sudden infant death syndrome. Although he speculated that a cardiac arrhythmia was the lethal event, he felt that the microscopic evidence in the lung of localized edema and hyperexpansion of other areas indicated either bronchospasm or laryngospasm. Handforth in 1959 cited intrathoracic petechiae as evidence of laryngospasm, which Beckwith has continued to cite to the present. Arguments against this theory include (1) the nonspecificity of petechiae in post-mortem examination, (2) the fact that unremitting airway obstruction that would be produced by laryngospasm does *not* produce petechiae in the experimental animal, and (3) the initial assumption that negative intrathoracic pressure would cause rupture of capillaries by increasing the transmural pressure is faulty.

Perhaps the first observed episodes of apnea preceding death were reported in 1965 by Stevens. Although he did not invoke any specific reflexes, his patients were not asleep, and the apnea could not be classified as sleep apnea. He described four infants with respiratory infection who were seen early during the course because of a near-miss episode with apnea, cyanosis, and unconsciousness. The first infant gasped and regained some respiration, and was then treated in a local hospital; by that time he looked relatively well. However, the child then developed rales and deteriorated rapidly over the next five hours and expired. His second case also was awake at the onset of apnea, limpness, and cyanosis. The mother administered artificial respiration, and the infant gradually responded. A seizure followed, but improved without therapy, and by the time the infant was hospitalized his general condition was thought to be good. However, a rapid deterioration followed, including repeated episodes of apnea with cyanosis, and death in six hours. Both of these cases, as well as the last two in this series had had a "cold" for two to seven days in duration, and they all were awake at the time of lapsing into apnea. They all had a very similar course, being relatively stable and in good condition by the time of arrival at the hospital, but with rapid deterioration leading to death in two to six hours after hospitalization. Although the severity of the respiratory infections ultimately were enough to explain death, Stevens emphasized that the severe apneic episodes had heralded the deterioration, rather than being attributable to the deterioration that followed. He rightly pointed out that had the infants died without observation during the first episode of apnea, they would have had relatively little pathology, and would have been diagnosed as sudden and unexpected death in infancy. Whether these infants might have had a tonic seizure related to fever at the outset is not clear; one certainly had a clonic seizure following the initial episode. The ability of seizures to cause apnea is well established (Deuel, 1973), presumed to involve activation of some reflex loops, but I know of no evidence as to the precise nature of these nerve tracts. It seems likely that seizure disorders, whether epileptic or a manifestation of fever, constitute a major sub-set of infants who have apnea, particularly those who develop apnea while awake.

Kelly and Shannon (1981) reported four infants with earlier demonstrated central apnea with sleep who later developed episodes of obstructive apnea, presumably true laryngospasm. Two of them had seizures, at least one of a primary nature, and three of them had central hypoventilation. Thus, the relationship of these infants to near-miss SIDS is not clear, particularly since the age of onset of the laryngospasm in all four cases was beyond the usual age for SIDS. The evidence for obstruction was based on the parents' inability to ventilate the infant successfully. Three of the four survived, although two of them, siblings, required emergency intubation by their parents. It is important to note that Kelly and Shannon have one of the largest patient populations on home monitors, and that the great majority of their typical near-miss SIDS infants with apnea respond to simple stimulation, and occasionally more vigorous mouth-to-mouth resuscitation. The four obstructed patients were the exception, and even they were not the hopeless situation prophesized by some.

The dive reflex has been well studied in diving animals, and appears to be an excellent defense mechanism for animals that earn their living by diving, such as seals. During the dive the animal is voluntarily apneic, although the apnea is probably also produced by reflex, since we were able to produce it in lightly anesthetized monkeys (French et al, 1972). (If anesthesia was not used, the stimulus produced an alarm reaction.) Bradycardia is almost immediate with the onset of the dive stimulus, a cold wet stimulus to the region of the trigeminal nerve. Vasoconstriction follows, but this may not be observed by simple blood pressure recordings, since the bradycardia may prevent hypertension from occurring. However, with atropine, the bradycardia may be blocked, and hypertension may then be recorded (French et al, 1972). The survival value of this reflex is particularly obvious for the diving animal, since it conserves the cardiac output and available oxygen for the coronary circulation and for the cerebral circulation. Wolf suggested that a malfunction of this oxygen-conserving reflex might be involved in sudden death, either in adults or in infants, resulting in a fatal arrhythmia, such as ventricular fibrillation (1966). We found that the dive reflex was indeed present in the infant but saw only a conservative cardiac adjustment with no worrisome arrhythmias with the apnea (French et al, 1972; Guntheroth, 1977). The worrisome aspect was the failure of the infant to resume breathing when the stimulus was removed.

In the second SIDS conference, I compared the Cushing reflex to the dive reflex (Guntheroth, 1970). Cushing (1901) had described a reflex with automatic increase in the arterial blood pressure paralleling an increase in intracranial pressure, opposing the tendency to collapse the arteries. Bradycardia was concomitant with the increase in pressure, and apnea. (Apnea was not described by Cushing because his experimental procedure in animals used a ventilator.

Guyton (1948) demonstrated apnea with cerebral ischemia.) The components of the Cushing reflex seem to parallel the oxygen-conserving reflex or the dive reflex, and probably have the same motor pathways, although obviously different afferent loops. The effect of these reflexes is conservative rather than destructive, and cannot reasonably be indicted as causing death, when the effect is to prevent or postpone death. In addition, the presence of bradycardia is a valuable warning, and can be successfully used for monitoring infants for apnea. The true apnea monitors are more difficult to maintain without false alarms, and as is obvious from the reports of obstructive sleep apnea, those that operate on the basis of chest movement would not trigger an alarm in spite of the absence of adequate air exchange, while bradycardia presents earlier with obstructive apnea than with central apnea.

Although not reported as having significance in SIDS, Harned and his co-workers (1970) were the first to report that fluid introduced into the trachea in newborn lambs would produce a profound respiratory depression. It had earlier been known that immersing the head of the newly delivered infant would maintain an apneic state (Karlberg, 1966), but this was thought to relate to trigeminal stimulation of the dive reflex. Recently, the same effect was shown by stimulation of the superior laryngeal nerve (Lawson, 1981).

In the Canadian conference on SIDS in 1974, Johnson reviewed the subject of laryngeal-induced apnea, work carried out in Dawes' laboratory. They were able to produce persistent apnea by instilling water—but not saline—in the larynx of newly born lambs, but in older lambs the apnea was usually transient, with a fairly prompt breakthrough of breathing following stimulation. Downing and Lee (1975) found in piglets that the laryngeal area was more sensitive to water than to milk, and that saline produced relatively little effect. They could block the laryngeal-induced apnea by sectioning the superior laryngeal nerve, or conversely, by stimulating that nerve they could produce the same reflex. They also observed the age-dependent nature of the strength of this reflex, gradually weakening after one month of age in the piglet.

In our studies of the premature and normal newborn with Holter monitoring, we frequently observed brady-cardia with various kinds of gastrointestinal stimuli, including stomach aspiration, defecation, and even feeding. More recently, a definite sub-set of infants with near-miss have emerged, who have gastroesophageal reflux (GER). Two groups independently reported a sizeable number of patients who presented with respiratory arrest that appeared to be stimulated by GER (Leape et al, 1977; Herbst et al, 1978). The atypical part of their presentation, relative to SIDS, is that they are more likely to develop the apnea while awake, thereby improving their chance of being diagnosed and treated. The reflex may involve the laryngeal reflex described above, or there may be a reflex stimulated by acidity in the esophagus, without actually reaching the laryngeal area. It seems likely that some of these infants were diagnosed at post-mortem in the past as aspiration of gastric contents, which accounts for a sizeable number of infants found dead in their cribs. Richards and McIntoch (1972) reported fourteen out of one hundred three cot deaths were found at post-mortem to have aspirated gastric contents. This would suggest a sizeable part of a population of infants dying of all causes might have had GER sufficient to produce some inhalation. Assuredly, from the reports, and our own observations of an infant with GER, choking or coughing is not a necessary part of the apnea, and in fact Herbst's group found only five of fourteen of their cases of GER had a history of vomiting. One of their patients subsequently died and was diagnosed by two pathologists independently as SIDS. Fortunately, most of this group, if diagnosed, respond to medical management with positional therapy or surgery. Leapes' group recommended surgery on all patients with respiratory arrest secondary to GER, although Herbst found good response to medical management in nine of fourteen patients. They specifically recommended against gastrostomy, and recommended fundoplication. The proportion of all SIDS that might have GER as a stimulus is unknown, but judging from the relatively non-specific complaints of some of the patients who were proven to have GER, it may be larger than earlier thought. Judging from the survey by Richards and McIntosh, there may be a 14% prevalence of GER in a population of SIDS cases. Jeffery et al (1980) studied twenty near-miss infants for GER, and found reflux in eighteen of twenty infants, usually during active sleep, but rarely in quiet sleep. For some unaccountable reason they did not report how many of these episodes of reflux were associated with apnea, if any. During the discussion of their presentation, Guilleminault reported that they had examined forty-four near-miss infants compared to two normal controls, and found only one of the near-miss babies had more episodes of reflux than the controls. Shannon also reported finding no relationship between reflux and apnea or bradycardia in a twelve-hour study of eighteen near-miss infants, including nighttime recordings. Walsh and his colleagues (1981) found in a group of infants with *both* GER and recurrent apnea that the two events were not temporally related in a majority of episodes. They suggested that these were "two manifestations of a more general developmental delay." There is little doubt that GER is capable of producing reflex apnea in certain vulnerable infants, and may account for a modest number of cases of SIDS. The vulnerability seems more related to the inability to overcome the apnea than the occurrence of GER, which appears to be almost universal at one time or another in the infant. Nevertheless, prompt detection and management of GER-induced apnea may be life-saving, and like seizure disorder, GER must be considered by the physician examining near-miss infants.

Hypoxic Apnea and Gasping

At the Canadian conference on SIDS, I commented that there appeared to be several reflexes and neurological disorders that could initiate apnea, but that the special vulnerability of the infant appeared to be a failure to arouse from sleep apnea, or to break through a respiratory depression that was particularly prolonged in the infant (Guntheroth, 1974). The specific danger of prolonged apnea was the risk of reaching hypoxic apnea, a stable "off-state" of the ventilatory control system found with very low arterial oxygen tension (PaO_2). We found in experimental animals that the point of depression in an otherwise healthy animal was close to a PaO_2 of twenty, regardless of whether the PCO_2 was high, as with asphyxia, or low with breathing a low oxygen atmosphere. There was a relatively brief interval between reduced ventilatory effort and the final apnea, which occurred at a PaO_2 of approximately 10 mmHg (Guntheroth and Kawabori, 1975). It is probable that there is some central depression at higher levels of PaO_2, particularly in the neonates and prematures, but ordinarily this is not seen because of the stimulation of hypoxic ventilatory drive via the peripheral chemoreceptors. In the past, this hypoxic apnea was not recognized as a stable—although brief— state, and was simply regarded as failure of the respiratory system. The importance of this stability with adequate circulation, but with bradycardia and vasoconstriction, lies in the ability to be resuscitated, either by the infant or animal's own gasping, or by medical help. The persistence of a stable cardiovascular system has been directly related to the amount of glycogen stored in cardiac muscle. This glycogen reflects the anaerobic life of the fetus, when the average arterial PO_2 is in the range of 25 mmHg. This ability of the myocardium to tolerate hypoxia is absolutely crucial; if the circulation ceases, a gasp will have no benefit without transportation of the increased alveolar oxygen to other vital centers such as the brain and the heart. The ability of the newly born fetus to survive with a heartbeat and measurable blood pressure and no oxygen is remarkable, and is demonstrated graphically in Fig. VI:1 of the delivered fetal monkey at term. Although gasping in the newly born animal is less dramatic in improving the organism's blood gases due to

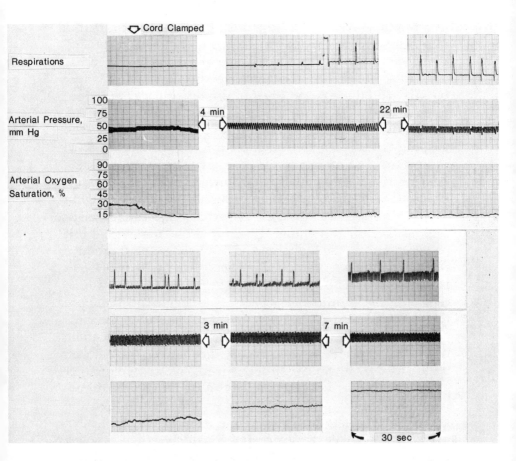

Figure VI:1 An infant monkey, delivered by Caesarian section, had its umbilical cord clamped at the time of the arrow in the first panel. The arterial oxygen falls and remains extremely low until the fourth panel (20 minutes after the third panel, and 50 minutes after the cord was clamped). Note the persistence of a strong heart beat with good perfusion pressure throughout. There are no regular respirations, only gasping, until the fourth panel. As the regular respirations are established, gasping gradually decreases in frequency. (Reproduced from Guntheroth: Neonatal and pediatric cardiovascular crises. *J Am Med Assoc* 232:168, 1975, by permission.)

fluid in the alveoli, the effect of a single gasp in an infant of a few days of age, or an adult is quite dramatic with a major pulse of oxygen appearing promptly in the aorta (Fig. VI:2). After only two or three gasps, the arterial oxygen has been raised to the point where hypoxic apnea is no longer present, and there is a gradual return of regular respiration, interspersed with gasping, which gradually slows in frequency as regular respiration improves. The effectiveness of gasping is very likely the explanation of the hiatus of SIDS during the first month of life. We suggested that the same reflexes and sleep apneas that occurred in the older infant, implicated in SIDS, probably occur in the first month of life as well, but are survived by virtue of successful gasping, resuscitating the infant. This would be undetected if it occurred during the night, and such episodes could produce the hypoxic changes noted at post-mortem by Naeye (1980). In the older infant, the resistance to hypoxia is much less, reflecting the diminished stores of glycogen and therefore limited substrate for anaerobic metabolism. When the gasp occurs, as is the case in the adult, it occurs with inadequate circulation, and the oxygen is not transported. This is well understood by first aid instructors who have known for over a century that a drowning victim must be given external respiration when pulled from the water. Even though the stimulus for apnea has been removed, and they still have a pulse, they have hypoxic apnea, which will not revert to regular respiration until the arterial oxygen content is restored.

In our 1975 study, we speculated that the gasping center was not dependent on the peripheral chemoreceptors, and was functionally separate from the ordinary respiratory neurons (Guntheroth and Kawabori). At the time there was surprisingly little in the medical literature on the gasp, and *Dorland's Medical Dictionary* did not even contain an entry. There was an early and relatively thorough study of the gasp which established its effectiveness in the newborn compared to the older animal, by Legallois (1812). Using a

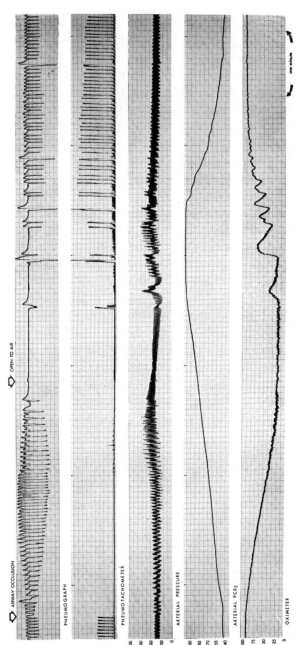

Figure VI:2 The airway of an anesthetized dog was occluded temporarily at the first arrow. Initially, the animal increased his respiratory efforts, as the arterial PCO₂ rose and the PO₂ fell. Respirations ceased after three minutes, and the airway was reopened. No respiratory effort occurred for 1.5 minutes, but blood pressure remained adequate, a state of hypoxic apnea. A single gasp occurred, producing a transient oxygen pulse. The second gasp produced better arterial oxygen, and a single normal inspiration, but respiration did not become regular for another minute. Gasping respirations gradually decreased in frequency, and the PO₂ and PCO₂ returned toward normal. (Reproduced from Guntheroth and Kawabori: Hypoxic apnea and gasping. *J Clin Invest* 56:1371, 1975, by permission.)

guillotine, he demonstrated that the center for the gasp was in the caudal portion of the medulla oblongata. Lumsden (1923) was able to produce gasping by sectioning the upper or middle medulla, and abolished all respiration, including gasping, when he sectioned low in the spinal bulb. Jansen and Chernick (1974) demonstrated that cyanide could produce a gasp response when placed directly on the central medulla, proving that the peripheral chemoreceptors were not necessary for that response. Hukuhara et al (1959) thought that the gasping center was suppressed by normal respiration. In our study, we found that the gasping did not occur until a PO_2 of less than 5 mmHg, but once gasping began, it would continue with decreasing frequency for some time after regular respiration had resumed, if the arterial PO_2 had been raised in the meantime; we therefore postulated a relatively independent neural apparatus for gasping. If there were interdependence, the relatively long interval of hypoxic apnea would have been ample time for disinhibition of the gasp center, if that were the mechanism. Recently, St. John and his colleagues, in neurophysiologic studies, found evidence that the gasp mechanism was distinct from the usual medullary mechanisms of automatic ventilation (St. John and Bartlett, 1981; St. John and Knuth, 1981).

Abnormal Ventilatory Drive

It may seem obvious that an infant dying, or almost dying of SIDS, with prolonged apnea necessarily has abnormalities of ventilatory control. Further, it would not be unexpected to find neuropathology in the part of the brainstem that controls respiration. The surprise may be the *lack* of abnormalities in both physiology and histology. Since function cannot be measured in the dead, the only hard data is obtained in survivors of aborted SIDS, the "near-miss." These studies of responsiveness to both carbon dioxide

stimulation and to hypoxic ventilatory drive have been analyzed in the chapter on near-miss. Although some survivors
have a definitely reduced response to both CO_2 and hypoxia,
it is by no means universal in that population; those with
abnormal ventilatory control were selected out of a group
that had had recurrent severe apneic episodes, and there
is a reasonable basis for questioning whether the abnormality of ventilation was the cause or the effect of the prolonged hypoxic episodes. Similarly, the abnormal brainstem
auditory-evoked potentials initially reported as highly
correlated with the near-miss infant have not been confirmed in other centers, and the specificity of these findings
has been challenged as to cause or effect. There are repeated
reports from varying centers, however, of near-misses who
survive intact and who have completely normal ventilatory
responses and completely normal BAEPs. If one looks at the
entire phenomenon of SIDS as a catastrophe occurring in a
period of biological vulnerability with the chief contributing
factors of immaturity, normal depression during sleep, and
a respiratory infection with increased airway resistance and
sleep fragmentation, it would follow that any weakness in
the ventilatory control would put the infant at even greater
risk. If, as some suggest, there is a genetic character to the
control setting of the respiratory system, and this was
relatively unresponsive, the risks would be greater. On the
other hand, there is a very clear difference in our experience
between the near-miss SIDS victim and a true congenital
Ondine's curse. One such infant was referred to us with
cyanosis, and possible congenital heart disease, who had no
heart disease except for acute cor pulmonale. This youngster
had had no complaints during the first four months of life,
but during the fifth month developed "croup," and was
admitted to a local hospital and placed in oxygen. Later he
was found to be less responsive and the oxygen flow was
increased, and within twenty minutes his respiration had
ceased. After resuscitation with a bag and mask he was
transferred to our hospital. Until he died at eight months of

age, this infant had *no* episodes of apnea, except for the one that precipitated his transfer. That episode was apparently due to reducing his hypoxic ventilatory drive when he was unresponsive to CO_2 (Beck et al, 1980). Although he hypoventilated while awake, it became much more severe when he went to sleep, but he never deteriorated to the point of hypoxic apnea. A trial of a wide range of medications was without success, and the only successful treatment short of placing him on a ventilator, which his parents refused, was conditioned avoidance of hypoxemia. This worked by virtue of awaking the youngster from sleep, although during the day when he was awake he was generally able to avoid hypoxemia sufficient to trigger the stimulus. Had this infant died earlier, before he developed the chronic cor pulmonale, his diagnosis would assuredly have been SIDS. In fact, at autopsy, there were no identifiable histologic changes in the brainstem.

As we observed in that chapter, the near-miss is a better defined and smaller group of disorders than the autopsy group of SIDS, since it is possible to distinguish abnormal functions such as seizures, gastroesophageal reflux, and central hypoventilation during life, but impossible after death.

Chapter VII

Miscellaneous Theories of the Cause of SIDS

The final mechanisms leading to death, or the theories of possible mechanisms, have been discussed under cardiovascular and respiratory headings. There seems to be an almost limitless variety of general disorders which require some consideration as entities, even though the final pathway of death may be an arrhythmia or apnea. Some of these theories have been suggested, one senses, as a kind of intellectual exercise with, "well, this *could* be *a* cause of SIDS." In a way, this reflects more on the ability of an autopsy to detect the true cause of death than it does on the credibility of the author who proposes the theory. The article "a" is a crucial consideration; if the author uses that phrase, it is very likely they are correct, and that sooner or later, an infant with that disorder will die, and will be diagnosed at post-mortem as SIDS. The use of the article "the" is another matter. There, the null hypothesis should hold, and some reasonable probability should be demonstrated by the author's hypothesis. If the author persists at length, defending the theory as *the* cause of SIDS, or even a substantial cause of SIDS, his judgment and even integrity may be questioned if the theory does not conform to the observed epidemiological facts, particularly expectations of frequency and prevalence. One must admire Shaw (1968, 1970) who proposed one of the most reasonable explanations ever developed, that respiratory infections block the nasopharynx at a time when the infant is dependent on the nasopharynx for breathing. The duration of obligate nasal breathing is within the first six months of life, and bilateral occlusion of the nasopharynx has been demonstrated to be fatal. Any adult suffering a serious "cold" can testify to the likelihood of nasal obstruction with a "cold." Unfortunately, the theory did not conform to the hiatus of SIDS in the first month of life, when obligate nasal breathing would create the greatest vulnerability. In addition, obstructions were not found at postmortem. His theory nevertheless stimulated work and thought so that his scientific contribution remains a major one in SIDS work. His graceful abandonment of the theory subsequently as science evolved stands as another major credit to this gentleman.

In the presentation that follows, we will begin with one of the earliest theories of cause of death—infections—taken here in the sense of an infection that killed directly or through the production of a toxin, rather than the concept of a trigger, associated with an infection mild enough but not lethal in its own right. That type of trigger seems to operate through apnea, following sleep deprivation or fragmentation (the total time in sleep might not be reduced, but broken up into less effective fragments.)

Lethal Infections

Prior to the era of routine bacteriological studies at post-mortem, infections were assumed to be a major cause of SIDS. Farber (1934) reported the isolation of pneumococcus in two apparent SIDS victims; he concluded that they had died of overwhelming septicemia, prior to anatomical changes that could be detected at post-mortem. Septicemia remains a cause of SIDS, when an autopsy is not performed, or when cultures are not obtained. In support of Farber's theory, are the four cases reported by Stevens (1965) of infants who presented with apnea and cyanosis who were resuscitated and seemed relatively well, with evidence of a minor respiratory infection, who progressed to a severe infection over the course of six hours, to death. In the early stages of a bacterial infection, in a child vulnerable to SIDS, triggering of apnea could occur, just as it does in the majority of SIDS victims who have only a mild viral respiratory infection.

Invasion of intestinal bacteria in SIDS was proposed by Reisinger (1965) based on a model of calves and a lethal disorder called "scours." In that situation, a massive invasion of E. coli occurs through the intestinal tract of calves and causes early death. Assuming that an autopsy has been performed and blood cultures obtained, this diagnosis would have been made; if it were a common cause of SIDS, the fact would be known long ago. Although E. coli produce an endotoxin, relatively large amounts are required for a lethal outcome, unlike botulism, which requires minute quantities for a lethal effect. For the production of a lethal amount of E. coli endotoxin, the blood stream would have to be heavily infected with E. coli, easily detectable at post-mortem.

Recently, a similar hypothesis was proposed for invasion of staphylococcus, with production of an enterotoxin (Trube-Becker, 1978). She postulated that *if* "bacterioenterotoxin poisoning occurred, that the subsequent changes would explain most of the findings at post-mortem in a true SIDS." She offered no explanation of how the staphylococci or other toxin-producing bacteria could escape detection by post-mortem culture.

The role of viruses has received substantial attention in recent years, particularly in the earlier conferences on SIDS, and the pathology and epidemiology have been covered earlier in this monograph. There are few, if any, experts in the field who would assert that the viruses are lethal *per se*, and consensus exists that they act in the fashion of a trigger, or by sleep deprivation. However, Raven (1977) suggested, without substantial evidence, that the viruses produce a hypersensitivity reaction. Dr. Raven has ample evidence of respiratory infection in her extensive post-mortem experience with SIDS, and although there seems little acceptance of this theory of hypersensitivity in relation to infection, there is probably more substantial basis for this suggestion than for several that will follow in the discussion of other hyperimmune reactions. The strongest argument against any of these is that there should be a range of severity in such disorders that would permit detection, treatment, and survival in a sizeable population, who would then be available to confirm the hypothesis. This has not been the case in the near-misses, who do not have findings of anaphylaxis, or of hyperimmune states. Immune deficiency, leading to overwhelming infection of either viral or bacterial origin, and to sudden death, was one of the earlier proposals, popular at the first Seattle Conference on SIDS. The assumption was not unreasonable, that the newly born infant was protected to some extent by maternal antibodies which would gradually disappear, and before the infant's own immune functions were fully competent, an infection could be lethal. This time course would fit the pattern of a hiatus of SIDS during the first month, with an increase in the second and third months, and then disappearing after six months as the child's immune mechanisms became fully competent. However, the immune globulins in victims of SIDS were actually somewhat higher than control infants, suggesting that they were stimulated by more infections than the average. This suggested not an immune problem, but a problem of greater exposure and therefore vulnerability. The assumption of immunologic deficiency has been applied to the lower prevalence of breast feeding in relation to SIDS. The theory (Gunther, 1975) implies that the *quantity* of immune globulins is not necessarily abnormal, but that the infant will fail to receive specific antibodies through the mother's milk, when artificially fed, and thereby be susceptible to specific infections. Although components of the theory are valid, namely that breast feeding is associated with a lower rate of

SIDS than for artificial feeding, and there is some transfer of immune components in breast milk, the final inference that an immune deficiency causes SIDS has not been established. One argument against the theory is the probability that the viral infection in SIDS was most likely transmitted from the infant's own mother, based on the number of chances of exposure. If she has the infection, she is not then immune, and breast milk would have no protective value. Only if the infection was introduced by a sibling, or father, or an outsider, could immune components in mother's milk have any protective value. In any case, it is important to remember that the viruses that have been associated with SIDS are not at all specific, and that the infection rate for the community, including many infants who do not succumb to SIDS, is very high, suggesting that the simple fact of a respiratory infection is not the problem, but the infant's response.

A disease basically of infectious origin that apparently masquerades at times as SIDS is infant botulism. The group in California handling this discovery performed admirably from a scientific and public health point of view. They established a new disease entity, infantile botulism, related it to sudden infant death, but also established that it accounted for only a fraction of the cases of SIDS. The bacteria, Clostridium botulinum, is ubiquitous, and ingestion of it or its spores causes no difficulty whatsoever in adults, nor apparently in most infants, particularly after one year of age. The toxin it produces is extremely potent, but it is not produced in the gut in the adult, and poisoning results from ingesting food that has previously been contaminated with C. botulinum and contains the toxin. Since infants ordinarily do not eat foods that would be contaminated with the toxin, no cases of botulism in infancy have been diagnosed during recorded medical history in California up to 1976. In that year, Midura and Arnon reported four infants from six to thirteen weeks of age who had symptoms consistent with botulism, and were found to contain toxin in their feces, in addition to C. botulinum. The symptoms were fairly striking, and more severe than is compatible with the usual story of a SIDS victim who was previously well, except for a mild "cold." These botulism victims had been generally well until the onset of constipation, poor feeding, diminished sucking and crying ability, cranial nerve palsy, loss of head control, and finally limb and respiratory muscle weakness. The important case was one infant who developed respiratory arrest in his mother's arms during hospitalization. The authors questioned whether SIDS might then be related to infant botulism. In 1978 they reported on their efforts at identifying either botulinum toxin or the organisms in victims of SIDS (Arnon et al). They analyzed serum, selected tissues, and bowel contents from two hundred eighty dead infants. They found C. botulinum in ten infants all of whom had died suddenly and unexpectedly, nine of whom had been classified as SIDS. In only two of these infants was toxin identified. One hundred and sixty age-matched healthy infants who served as controls showed no instances of fecal organisms or toxin, except for one specimen containing only the organism. The final estimate was 4.3% of cases identified as SIDS at autopsy were possible cases of infant botulism.

In a research news report in *Science* (Marx, 1978), these findings were reported, with comments from Beckwith who thought the symptoms of botulism was quite atypical, since most of the SIDS victims he had studied had been active, with no evidence of hypotonia prior to their demise. Peterson was quoted, relative to some results he had obtained (subsequently published in 1979), from thirty SIDS victims and six controls. They found the bacteria but not the toxin in only one of the SIDS victims. Peterson speculated that although deterioration in the specimens might have led to an underestimation of the presence of toxin or bacteria, the opposite might be true—that deterioration of the specimens may have permitted growth of the C. botulinum as a contaminant that was unrelated to the infant's death. On the face of it, Peterson's study revealed approximately the same prevalence of C. botulinum as was found in the California study, 3 to 4%.

The California group reported that 30% of infants hospitalized with botulism had been fed honey before they became ill, and they were able to find the spores of C. botulinum in 10 to 15% of honey samples. They very reasonably suggested that infants under one year of age not be given honey. In summary, a small percentage of SIDS victims may well be victims of botulism, which qualifies botulism as *a* cause of SIDS, but assuredly not *the* cause.

Hyperimmune Reactions

The most celebrated theory relating to sensitization was that of the British scientists who proposed that SIDS was an anaphylactic reaction to cow's milk, regurgitated from the stomach during sleep (Parrish et al, 1960). Their animal model involved guinea pigs in which it is rather easy to produce an anaphylactic reaction. When they sprayed the upper airway of sensitized guinea pigs, respiratory arrest occurred and a quick, struggle-free death followed. They reported that this rarely occurred in the unsensitized animal. This theory received much attention in the following years, and was a major point of debate during the first Seattle Conference on SIDS in 1963. By that time, two centers had reported no greater rise in antibodies in SIDS infants than in healthy controls, and in fact found that they were somewhat lower in SIDS (Gold et al, 1961; Coe and Peterson, 1963). Parrish's theory was not without merit in the sense that almost every epidemiological study of SIDS has found a lower prevalence of SIDS in breast-fed infants than for those artificially fed. Also, the special case of gastroesophageal reflux must be considered, although the British group reported no apnea in animals that had not been previously sensitized to cow's milk.

An anaphylactic reaction causing SIDS due to a "nephrosis peptide" was suggested by Stowens et al in 1966. The reasoning was that in anaphylaxis experimentally induced in animals, anatomical changes were similar to those found in SIDS, including an abnormal protein in the urinary system. The initial insult was suggested to be the absorption of undigested protein. In contrast to Stowens' earlier proposal of a reflex mechanism of death, the theory on the nephrosis peptide has "failed for the want of a second."

Immunization reactions to pertussis as well as other ordinary childhood immunization has been suspected as a cause of SIDS. Without question, on rare occasions pertussis can produce catastrophic neurological problems. Lenard et al (1977) reported sixteen cases of neurological catastrophies and/or death after pertussis immunization, and three of those were diagnosed as SIDS, whereas several of the others had a typical pertussis encephalopathy. Considering the vast number of infants who are exposed to immunizations world-wide, the fatalities are certainly rare, and overall, the protection of the "herd" seems to warrant the very small risk to the individual. There remains in my mind the question of whether it is really important to start the immunizations for *all* infants at two months of age, as opposed to six months of age, at which time there is much less risk of SIDS. It seems likely considering all of the non-specific triggers identified in sleep apnea, that the mild febrile reaction common in infants after immunization might lead to sleep deprivation or fragmentation, and lead to SIDS. Although it would be a disservice to most children to eliminate the immunizations because of fear of SIDS, postponing rather than eliminating is a question that should be analyzed objectively for each child. This is particularly true in the relatively affluent cultures where herd immunity offers substantial protection by reducing the chances of contact with infected individuals. Transmission through immune individuals does not occur.

Raven for some years argued that, on the basis of many crib deaths studied in Detroit, the cause was "primary acute interstitial pneumonitis" (1967). She also emphasized that many of the infants were not perfectly normal, as was commonly held, and in her study of nine hundred fifty cases, 40% showed "a history of prematurity, low weight, or some other handicap at birth." She found only 70% of the cases suggested a viral etiology. Although her reports have not been treated with the respect that the numbers alone should have commanded, the difference really seems to be one of emphasis. Dr. Raven has suggested that the post-mortem findings that she observed could cause death, whereas most pathologists not only did not regard the histologic changes as lethal, they defined SIDS in such a way as to exclude that possibility. In fairness, it would appear that her observations were correct, and her conclusions overdrawn, but nevertheless helpful in establishing the role of viral respiratory infection as at least a trigger of SIDS. More recently, Raven and her co-workers (1978) have suggested that the lethalness of these infections might be through a hypersensitivity reaction. Unfortunately, proving that immunoglobulins are present in tissues at necropsy is not equivalent to proving an anaphylactic reaction as the cause of death.

A similar criticism must be applied to the theory of anaphylaxis and the house dust mite. The mite is apparently ubiquitous, although why it should be lethal only from one month to six months of age is not clear. The "epidemic" of articles suggesting this relationship began in 1971 in New Zealand (Helson, 1971), and spread rapidly to Australia (Mulvey, 1972), and with Turner and co-workers as a vector, to the British medical press (Turner et al, 1975). They reported that serum IGE antibodies to D. pteronyssinus were found in 37% of SIDS victims compared to 7% of matched controls. They also found antibodies to cow's milk and to aspergillus at twice the frequency for SIDS as in control infants. They concluded that anaphylaxis due to one or more allergens was the immediate cause of death in SIDS or at least one of the factors. Actually, there is no substantial evidence for anaphylaxis to *any* known allergen in SIDS.

Although a hypothesis might suggest that the majority of these reactions occur at night, and are therefore unobserved, the probabilities are that hypersensitivity reactions will occur in a graded fashion, and therefore some near-misses should be available for confirmation of the theory in subsequent studies. This was the case for botulism, which now can be ranked as *a* cause of SIDS, but to my knowledge, there has not been a single near-miss of hypersensitivity reported in the world's literature.

Deficiency States

Deficiencies as a cause of SIDS started with artificial feeding, and specifically involved hypoglycemia and dehydration. There were well-documented individual cases of dehydration from inappropriate mixing of dried milk, common during World War II. Francis Camps, introducing the 1970 British Conference on Cot Deaths (Camps and Carpenter, 1972), recalled that very early a pathologist had made a public statement that "dried milk kills babies." Porter, in this symposium, suggested that the artificial formula induced hypoglycemia by a complicated metabolic pathway. This theory has not been substantiated, either in terms of frequent occurrence of hypoglycemia or by genetic studies. Sturner and Susa (1980) found the glucose concentration in the vitreous humor, and the liver glycogen content to be similar at autopsy in SIDS and controls. However, hypernatremia and uremia were found by Emery and colleagues (1974) to have a substantial prevalence in SIDS, almost half in Sheffield, measured by post-mortem studies of the vitreous humor. Although some of these infants had had gastrointestinal upsets, as a reasonable cause of dehydration, Emery postulated that the underlying cause was a high rate of artificial feeding for these victims. In most instances, the mother was using powdered milk, reconstituting it in a more concentrated form than it was intended, based on a well-intentioned idea of enhancing growth. Fortunately, a campaign was begun in Sheffield shortly after the results were discovered to convince mothers of the dangers of concentrated formula. In the period from 1969 to 1978, there was a virtual disappearance of deaths with hypernatremia in the group of cot deaths (Sunderland and Emery, 1979). They attributed their success to the gradual reduction in the incidence of gastroenteritis, with emphasis on good hygiene, in addition to the removal of the high-sodium milk-solid preparations, and an increased incidence of breast feeding, following their local campaign. Although deaths with hypernatremia had disappeared, cot deaths continued, although at a lower rate, from an average of approximately four per one thousand live births, to a recent average of two per one thousand live births.

Other electrolytes have been implicated, probably all of them at one time or another, by one authority or another, as contributing to SIDS. The first appears to be by Maresch (1962); he felt that electrolyte imbalance caused myocardial dysfunction, and wrote a series of papers suggesting a role in SIDS for dietary insufficiencies, including rickets. Magnesium has been a particularly rich vein, producing papers on the cause of SIDS. Caddell, in particular, has vigorously pursued magnesium deficiency as a cause of SIDS, beginning in 1972. To counter the growing number of centers that did not find low magnesium in the vitreous humor, she dismissed that evidence on the grounds that "the vitreous magnesium did not reflect the known degree of magnesium deficiency in experimental animals." To make matters more convenient for the theory, she also contended that plasma magnesium values were unreliable. This left only her loading test of live patients with parenteral magnesium as the sole criterion of whether magnesium deficiency existed or not. Needless to say, that invalidated any postmortem decisions as to magnesium deficiency in her opinion. In defense of her theory, the ability to produce apnea and bradycardia with an experimental magnesium-deficient diet is a reasonable model, and the post-mortem findings in the animals were similar to those found in SIDS (Caddell, 1978). Also, a physiological method of producing magnesium deficiency was found in multiple pregnancies for rats, and when human multipara were tested with parenteral loading of magnesium, they were found to retain a high percentage, and therefore to be magnesium-deficient. In her 1978 report, Caddell briefly mentions twenty-five near-miss infants; she found that they retained 60 to 100% of the parenteral loading dose. Curiously, some of them had received magnesium therapy prior to the load test. There was also a cryptic comment that "*some* other infants with similar episodes had lower retention of the magnesium loads" (emphasis added). There was also a caviat at the end that, since magnesium "operates in conjunction with other minerals in the body, we would expect to find an associated mineral imbalance," not actually demonstrated.

A thorough study by Blumenfeld and colleagues (1979) of post-mortem vitreous chemistry in SIDS victims compared to other children dying in the same age group revealed magnesium concentrations that were actually higher in the SIDS victims. They concluded that the chemistry measurements post-mortem did not aid in the diagnosis of SIDS, a commendably restrained conclusion for an excellent analysis. The same cannot be said for an unfortunate communication in *Lancet* (Chipperfield and Chipperfield, 1979). In an amazing structure of hypothesis and unproven facts, they began with an assertion that magnesium concentration in heart muscle was low in ischemic heart death. Secondly, they quoted Caddell as showing that magnesium deficiency could cause cot deaths. Thirdly, in seven infants dying of cot death they found a magnesium concentration in heart muscle of one hundred seventy-nine, compared to adult controls of one hundred eighty-six, with a single standard deviation of twenty-one and twenty-five, respectively. They do not comment on the significance of that difference, but rather emphasized a significant difference in potassium and calcium concentration in the heart muscle from cot deaths. They then list as evidence a ratio of magnesium to calcium as a contributory cause of sudden cardiac death in cot deaths, and cite for support a report by Guilleminault et al (1976) as further evidence of cardiac abnormalities. (The only cardiac arrhythmias of an ominous nature were observed by this group in an adult, and the arrhythmias seen in the near-miss infants were of the oxygen-conserving type.)

Selenium and vitamin E have been implicated in SIDS (Asher, 1975; Money, 1971), but subsequently were dismissed by Schrauzer et al (1975) for San Diego County, if not for New Zealand!

The suggestion that a simple vitamin D deficiency was involved has recently been eliminated (Hillman et al, 1980). Thiamine was proposed as a vitamin deficiency that could account for sleep apnea by Read (1978), but Peterson and his co-workers (1981) found no evidence in favor of that suggestion by studying erythrocyte transketolase. A rather fanciful indictment of ascorbic acid deficiency as a cause of SIDS, among many human disorders, was detailed by Stone in 1979. He correctly pointed out the unfortunate inborn error of metabolism that the human has carried for thousands of years—the inability to produce ascorbic acid from carbohydrates. In a mathematical analysis that would please Pauling and the manufacturers of vitamins, Stone calculated that the average 70 kg goat produces over 13 grams of ascorbate daily. Stone extrapolates to the need for very large quantities of ascorbic acid for the human, and asserts that the usual quantities recommended for human daily requirements result in a continued state of mild scurvy. No substantive evidence relating to SIDS was offered.

The most recent vitamin deficiency allegation is by Johnson et al (1980), who found that chickens made biotin-deficient died unexpectedly when exposed to stress. They reported that the levels of biotin in livers of infants who died of SIDS were significantly lower than those of infants of similar age who died of explainable causes of death. No refutation has appeared yet, but if the course is similar to other alleged deficiencies, if should not be long coming. Although I have no hard data whatsoever on the subject of biotin deficiency in chickens or in the livers of SIDS victims, I did attempt to produce biotin deficiency in rats as a student laboratory exercise at Harvard Medical School, and I can report that to produce a diet deficient in biotin requires an incredibly narrow range of food sources. Recently, an eleven-year-old retarded boy was found to be biotin deficient as a result of a diet of raw eggs, which contain avidin, a biotin-binding protein (Sweetman et al, 1981). These authors state that "biotin is widely abundant in foods and is produced as well by intestinal bacteria so that its deficiency is rare."

Endocrine deficiencies as a cause of SIDS have had an occasional advocate. Geertinger (1976) was unable to find parathyroid glands in patients dying of cot death. This was refuted by several centers, and the embryological basis was also flawed. Since the thymus is intimately related, developmentally, the absence or hypoplasia of the thymus should be obvious, and the infants should have had tetany at an early age. Congenital adrenal hypoplasia was reported as a cause of sudden infant death by Russell et al (1977). However, the report involved a nine-month-old infant, and as has been emphasized repeatedly, the finding of a true disorder of this sort automatically removes it from the category of SIDS. Assuredly, an infant dying at nine months is highly suspect of having some cause of death other than SIDS.

Hypothermia and Hyperthermia

Possible deficiencies of thermal homeostasis have been proposed as explanation of SIDS, through hypothermia. The proposal by Cornwell (1979) is that there is an abnormality of the adrenergic system resulting in diminished non-shivering thermogenesis. The proposal assumes genetic factors, although the epidemiology of SIDS is not consistent with an ordinary dominant or recessive inheritance.

Overheating is postulated as causing at least some unexpected deaths in infants (Stanton et al, 1980). The inference was from histological changes in the small intestines that were similar to those described in heatstroke. The interaction proposed is between a fever initiated by an infection, and excessive bed clothing. Obviously, any infant is relatively at the mercy of the elements, and parental judgment of what is necessary for clothing, and it seems likely that on rare occasions an infant will be brought to death or near death from either extreme of temperature, but no one would seriously suggest that this is *the* cause of SIDS, or for any substantial part. However, there may be a more indirect role for hyperthermia increasing the susceptibility to sleep apnea, discussed in that section.

Abnormal Thyroid Levels

In November, 1981, Chacon and Tildon reported elevated levels of tri-iodothyronine (T_3) in victims of SIDS, but relatively normal thyroxine (T_4). In contrast, levels from autopsied infants with known cause of death were normal, except for three infants with acute respiratory infections. Although the authors acknowledged the possibility that the elevated T_3 was secondary to other pathological events, they obviously favored the idea of a primary role. They suggested that post-mortem findings of an underdeveloped vagus nerve (Sachis et al, 1981), increased muscle mass in the pulmonary arterioles (Naeye, 1973), and the abnormal cardiopulmonary functions in aborted SIDS patients (Leistner et al, 1980; Haddad et al, 1979) could be attributed to hyperthyroidism. Chacon and Tildon rejected a primary role for hypoxia in the elevation of T_3 because Moshang and his co-workers (1980) found lowered levels of T_3 and T_4 in children with cyanotic congenital heart disease.

An alternative to primary hyperthyroidism that is compatible with elevated T_3 and normal T_4 involves the role of the thyroid in cold stress and fever. An excellent review of neuroendocrine thermoregulation was prepared by Gale (1973); several relationships with aspects of SIDS postmortem findings come to mind after reading this review. Of cardinal significance is the mechanism by which the body develops and sustains a fever: "resetting upward of the regulated temperature (of the body) in the preoptic anterior hypothalamus (POAH)." This phenomenon can be studied very precisely by cooling or warming the hypothalamus in primates. In this paradigm of fever production shivering and non-shivering thermogenesis are achieved by neuronal control enhanced by secretion of thyrotropin and corticotropin. A more sustained challenge to thermogenesis, chronic cold exposure in animals, utilizes similar metabolic mechanisms. Hillier (1968) found that mature animals exposed to cold increased their consumption of both T_4 and T_3. This deiodination was enhanced by epinephrine and norepinephrine, with greater effect from the latter. Relative to the specific findings of Chacon and Tilden of increased T_3 but no increase in T_4, animals chronically required to increase heat production preferentially increase T_3 and plasma T_4 is unchanged or even decreased (Dulac and Jobin, 1972). This is in contrast to thyrotoxicosis which produces a marked rise in T_4 (Ingbar and Bass, 1957). The relationship of T_3 to T_4 levels in SIDS does not then suggest a primary disorder of hyperthyroidism.

Studies in primates and in man of infections with fever established the secondary effects on thyroid metabolism. Woeber (1971) reported that the clearances of labeled T_4 and T_3 from peripheral pools were accelerated. He did not measure the serum T_3, but found serum T_4 level unchanged. Gregerman and Solomon (1967) in human patients with bacterial pulmonary infections found a greatly accelerated disposal rate of both T_4 and T_3 during the acute phase of these illnesses.

The mechanisms of thermogenesis, whether as a febrile response to infection or to cold exposure, have some common features with other known pathologic and epidemiologic features of SIDS. Naeye (1974) found delayed replacement with white fat of the periadrenal brown fat at autopsy of SIDS victims. Although he attributed this delay to chronic hypoxia, the chief function of this brown fat is nonshivering thermogenesis. The infant has a well-developed ability for this form of heat production, which is enhanced by norepinephrine and thyroid hormone acting synergistically (Gale, 1973). It is possible that the persistence of brown fat and elevated T_3 levels in SIDS victims are manifestations of febrile episodes, or chronic cold exposure. The former is consistent with elevated gamma globulin levels reported by Valdes-Dapena (1963) and the consistent epidemiologic and pathologic findings of minor infections in the victims. The possibility of a contribution from chronic cold exposure in some cases is suggested by the greater rate of occurrence of SIDS in winter, although that association may only coincide with greater frequency of respiratory infections. The evidence of increased sympathetic activity in aborted SIDS could also relate to thermogenesis (Haddad et al, 1979). The role of abrupt rise in body temperature on sleep apnea was presented earlier.

Toxicology

Deliberate poisoning is a remote possibility that cannot be ruled out without a toxicologic study (Finkle et al, 1979). In a review of sixteen cases of "chemical child abuse," Shnaps and co-workers (1981) found the assailant to be the mother in all, in contrast to physical abuse which usually involves the father or another man. The mother was subsequently judged "mentally disturbed" in eleven cases, but only once was that known to the medical staff during the child's evaluation. Four of the sixteen cases were infants in the SIDS age range; salt was the agent twice, and aspirin and chlorpromazine once each. Although three fatalities resulted, homicide was never the intent; usually, the abuse was an attempt to escape severe physical or emotional problems.

To place poisoning in the context of infant death, Smialek and Monforte (1977) studied 130 cases of sudden death in infants, including 102 concluded to be SIDS. Six positive toxicologic results were found but in five of those, the drugs had been prescribed for a variety of illnesses. None of the SIDS cases were concluded to be related to the toxicologic findings. They concluded that the likelihood of positive toxicologic findings were sufficiently remote that there should be no delay in informing the family of the diagnosis of SIDS after the post-mortem examination, rather than wait for a full toxicology report. That does not mean that toxicologic studies should not be done if there are grounds for considering that possibility, but that study can quietly proceed and the question re-opened in the event of positive findings without burdening the great majority of families who are neither homicidal nor negligent.

Cerebral Ischemia

We have reviewed—and dismissed—the theories of airway obstruction due to extremes of posture. A variation on this theme but with a vascular mechanism was recently reported (Gilles et al, 1979). They found relative ease of displacement of the vertebral column relative to the skull in infant cadavers. They were able to invert the posterior arch of the atlas through the foramen magnum, during extension of the head on the atlas, and observed that this would compress the vertebral arteries bilaterally. They went on to suggest this as a possible cause of SIDS. The ability to do things with force on a cadaver should not be easily translated into a subtle mechanism of death such as is found in most instances of SIDS. It is not clear how the authors propose that the infant will somehow decompress prior to death, so that the autopsy would miss this extreme dislocation. The other objection to this theory is that occlusion of the vertebral artery is very unlikely to produce lethal cerebral ischemia. Particularly in infants with very compliant blood vessels, collateral circulation through the circle of Willis, from the carotid arteries, will easily take up the deficiency produced by vertebral artery compression. It is a common practice in cardiovascular surgery of infants and children to sacrifice the vertebral artery in the process of creating a shunt in tetrad of Fallot. This Blalock-Taussig procedure may have to be repeated on the contralateral side, resulting in bilateral, permanent interruption of the vertebral arteries, and I know of no instances in childhood or infancy in which a cerebral catastrophe followed. (There are rare reports of problems in adults of that complication). In short, the studies of Woolley again should be reassuring to us, against continued new theories of extreme posture causing sudden death; it is extraordinarily unlikely.

Chapter VIII

Maternal Factors in SIDS

One of the most difficult areas to discuss in SIDS is the evidence of an epidemiologic nature that indicates certain maternal characteristics cause a statistical increase in the rate of SIDS. There is an unfortunate possibility that the mother of a SIDS victim, who was perfectly loved and cared for, will feel that these comments are an insensitive accusation. In agonizing over this decision with parents of a SIDS victim who have supported research on this subject, I was encouraged by their response. They recognized the need for factual information to assist in preventing the tragedy, and secondly, they personally felt no anxiety about such information, knowing that their infant died in spite of receiving the best emotional and physical care. Just as we must face the difficult problem of child abuse, an intentional hurting of infants and children, the goal of preventing crib death seems to justify the exploration of this subject in depth. There is also the requirement of science that we look at the facts, and not suppress those relationships that are real, if uncomfortable in their implications.

It is reasonably clear that SIDS represents a peculiar vulnerability of the infant in the first few months of life, and that the precipitating event or events may vary substantially in variety and severity. Similarly, there is obviously a wide range of robustness of infants, some succumbing after a mild respiratory infection, and other infants surviving relatively major challenges to the life force. It then is not surprising that any characteristic relationship that weakens the general vitality of an infant would make him more vulnerable to SIDS, without directly *causing* SIDS. This role of a contributing factor, rather than etiology, is what we wish to explore in this chapter.

We will begin by considering some of the most obvious, extreme examples, where the maternal deprivation is most obvious, to establish that contribution in the extreme before considering the subtle problems.

Maternal Psychoses and Sociopathic Behavior

Asch's contention (1968) that a substantial number of SIDS victims were the victims of post-partum depression and infanticide was never seriously accepted by most individuals familiar with the field of SIDS for the same reason that we have referred to repeatedly, that *a* cause for sudden and unexpected infant death is not the same as *the* cause. However, there are well-documented tragedies of women who are pathologically depressed after delivery to the point of suicide; Asch analyzes the psychodynamics to show that the infant is seen in the disturbed mind as an extension of the mother's own self, so that the destruction of the infant is a symbolic suicide. Not infrequently, maternal suicide accompanies the infanticide. In any case, the psychotic behavior of the mother is relatively plain to see and this cause of SIDS would be obvious and could not account for any substantial part of the overall problem.

Non-psychotic but socially unacceptable maternal behavior can be shown to affect the rate of SIDS, specifically in drug-dependent mothers. Pierson and colleagues (1972) reported three sudden and unexpected deaths out of fourteen infants born to women in their methadone maintenance program. One of those deaths was not proven at autopsy, but even two out of fourteen is a high prevalence, compared to the two per thousand in the usual population. A more conventional epidemiological study was performed in 1978 (Rajegowda et al) of a wider range of narcotic-dependent mothers. They found an incidence of SIDS 5.5 times that of the general hospital population, and 8.7 times that of the neighborhood in New York City. Another study, from Detroit, found a ratio of 5:1 for SIDS in infants of drug-dependent mothers, compared to a control population from the same hospital (Chavez et al, 1979). Of interest, in relation to the mechanism of death, was that the deaths occurred after withdrawal problems were completely over, and the authors concluded that withdrawal could not be implicated in these sudden infant deaths. The authors also commented that careful autopsy failed to reveal any evidence of physical abuse. Olson and Lees (1980) studied nine infants born to mothers maintained on methadone and found most of their respiratory behavior was normal, but that they had a flattened ventilatory response to carbon dioxide in the first fifteen days. Only one infant still had an abnormal response by thirty-one days, and none died. The authors suggested that the abnormal ventilatory response might be causally related to the reported increased rate of SIDS, but the time of the ventilatory abnormality was not appropriately related to the known time of SIDS deaths, having returned to normal by the time SIDS would be expected, after one month of age. Considering that the deaths occur at a time when there appears to be no further functional abnormality in the human infant, another very significant possibility is that the infant of drug-dependent mothers receives less than normal attention, not abuse, but simply a diminished awareness and interaction with the infant.

Epidemiological Characteristics of Mothers of SIDS Infants

Although none of the differences between mothers of victims of SIDS compared to a normal population are strong enough to predict effectively, there are differences which are statistically significant, and many of these differences are found repeatedly in different countries and different regions. The mothers of SIDS victims tend to be younger, and of particular interest, they are usually multiparous, and therefore, not inexperienced. They tend to be poorer than average, and there is always a higher prevalence among black than white mothers. The mothers usually seek less medical care, both for themselves during the pregnancy and for the infant. One of the most striking findings from Sheffield, England, as the best single predictor of death in infancy was the failure of the mother to bring the baby to the first follow-up clinic (Protestos et al, 1973). The same group found that a major contributor to post-neonatal deaths was the failure of the mother to recognize a serious health problem (McWeeny and Emery, 1975). They attributed this failure in part to a general inability of some parents to recognize the importance of symptoms, but also, a negative attitude on the part of these parents towards health services. They commented that the parents of some of the cot death victims had very little initiative or persistence required to obtain general medical care.

Steele and Langworth (1966) were probably the first modern writers to suggest certain problems of "mothering" that emerged from their study of eighty cases of SIDS in Canada. They found that artificial feeding as opposed to breast feeding was associated with a higher incidence of SIDS. They found a higher incidence in women who married young, and whose first pregnancy occurred at a younger age. They found that the mother's first prenatal visit was later in the pregnancy leading to a SIDS, than for the normal population, and finally they found a higher rate of cigarette smoking in the mothers of SIDS victims. Although the level of statistical significance was striking, ranging from .05 to less than .001, the actual ratios were not as striking. For example, in the mothers who had infants who died of SIDS, the ratio of smokers to non-smokers was 2.2:1, whereas the control was only 1.5:1. The same is true for the other variables that identify a population difference, but when applied to the individual family, have little value in prediction. The particular issue of breast feeding versus bottle feeding has been an emotional subject, perhaps because it is one of the few differences that reflect an opportunity for choice for the mother. In most epidemiologic studies, a substantially higher percentage of SIDS victims have been bottle-fed than breast-fed. This led to the earlier British theory of death due to anaphylactic reaction to cow's milk. Although this anaphylaxis theory has never advanced beyond the level of a hypothesis due to lack of substantial evidence, the statistics on breast feeding are persistent (Carpenter and Shaddick, 1965; Mason et al, 1980; Carpenter and Emery, 1977). I have found only one study that failed to find any difference between breast feedings and artificial feeding in the incidence of SIDS (Schrauzer et al, 1975). Without doubt, there is no absolute protection against SIDS by breast feeding, and for the unfortunate mother who is psychologically or physically unable to breast feed, the implication that she is placing her infant at risk for SIDS is one capable of causing great guilt. Yet, the statistics are there, and considering the increased opportunity for gastrointestinal infections due to improperly prepared formulas, either through errors in strength or contamination, very few pediatricians would argue that breast feeding was not a desirable method of nutrition, and would argue for its theoretical immune advantages. A subtle problem emerges, that of an unhappy or depressed mother, such as an unmarried mother with an unwanted pregnancy, who unconsciously finds it difficult to nurture that infant in a loving manner, including breast feeding. A lack of strong maternal-infant bonding may be a very powerful force to which we will return. Certainly, many of the statistical descriptors of mothers of SIDS contain the ingredients for a tired and depressed mother, who would be less capable of strong bonding.

A hint of the role of mothering may be seen in the repetition rate of SIDS in families, which is six to ten times higher than in the average population. Yet studies of monozygotic and dyzygotic twins and studies of first cousins indicate that there is no inheritance operating in a Mendelian sense. The higher rate in a family, without a substantial genetic contribution, leaves an environmental factor a strong possibility, and the single most crucial element in the infant's environment is quite clearly his mother.

The dependence of successful breast feeding on the attitude of the mother is borne out by the study in Sheffield by Carpenter and Emery (1977). In their final results of studies of infants at risk for sudden death, not only was breast feeding associated with low risk, but the stated *intention* of the mother to breast feed at the time of discharge from the maternity hospital had a beneficial effect, statistically.

Cigarette smoking, first identified by Steele and Langworth (1966), remains in every study as a significant factor, including one whose authors found no significant relationship for breast feeding (Schrauzer et al, 1975). Peterson (1981) suggested that even the earlier report of slowed post-natal growth in the victims of SIDS might be explainable on the basis of maternal smoking, since the effects are quite similar. As with many other epidemiologic facts, the association between cigarettes and SIDS is not necessarily a causal one, but could reflect a response to stresses on the younger mother who has inadequate resources, both emotional and physical, to handle her responsibilities for a totally dependent infant. An alternate explanation for the low birth weight, statistically associated with SIDS, has been suggested—the short pregnancy interval. The short pregnancy interval leaves the mother depleted in terms of mineral resources, as well as emotionally, and very reasonably could account for the small size at birth (Spiers and Wang, 1976).

Finally, there is the distressing similarity of the epidemiology of SIDS to child abuse, including the fact that sudden infant death syndrome is more frequent in these families, even though thorough investigations have ruled out abuse in the specific reports (Roberts et al, 1980). In particular, young maternal age, premature delivery, and increased neonatal morbidity are common to both child abuse and SIDS. Babies from abusing families fail to thrive, and Roberts et al suggest that a major feature is the failure of bonding between mother and the infant in these families.

Although these statements can be substantiated from a statistical point of view, they have very weak predictive power in any individual family or situation. Many victims of SIDS can be shown to have been breast fed, to have had a mature, married mother with great enthusiasm for the pregnancy and infant, and who did not smoke cigarettes, but still suffered the tragic loss of sudden infant death. The only reasonable inference is that sudden infant death is a major disorder of infancy, and any additional vulnerability of an infant through unskilled or emotionally uncommitted mothering will increase the chances of the infant succumbing to SIDS or any other disease. On the other hand, this epidemiology offers very real opportunities for reducing the chances of SIDS by improving the care of the mother and infant, including the emotional as well as the physical well-being.

Epidemiologic Characteristics of SIDS Infants

Characteristics of the infants who die may be examined for the same kind of evidence we have looked at in their mothers, that might suggest an increased vulnerability. The infants, as a whole, who succumb to SIDS are smaller at birth, but of more significance, gain and grow less well than a matched control group (Emery, 1959; Peterson et al, 1974; Naeye et al, 1976). Naeye and his colleagues reported other abnormalities, including difficulties with respiration, feeding, and temperature regulation. Although Naeye attributed these to neurological deficits or brain dysfunction, these are also characteristic of depressed or deprived infants and even animals. Naeye and colleagues reported the behavioral characteristics of SIDS victims (1976). The data were collected retrospectively, and are to that extent suspect, but they revealed a remarkable similarity, with statistical significance. The parents recalled that the victims had "less intense reactions to environmental stimuli, were less active physically, were more breathless and exhausted during feeding, and had more abnormal cries." If one looks at the first two characteristics in a broader emotional or psychological point of view, the similarity to the description of a depressed individual is evident. Although depression ordinarily is thought of as a characteristic of an older child or adult, the existence of the non-verbal state of the infant does not eliminate the possibility. A fascinating description of depression in a three and one-half month-old child was reported by Gaensbauer (1980) based on an infant who suffered repeated losses of a mother-figure. Quoting the description of this infant, "pathognomonic signs of anaclitic depression that were present in her case include the sad facies, withdrawal, apathy, psychomotor retardation, absence of pleasure, and a tendency toward irritability and distress." This infant's mood disturbance was not a transient one, but persisted for several days, even after adequate caretaking was re-established.

The effect of maternal deprivation, or even impaired maternal-infant bonding has been shown to affect the physical status of infants as well as emotional status (Rutter, 1972; Bowlby, 1973; Klaus and Kennell, 1976). Klaus and Kennell, for example, showed that severe impairment of maternal-infant bonding could result in failure to thrive and even "the battered child." Spitz (1945) reviewed the early literature on maternal deprivation syndrome, and found that the syndrome could develop despite excellent nutrition, impeccable sanitary conditions, good health care, and in the absence of overt abuse. He found that despite such physically favorable conditions, 37% of orphans confined in one institution under such a regimen died before reaching their first birthday! Ironically, the "sterile" milieu that was aimed at preventing infectious diseases killed more infants than when they were exposed to a more casual physical contact in comparable institutions, with effective mother-figures. Children who are deprived during infancy of maternal-infant bonding develop a syndrome characterized by extreme short stature and marked delay of skeletal maturation, resembling idiopathic hypopituitarism, accompanied by psychological abnormalities (Silver and Finkelstein, 1967; Powell et al, 1967). These children are not malnourished, but have normal or greater than normal weight for their stature. Some instances are found in families of higher socioeconomic status, where there is inadequate "mothering" resulting from a depression or other psychiatric difficulty (Colman and Provence, 1957; Elmer, 1960). Some of these cases document impaired development as early as three months of age (Colman and Provence, 1957; Menking et al, 1959). The syndrome has received attention even in the lay press, as "psychosocial dwarfism" (Restak, 1979).

Even rats suffer with a reduced long-term viability when deprived of their mothers. Ader et al (1960) found that rats separated from their mothers only seven days prematurely showed increased susceptibility to gastric ulcers as adults when placed in a conflict situation, and even showed increased susceptibility to transplanted tumors (Ader and Friedman, 1965). The surviving rats suffer greater mortality and a smaller adult weight, and of particular interest, the maternal behavior of the females is severely affected. The offspring of the deprived mothers in turn gain weight more slowly and suffer elevated mortality (Thoman and Arnold, 1968). Monkeys raised in total social isolation frequently develop anorexia and succumb more readily, and the surviving monkeys are "hypoactive, non-exploratory, and engage in high levels of self-clutching, withdrawal, and repetitive stereotyped responses" (Sackett, 1968). The physiologic changes that accompany separation of the infant monkey from his mother are a decrease in heart rate, body temperature, total sleep time, REM sleep time, and the number of REM periods (Short et al, 1978). Infant rats also have similar responses with a 40% decrease in cardiac and respiratory rates, even when the body temperature is maintained, and after adequate nutrition is supplied (Hofer, 1970).

Biochemical and endocrinologic changes can be found with separation of infant rats from their mothers. As little as one hour of separation resulted in a 50% reduction of ornithine decarboxylase, an enzyme crucial for organ growth and differentiation in the brain and hearts of rat pups (Butler et al, 1978). Surprisingly, control pups left in the presence of a mother with ligated nipples showed no decline in enzyme activity, but pups left in the presence of an anesthetized, lactating mother did experience the fall in ornithine decarboxylase. This experiment seems to rule out nutrition and feeding as the explanation, and implicates active mothering behavior as the crucial factor. The reduced enzyme activity depresses serum growth hormone (Kuhn et al, 1978), consistent with observations of deficient pituitary functions in human maternal deprivation syndrome (Powell et al, 1967).

Central catecholamines are also depleted with maternal deprivation (Welch and Welch, 1971). Mice isolated for prolonged periods, in addition to displaying abnormal behavior, display lower rates of turnover in their central catecholamines, and have increased vulnerability to toxic effects of sympathetic drugs. Behaviorally, animals depleted of central catecholamines with reserpine show behavior and physiology very similar to that observed with separation reactions in the same animals (Kety and Schildkraut, 1967).

Even the adult responds with a variety of illnesses with relatively subtle stresses, identified in the work of Holmes and Masuda (1973). In this classic, they were able to quantify stresses of ordinary life-changes, such as marriage, divorce, birth of a child, loss of job, and to quantify the total effect of these life-changes in a period of time, and successfully predict illness and injury. There seems little reason to expect an infant's health to be immune from life-changes, such as the prolonged absence of his mother, or sleep deprivation.

One of the most hopeful findings related to the problem of mothering are those reported by Carpenter and Emery and their colleagues in Sheffield. They found that remarkably non-specific intervention aimed at improving infant care produced a notable reduction in infant mortality, including that of SIDS (Prostestos et al, 1973; Carpenter and Emery, 1974; Emery and Carpenter, 1974; Carpenter and Emery, 1977; and Carpenter et al, 1977). Their efforts in prediction of the infant at risk of dying in infancy led to an increased effort directed at the mothers of the group at risk. The interventions consisted only of extra post-natal follow-up exams and bi-weekly home visits from a public health nurse. Among high-risk infants whose families received this special attention, the rate for SIDS was 3.2 per thousand, while among a control group of similar high-risk infants who did not receive the additional post-natal attention, the rate was 10.6 per thousand. They felt that the health visitors prevented some deaths simply by offering support and suggestions relating to nutrition and hygiene, and by alerting health and social workers to urgent medical or domestic problems. The incidence of non-SIDS death was also lower in the group receiving support, and the possibility of simply improved relations between the infant and the mother was enhanced by the approval and attention of the health visitor. A similar effect has been found in this country (Kempe, 1976). His group identified families at risk for child abuse and neglect. No incidents of abuse or neglect were detected in twenty-five high-risk families visited by health workers, compared to five incidents requiring hospitalization including one death, among twenty-five high risk families not visited (Krugman et al, 1978).

The other obvious targets for preventive work that should reduce overall mortality and morbidity, as well as the rate of SIDS, would include family planning with better spacing between infants, the avoidance of unwanted pregnancy for both unmarried and married women, and improved prenatal and post-natal care with appropriate counseling and emotional support. These should be easily available and should include an outreach program to reach those very women most in need of support who are depressed and lack initiative. This does *not* imply that SIDS is a disease of neglect, but that SIDS is only one of many threats to the life of a vulnerable infant; the better the maternal-infant bond, and the better the physical and emotional well-being of the mother and infant, the better the chance that the child will survive this period of vulnerability without falling victim to SIDS.

Chapter IX

Management and Prevention of SIDS

The Dead Infant and His Parents

The immediate management of the victim of SIDS also involves the parents. No matter what may be defined as the minimal requirements of management, the reality of the individual situation will vary markedly from one geographic area to another, depending upon the resources available, the awareness of the problem by the health personnel involved, and even the socioeconomic status of the family. Some of the "deficiencies" in management may be fairly attributed to inadequacies of our health-care system, but others may reflect flexibility and good common sense. In general, an infant dying suddenly and unexpectedly is a "coroner's case" by law, since the deceased will not have been under the immediate care of a physician for any disorder expected to be lethal. Such laws were intended to detect deliberate or negligent homicide, and were not really aimed at the death of an infant, although that age group should surely not be excluded from the protection of law. The fact that the protection of the law may lead to accusations of culpability, and even trial, should not be used to discredit those required to enforce such laws. It is understandably a trying experience to face accusations of this sort, whether guilty or innocent, and even for the truly guilty there may be extenuating circumstances. It is undoubtedly tragic that society must have laws to protect children and adults from abuse and neglect, but the frequency of child abuse is unfortunately many times that of SIDS. An insensitive investigator is obviously regrettable in terms of the hurt to the innocent parent, but a flaw in the system does not justify its suspension or inactivation by special interest groups who are more preoccupied with the feelings of the parents than with the protection of the child by society. To me, as a pediatrician and a parent, the helplessness of the infant demands a greater priority on balance, before the feelings of the parent. There is still no need for brutal insensitivity during any investigation of a sudden death in an infant, but there remains the need for a reasonable investigation. It is probably therapeutic, in fact, to have a reasonably thorough investigation, culminating in an honest and factual reassurance to the parents that the infant died of crib death. In most cases, this investigation will be centered around an autopsy, performed by a competent pathologist. The extent of a post-mortem examination will reasonably vary although there are certain minimal screening procedures for the examination that should always be performed. Depending upon abnormal findings, further investigations, including x-rays, toxicologic examination, microbiology studies, histochemical studies, and of course microscopic slide preparation may be required.

There are definite problems in obtaining an autopsy in some situations. Transportation may be a genuine limitation in large parts of the country that are sparsely settled. It may be quite unsettling to young parents to be asked to drive the remains of an infant several hundred miles to a facility for post-mortem examination, and it may seem shocking to them to find out that the hospital expects to be reimbursed for the expenses of the autopsy, including the services of the pathologist. If microscopic slides are involved or other more extensive studies, the cost may be substantial, and more than many can afford. Health insurance plans rarely include more than a token amount for such an examination, and only teaching hospitals have been willing to subsidize the post-mortem examinations for the value in teaching and in advancing knowledge. Presumably, if the coroner orders the autopsy, the expense is borne by some part of the government, which may be an advantage to the family.

In brief, a thorough autopsy is generally a requirement for the management of SIDS, but I do not see this as mandatory in every circumstance, and I accept as valid a decision by the primary physician, on the basis of knowing a family well, after inquiring about the circumstances of death, to conclude that he has a valid basis for the diagnosis of SIDS, without an autopsy. Of course, there is an important distinction between what is adequate for an individual death, and what is required for research or epidemiologic analyses. The scientist, like a law enforcement officer, is required to be skeptical and inquiring. In this regard, skepticism must be maintained even toward the autopsy, and the ability of the autopsy to establish the cause of death. It cannot be overemphasized that the autopsy diagnosis of SIDS is one of exclusion of lethal disorders.

If an autopsy is performed on an infant, a prompt report to the parents is of great importance. I agree with the recommendation, made many times by many authorities, that it is not necessary to wait until all of the microscopic slides have been processed, or other investigations completed, before a tentative report is provided to the parents. The statistics alone, not to mention a tradition of presumption of innocence, require an early reassurance to the parents. This presumption and sensitivity does not preclude more thorough investigation subsequently, nor should it deter prosecution if the findings subsequently suggest neglect or abuse. But the overwhelming majority need not suffer long delays while a quiet and thorough investigation is continued.

The management of the surviving parents and any children in the family presents a major opportunity for prevention of subsequent psychopathology. As a pediatric cardiologist, I have had substantial experience with parents who have lost children and infants. Although the grief is strong, there is usually a degree of calm acceptance, with great comfort taken by the parents from the confidence that they had done everything possible for the child. In addition, they almost invariably knew in advance of the illness, or surgery, and of the potential for loss of the infant or child. These two considerations—expectations of the possibilities of death, and the opportunity to place the infant in the care of a physician—are denied to the parents of SIDS victims. I have been impressed with the difference that this makes in the ability of the parents of the two kinds of infant deaths to handle the grief. The disturbance to the family seems much longer in duration, with more opportunities for pathological expressions of grief. Dr. Erich Lindemann made a very basic but practical analysis of the effects of that normal grief in survivors of the Coconut Grove fire in Boston (1944). He described the sequence and characteristics of the normal grief "work," a kind of debt that could be postponed but could not be avoided. Attempts to avoid the grief, including various devices to avoid the reality of the loss, created protracted grief, frequently expressed in abnormal ways, destructive to the life of the bereaved.

The basic emotional responses to SIDS are not dissimilar from any other grief reaction, except for intensity and duration. Smialek (1978) found, in three hundred fifty-one families with an infant who had died suddenly and unexpectedly, immediate reactions that include "shock, disbelief, and denial; negativism, hostility, and anger; self-reproach and guilt; demonstration of former unresolved grief; verbalization of previous fears of loss; and sometimes, even, relief." Although the emphasis is appropriately on the maternal response, SIDS also may profoundly affect the father. Mandell and his colleagues (1980) suggested that the impact on the father may be more difficult to deal with, insofar as men are expected to be "stoic and less emotional," and this attitude in both the father and in the health professionals may interfere with the full expression of grief and the ability of the health-care providers to assist in the normal expression of that grief. They found certain male patterns of behavior following SIDS, such as increased work (keeping busy), diminished feelings of self-worth, self-blame for lack of involvement with the infant, and as suggested, a limited ability to ask for help.

Observations on health-care professionals exposed to sudden infant death in a hospital setting demonstrates remarkably similar responses from those individuals: i.e., "shock, disbelief, anger, guilt, fear, blaming, sadness, and behavioral manifestations" (Friedman et al, 1979). For both the health-care professionals and the parents, the common stimulus includes surprise and "failure" to prevent the death. The fact that the infant had been only briefly hospitalized suggests that close attachment was not a major factor in the reaction of the professionals to the infant's death, but the thread of surprise and perceived guilt seems to connect the two groups.

Although most reports of the effects on surviving family members are unquantified or even anecdotal, one report gives more accurate measurements of the effects (DeFrain and Ernst, 1978). They found, by questionnaire, that SIDS was the most severe crisis the majority of the parents had ever experienced. The families reported that it required an average of eight months to regain the level of family organization that preceded the death, and sixteen months to regain their former level of personal happiness. They found that the tragedy seriously affected the relationships between family members, and perhaps most ominous, 60% of the parents of SIDS victims could not be found for participation in the study, although only two and a half years had passed after the SIDS event.

When excessive guilt becomes involved in the process, even if totally unrealistic, the psychopathology may become severe. For example, older siblings of a SIDS victim who were understandably jealous of the new infant who

occupied the mother's time and affection very commonly
have wished that the infant did not exist, and may even have
had fantasies of the infant's death. Even the best of mothers
may have occasional periods in which the new infant is
seen, temporarily, as a source of disruption to their aspira-
tions and their emotional and physical well-being. It is
inevitable that those earlier, innocent sentiments will be
remembered with guilt after the sudden death of the infant.
I would go so far as to say that for ordinary human beings,
this ambivalence toward the infant is almost universal, and
may account for the very wide-spread disturbances that
can follow crib death. As with any other emotional problem,
the basic structure of the individual's ego, and the support
available from others, such as spouse, minister, physician,
grandparents, and friends, may be very crucial. The primary
care physician should be aware of this vulnerability of
the parents, particularly the mother, and should plan to
meet with the parents, whether asked to or not, to explain
the facts known about SIDS, the likelihood or unlikeliness of
recurrences, and the blamelessness of parents and siblings.
The siblings should be particularly thought of by the pediatrician, and both they and their parents reassured as to the
normal and universal nature of ambivalent feelings toward
an infant, with reassurance that these did not contribute
to the death of the infant. It is here that I think the
parents' organizations are so important. There are four major
organizations; the National Foundation for Sudden Infant
Death Syndrome (8240 Professional Place, Landover, Maryland 20785): the International Guild for Infant Survival (7501
Liberty Road, Baltimore, Maryland, 21207); the Canadian
Foundation for the Study of Infant Deaths (4 Lawton Blvd.,
Toronto, Ontario M4V 1Z4); and the Foundation for the
Study of Infant Deaths (4 Grosvenor Place, London SWIX
7HD). There are chapters of these organizations in many
communities, and the support from a group of parents who
also have lost infants through this tragedy appears to be
particularly helpful, perhaps more than a single, brief coun-

seling session with a physician or psychiatrist. The effectiveness of groups dealing with various health problems has been recognized for many years, beginning with Alcoholics Anonymous. In my general pediatric training, I was impressed with the value to parents of leukemia victims of informal parent groups; the individual family is unlikely to know anyone who has had the particular tragedy that struck them, and the response "why us?" expresses the family's sense of isolation and resentment. Seeing other parents cope with the tragedy provides, at the least, reassurance that the tragedy can be survived. The involvement of the bereaved, sooner or later, in the work of the organization is also an important part of the therapy. As I have suggested earlier, it is natural for the group to emphasize that the disease of SIDS cannot be prevented, as part of the reassurance to the family, and I sincerely believe that that is true in the great majority of instances of SIDS. However, a distinction must be made between the individual grieving family, and our national attitude toward this disorder, which must place *prevention* of SIDS as a higher priority. I think that most parents, after the normal grief work, are capable of distinguishing between what might have been and what was, and will follow the example of Carolyn Szybist, the recent Executive Director of the National SIDS Foundation, who coped with her grief, and in a very positive manner, worked toward the future for the protection of as many infants as possible.

In addition to the parent organizations, federal funding of a program by the Department of Health and Human Services established counseling programs around the country, aimed primarily at assisting families to deal with the death of their infants. Although the parent organizations lobbied vigorously for the funding of these programs, judging from copies of correspondence that I have received, it is clear that there is a certain amount of fighting over turf, which seems sad, given the common cause. Again, the desire of a relatively few physicians to dictate the methods and basic assumptions for all smacks of zealotry with all of its inherent dangers. One is reminded of the earlier days of the parent organizations, in which they used the television and lay press to publicize the disorder of SIDS and to demand better funding of applied research toward prevention of SIDS. Having raised the level of consciousness of the public to this very real boogeyman, some of these individuals then sternly castigated the press and "irresponsible" scientists when reports of new observations or theories came forth. Having raised the spector of losing an infant in the night, they continued to insist that nothing could be done to prevent it, and that individuals with theories as to cause, or even worse, prevention, were cruel and perhaps even money-grubbers. My own conviction is that the truth is not alterable by wishes, and attempts to control the flow of information, no matter what the excuse, is a benighted act of paternalism, or worse. If parents are encouraged in this fatalism about SIDS, the question of culpability of those leaders who foster that approach must be weighed in subsequent deaths of infants.

Counseling of parents should also include discussions of future pregnancies, particularly the timing of them, and the likelihood of a recurrence of SIDS in the future. Mandell and Wolfe (1975) warned that a common urge in bereaved mothers of SIDS victims is to attempt to quickly "replace" the lost child. They found a high rate of infertility, and a high rate of spontaneous abortions. If successful, in an early pregnancy, the mother runs the risk of carrying the infant in a state of physical depletion, to say nothing of emotional depletion, and paradoxically, may increase the chance of recurrence of SIDS, in a non-specific way. The recurrence rate is five to ten times higher than for a family who has had no previous SIDS victims, but still only 2%. Several studies have established that SIDS is not inherited in a simple Mendelian fashion, neither dominant nor recessive, nor is there a true sex linkage, except for the generally higher mortality of male victims. Thus, the 2% recurrence rate is not a genetically determined recurrence, but presumably an indication of the existence of risk factors that make the infant more vulnerable to SIDS. These risk factors have been dealt with earlier, and it cannot be over-emphasized that each of these seems weak, by itself, and can most logically be regarded as contributing factors in a vulnerability that is probably universal.

The Management of the Near-Miss

As we have considered in the chapter on the near-miss, their epidemiology is undistinguishable from the dead SIDS victims. The near-miss infants who have subsequently died have been diagnosed at autopsy as SIDS. There are over four hundred cases of near-miss in the literature now who have been observed medically to have prolonged apnea with cyanosis as the precipitating event that caused them to be listed as near-miss SIDS. As with any disease, one would logically expect a range of severity in expression which makes the existence of a near-miss form of SIDS extraordinarily probable, unless of course, the definition is arbitrarily constructed to exclude the living. This probability led Dawes to challenge the proponents of the milk hypersensitivity theory to produce a near-miss infant who could be demonstrated to have the appropriate antibodies, eosinophils, and other laboratory manifestations of that hypersensitive state. The same requirement applies to the long Q-T syndrome and other theories of cardiovascular mechanism for SIDS. Froggatt, although having been the first to raise that possibility, was forthright in subsequently pointing out the rarity of symptomatic arrhythmias occurring early in the long Q-T syndrome (Froggatt and Adgey, 1978). In an earlier paper (Froggatt and James, 1973), they also pointed out that the inheritance of SIDS did not in any way match the inheritance of either of the two long Q-T syndromes, and that even if one postulated spontaneous mutations, the rate would have to be at a "rate of many hundreds of times greater than any yet postulated for man." They concluded that in an individual case of cot death a role for arrhythmias could not be ruled out, but the data known did not support the idea that arrhythmias were a prominent cause of SIDS. A most striking consensus occurred in a workshop in Washington, D.C., in 1975, organized by Eileen Hasselmeyer for *all* SIDS research grantees and contractors for the National Institute of Child Health and Human Development. In a session that I was invited to chair, I asked for a show of hands of these investigators from all over the US, Canada, and Europe, as to whether they thought the primary event in SIDS was apnea or cardiac arrhythmia. Not a single hand was raised for a cardiac mechanism; almost all present voted for apnea, although about 10% took an agnostic position. This is particularly striking since there were relatively few near-misses that had been studied and reported in 1975, compared to over four hundred now.

Considering that the two final pathways to death are necessarily either cardiac or respiratory arrest, to ignore the four hundred published cases of near-miss due to prolonged apnea as unrelated to SIDS appears to be doctrinaire, to put it charitably, reminiscent of the tobacco industry continuing to assert that the causal relationship of smoking and cancer of the lung cannot be definitively proven. While it is true that probability of a statistical sort is not the same as a proof of cause and effect, probability is the only practical basis for most of medicine.

The controversy about the relationship between prolonged apnea and SIDS has become somewhat precious, and fortunately, some wise individuals have ignored the implications and simply proceeded to act on behalf of those infants fortunate enough to have survived an episode of prolonged apnea with cyanosis. The American Academy of Pediatrics has endorsed a relatively brief statement on management of prolonged apnea (Task Force on Prolonged

Apnea, 1978). The report was simply titled *Prolonged Apnea*, and in the opening paragraph acknowledged that at least "some victims of sudden infant death syndrome have succumbed to unrelieved prolonged apnea." Specific etiologies mentioned as important to rule out included "seizure disorders, severe infection, significant anemia (especially in infants who were pre-term), gastroesophageal reflux, hypoglycemia, and other metabolic disorders, and impaired regulation of breathing." At a later meeting, Guilleminault and Korobkin (1979) summarized the recommendations of several centers who were actively involved in studying or managing infants with the near-miss. The group consensus was that a period of cessation of air exchange greater than fifteen seconds in the first six months of life was abnormal, although for premature infants, up to twenty seconds was within the range of normal. They warned, however, that apnea exceeding even ten seconds in duration in the age range of one to six months was sufficiently exceptional that a careful evaluation of that infant was indicated. The group recommended a detailed history and medical evaluation for these patients with near-miss, or prolonged apnea, and Table IX:1 presents this in its entirety. The history includes the infant's past medical history and a special family history, including details of the maternal health during pregnancy.

The group recommended that the near-miss infant be given a complete physical examination including a careful neurological examination, and a developmental assessment. Although there was not unanimous agreement, the consensus was that a minimal work-up should include a chest x-ray, an electrocardiogram, electroencephalogram, complete blood count, blood glucose, blood electrolytes, including calcium and phosphate, and some measurement of respiratory function. These studies were considered to be screening tests, and if indicated by the history, physical examination, or the screening laboratory evaluations, further examinations should be considered including those listed on Table IX:2. These studies relate logically to the

Table IX:1
Suggested History for Near-Miss Infants*

I. The Event
  A. State of the infant
    1. Awake
      a. coughed prior to apnea
      b. vomited prior to apnea
      c. choked prior to apnea
      d. stiffened prior to apnea
      e. other; e.g., strange cry
      f. combinations of the above
    2. Asleep
      a. vocalization prior to apnea
      b. noisy respiration
      c. no sound
      d. cough, choke
    3. State unknown
    4. Relationship to feeding
  B. Appearance of the infant
    1. Color
      a. pale—circumoral or total body
      b. blue—circumoral or total body
      c. red
      d. gray
      e. unknown
    2. Tone
      a. limp
      b. stiff
      c. normal
      d. unknown
    3. Abnormal posturing or movements
    4. Temperature
      a. febrile
      b. cold
      c. normal
      d. unknown

*Reproduced from Guilleminault and Korobkin, 1979, by permission.

C. Intervention
   1. Mouth-to-mouth resuscitation given
      a. once
      b. more than once
   2. Vigorous stimulation given
      a. once
      b. more than once
   3. Little or no stimulation given
      a. once
      b. more than once
   4. Estimated length of time between onset of event and intervention
   5. Estimated length of time between intervention and
      a. re-establishment of respiration
      b. normal behavior and appearance
D. Condition / response of the infant after intervention
   1. Regurgitation
   2. Abnormal breathing
   3. Blood in mouth or nose
   4. Second or repetitive events
   5. Normal
   6. Unknown
E. External conditions prior to event
   1. Acute (<48 hours)
      a. sleep disruption, deprivation, or disorganization
         (1) sleeping at home in crib or elsewhere
         (2) maintaining usual routine of bedtime and naps or not
      b. changed state of health
         (1) new symptoms of upper respiratory infection
         (2) recent immunization
         (3) recent medication
         (4) other illness
      c. change in behavior
         (1) irritability
         (2) lethargy
      d. change in eating pattern
         (1) new foods
         (2) different feeding schedule

Table IX:1 (Continued)

    2. Chronic (>7 days)
       a. perspiring
          (1) head
          (2) total body
       b. snoring
       c. respiratory stridor
       d. sobbing in sleep
       e. excessive sleep
       f. reduced total sleep

II. Special Past Medical History (Note: This is in addition to the standard medical history)
  A. Sleep history
    1. Typical sleep routine
       a. usual time infant goes to sleep and wakes up
       b. usual naps
       c. sleeps through night or not
       d. duration of longest usual sleep
    2. Respiration in sleep
       a. respiratory noise asleep (see E2)
       b. no respiratory noise
  B. Respiratory difficulties awake
    1. Noise
    2. Nasal congestion
       a. chronic
       b. acute
    3. Chronic cough
    4. Other
  C. Breath-holding spells
  D. Chronic perspiration
    1. Head and/or body
    2. Awake or asleep
  E. Frequent spitting up
    1. Amount
    2. How long after feeding
  F. Feeding problems
  G. Colic
    1. About how many hours per day
  H. Developmental anomalies

    I. Immunizations

    J. Medications

III. Special Family History (Note: This is in addition to the standard family history)

    A. History of SIDS verified by post-mortem examination
1. Immediate family
2. Remote family
3. Unexplained death in infancy or childhood with post-mortem examination
4. History of sudden death in adults

    B. Maternal health
1. Asthma
2. Diabetes
3. Hypertension
4. Obesity
5. Pregnancy history and birth order
6. Drug history
   a. cigarettes
   b. alcohol
   c. other drugs
7. Infections during pregnancy
8. Bleeding during pregnancy
9. False labor

    C. Parental significant health-related behavior
1. Drug addiction
2. Alcohol abuse
3. Smoking—amount in child's environment
4. Other drugs

    D. Snoring
1. Parents
2. Siblings
3. In mother during pregnancy

    E. Apnea
1. Parents
2. Other family members

    F. Syncope in family members

    G. Pallid breath-holding among siblings

    H. Heart disease

    I. Epilepsy

Table IX:2
Minimal Workup Required for "Near-Miss" Infant*

Complete physical examination
Complete neurological examination, including developmental
assessment using scales such as Amiel-Tison, Bailey, or
similar; scores should be systematically recorded.
Chest X-ray film
Electrocardiogram
Electroencephalogram
Complete blood count
Blood glucose, electrolytes, calcium, phosphate
Some measurement of respiratory function (e.g., end tidal
PCO_2)

If indicated by the initial evaluation (but *not* mandatory), the
following examinations should be considered:

Sepsis workup
Nose and throat cultures
Barium swallow
Blood gases if infant seen soon after "near-miss" event
Blood gases drawn while asleep
Computed tomography brain scan
Esophagoscopy
Esophageal pH monitoring for 24–48 hr.
Further cardiological evaluation (e.g., echocardiogram)
Lumbar puncture
Otolaryngological   consultation   including   laryngoscopy,
bronchoscopy
Hospital monitoring of respiration and heart rate for at least
24 hr. —and with hard copy, if possible—if the acute
episode was very recent.

*Reproduced from Guilleminault and Korobkin, 1979 by permission.

specific etiologies listed above, developed by the task force on prolonged apnea.

The commentary (Guilleminault and Korobkin, 1979) on polygraphic monitoring of the near-miss infant suggests that the monitoring with a hard copy should be performed within the first seventy-two hours after a near-miss event, should include a portion of the normal sleep cycle of the infant; variables suggested for recording were two channels of electroencephalogram, the electrocardiogram, electromyogram (chin), the electrooculogram, respiration (preferably including channels permitting the identification of central versus obstructive apnea), oxygen saturation, and if possible, a video recording of overall activity. Guilleminault and Korobkin properly emphasized that some studies that are essential for research programs on the etiology and longitudinal history of near-miss episodes in infants were not necessarily required for a hospital routine oriented toward cost-effective management. I would agree, and submit that excessive "requirements" of highly technical studies, such as a complete sleep study program, will actually interfere with adequate care of these infants on a country-wide basis since they are simply not available in any but a few major centers, and many young families lack the resources to travel to those centers, let alone pay for the work-up. Clearly, the standards for such centers of excellence should not be imposed on the average health care providers, since they will likely intimidate the physician from a less complete but probably adequate work-up and management.

Home Management

Home management of survivors of near-miss episodes appears to be the most controversial part of a generally emotional subject. From my point of view, I am surprised at the controversy in an area of management where the choices are so clear-cut, and the alternatives so distasteful. I first suggested monitoring of the infant at risk in the second Seattle SIDS meeting (Guntheroth, 1970). At that point it was based on two considerations: (1) that the instrumentation existed for monitoring both respiration and heart rate (Daily et al, 1969), and (2) that apnea and cardiac arrest were the only reasonable final pathways to death. When I actually began to monitor infants at home, it was based less on a conviction that home-monitoring would assuredly prevent SIDS, but more a way of reducing the anxiety of parents who would otherwise be sent home to take care of an infant who had already had an episode of prolonged apnea, with no help. The infants had been referred to me initially as a cardiologist, because of the tentative diagnosis by a referring physician of cyanotic congenital heart disease. After a careful cardiologic work-up, we concluded that the infant had no heart disease, and that the history suggested that the infant had been apneic, and that that was the cause of the cyanosis. After explaining this to the parents, the mother of the first patient asked what the chance of recurrence of the episode was, and the only information I had at that time was approximately 20%, based on a local estimate. The mother indicated reluctance to take the child home, with that kind of threat hanging over the child's head like the sword of Damocles. However, keeping the infant in the hospital for two or three months seemed unhealthy psychologically, and we persuaded the local General Electric representative to provide a GE apnea monitor for the family for several weeks. That infant had several further episodes of apnea at home, all successfully managed by the parents. Fortunately, these episodes decreased in frequency, and by the time the child was six months old, the parents had no apparent reluctance in giving up the monitor. In discussing their experience, I presented to them the hypothetical objection that monitors would make parents anxious, and their response was a firm dismissal of that theory, and suggested that they would have found it difficult to have kept their wits over those months without something that would allow them to sleep at night.

The choice then seems to be not whether a monitor will make a parent anxious, since the event of the prolonged apnea would certainly take care of that, but whether a monitor will improve or diminish the sense of security felt toward their infant at home.

A home monitor, no matter how perfect, does not guarantee survival of the infant (Kelly et al, 1978). For the survivors, and the family members, the impact of the apnea monitor on family life is substantial, documented by Black et al (1978). Performing noisy tasks such as using the carpet sweeper posed threats to the infant since the monitor alarm might not be heard. The mother frequently felt hopelessly chained by a very short tether to the monitor. As the infants grew older they began to use the monitor as a means of manipulating the household, some apparently deliberately removing the electrodes in the morning in order to get the mother's undivided attention. These very real considerations became a major issue for those of us on the Task Force on Prolonged Apnea (1978), and the argument repeatedly returned to the problem of a choice between real alternatives of management. The *first* choice would, of course, be that there be no infants who had prolonged apnea and therefore there would be no anxiety on the part of the parents. However, given an episode of prolonged apnea in an infant, all of the group agreed to the statement that "twenty-four-hour surveillance is critical to the management of prolonged apnea." Some members preferred that this be done in a hospital, but all finally agreed that it could be done at home or in a long-term care facility or foster home. For most of us, the home seemed the most appropriate place for care of an infant for a period of weeks or months, and then the question was whether an electronic monitor would be a useful adjunct to the twenty-four-hour surveillance. Although the phrase "may be useful" was finally adopted, it is still difficult to imagine that having parents sit up at night, without a monitor, could be a reasonable or less anxiety-producing alternative.

The Task Force did not speak to the issue of type of monitor, except to acknowledge that either heart or respiratory rate could be monitored. There continue to be differences of opinion depending upon the individuals in charge of monitoring. Initially, we used a large and relatively cumbersome monitor for respiration and heart rate, which operated from household electrical outlets. The number of false alarms, particularly from the respiratory part of the monitor, seemed excessive, and judging from our experience in the hospital intensive care units, when monitors produce frequent false alarms, the tendency is for the nurse or physician in attendance to disable the alarm, and depend on a visual signal that is less disturbing. Unfortunately, it is more difficult to do other activities when watching for a visual alarm, and the absence of the audible signal may endanger the subject if the caretaker is involved in some other activity. We decided to try our heart rate monitor that we had originally purchased for our animal laboratory, made by Parks Electronics (12770 SW 1st St., Beaverton, Oregon 97005). This is a compact instrument, operating on flashlight batteries, which last several weeks; the independence of power supply and its light weight permit great portability. The cost is remarkably little, such that one could purchase several of these for the price of the more complete units with respiration and heart rate, which would permit a standby unit at a reasonable cost. The operation of the unit is simple, requiring only a setting of the rate which will produce an alarm; the instrument has a modest time-delay, so that very brief transient episodes of bradycardia will not produce an alarm. A psychological advantage to the heart rate monitor is that it makes a gentle click with each heart beat, audible for several feet from the monitor. This removes an ambiguity that is inherent in the respiratory monitors; quiet during the night could mean either that the monitor is working and that the baby is breathing, or that the instrument is not working, which inherently includes the possibility that the infant might be dead, in spite of the silence. The cardiac monitor on the other hand provides an audible signal that all is well in the middle of the night, in addition to the absence of an alarm tone. Although our choice was initially based on practical considerations, the bradycardia monitor was soundly based on observations (Daily et al, 1969; Ingman et al, 1970; French et al, 1972; Katona and Egbert, 1974). With the reports of obstructive apnea with sleep (Guilleminault et al, 1975), a positive advantage emerged for a heart rate monitor over respiration of the impedance variety, since most of these respiratory monitors depended upon chest wall movement, which continues in obstructive apnea even though there is no exchange of air. The obstructive apneas require either an esophageal pressure, or an airflow monitor taped near the nose, in order to be detected. The addition of a transcutaneous PO_2 electrode was suggested by Lucey et al, (1977), but primarily as an adjunct to the study of near-misses in hospital. As Nelson points out (1978), these PO_2 units are expensive, and have wide swings in oxygen tension with relatively innocuous maneuvers. In the issue of *Pediatrics* that presented the Task Force recommendations on prolonged apnea (chaired by Nelson) there was also the report of Kelly et al on their monitoring at home of near-miss infants, and an editorial comment by Nelson which was surprisingly nihilistic. He cited the difficulties in monitoring, with emphasis on the unreliability of impedance respiratory monitors and the impracticality of the transcutaneous oxygen monitors, but said little about the simpler cardiac monitor. There was a brief, implied criticism of the cardiac monitor that suggested it was a belated warning, but the studies by Guilleminault suggest that the bradycardia in fact follows the hypoxia quite well, and ultimately that should be of more concern than brief respiratory pauses. Nelson also criticised the home monitoring as having failures, citing Kelly's figure of 11%. However, that group described numerous episodes of apnea that were successfully overcome, in almost every patient monitored. It must be realized that this was a group of patients with particularly severe episodes, and if one included the entire population, the mortality was only 7%. Nelson went on to question the validity of parent observations, doubting whether the infants really required resuscitation at all. He concluded by advocating prayer as a method of managing the risk of a repeated episode of near-miss; I admire *his* religious faith, but I believe most parents, given the choice, will choose modern technology over sleeplessness and faith.

Without question, there is an entity in pediatrics, described as the vulnerable child syndrome. These children are over-protected, and are not allowed to grow up with the usual freedom to explore and learn (sometimes painfully). It is legitimately of concern that a near-miss infant may suffer that fate from well-meaning but still over-protective parents. This has been used as an argument against monitoring, although it seems unlikely that the vulnerability arises from the use of the monitor, rather than the original episode of prolonged apnea. Nevertheless, it was our policy when we provided parents with the home monitor to reassure them at the outset that the disease was a disease of the first five or six months. After that, the child was expected to be normal in every way. When there are no episodes of severe apnea for a one-month period, the monitor is removed from the home. I am content that the monitoring has produced no long-term ill effects in the behavior of the child. Unfortunately, there are some patients in the group of prolonged apnea who may have a different disorder, central hypoventilation. These infants are a subset, and although they are at risk of death during infancy, they are not typical of most of the near-misses. For those patients, monitoring may be required for a much longer period of time. Some of them may even unwittingly be conditioned toward apnea, or at least setting off the alarm, since either will produce a prompt response from mother or father, who will be, of course, greatly concerned. It is difficult to imagine a more effective attention-getting device for an older child. In those instances in which the child appears to have a normal ventilatory response at rest, with no CO_2 retention during normal sleep, serious consideration should be given to a biofeedback system which provides an aversive stimulus, such as a light shock, for apnea. We used such a device successfully on an infant with congenital Ondine's curse (Beck et al, 1980), but eventually abandoned the use because it completely disrupted sleep. Each time that infant went to sleep his arterial oxygen saturation dropped as his ventilation dropped, without apnea, and the alarm stimulus would awaken the infant and thereby restore oxygenation. The stimulus worked well during the day, but the continued shock during sleep seemed too cruel to us and his parents, so that the conditioning was abandoned, and the infant died soon thereafter.

The Task Force (1978) on Prolonged Apnea were all in agreement on the final recommendation for management of the infant with prolonged apnea: "Pediatricians must keep in mind that there is a significant psychological impact on all members of the family of an infant with prolonged apneic spells, whether or not monitors are included in the management plan. Families, including siblings, should be evaluated and their strengths, weaknesses, resources, and needs assessed before decisions are made and implemented. Community resources, appropriate to the family's identified needs, should be mobilized. In addition, the physician should emphasize to the family the normal aspect of their infant's development so that they may be recognized, and may be enjoyed and nurtured, and the parent-infant bonding strengthened. The emotional and physical needs of siblings require comparable attention."

Prevention of SIDS

Education

Better education of health care providers will not immediately change the incidence of SIDS, but it has demonstrably changed the effects of how we handle the survivors of an incident of SIDS, with sensitivity, and counseling over a tragedy. In this day and age, this education should include emergency medical technicians, firemen, and policemen so that they are aware of SIDS and that in most cases, there is no culpability. We are equally convinced of the need for a quiet observer's role for those individuals, vigilant for evidence of child abuse, but sparing the great majority who are innocent. I believe that this is possible and must be done, since both the parents of the genuine SIDS case and the future victims of child abuse are worthy of our efforts. In terms of the lay public, I believe that full reporting of all facts is warranted and that a paternalistic censoring of what is appropriate news for the lay press is ill-advised, just as news management was wrong for political purposes. It is obvious to most individuals that there are many "break throughs" in science, and only a few survive the test of time, and peer judgment. It does not require long for even a child to discern that what is advertised on television has little relationship to the product purchased and brought home for close inspection. From the point of view of the physician and scientist, the single most important lesson from the literature is that *a* cause of sudden death in infancy is not *the* cause of SIDS. This necessarily implies that many instances of SIDS, by autopsy standards, will eventually be shown to be other entities. These entities will almost certainly remain a minority of the cases of SIDS, and the core of this tragedy lies in a developmental problem—apnea, or more precisely, failure to arouse from sleep apnea.

General Maternal and Infant Welfare

Statistics from several countries over many years support the contention that deaths due to SIDS parallel infant mortality for that time and place. A general improvement of nutrition of the mother and of the child, encouraging breast feeding, discouraging cigarette smoking, improved housing (at least to the point of avoiding excessive crowding of people which increases the transmission of respiratory infections), are all improvements that will result in a reduction in SIDS, as well as in all other forms of infant mortality. On an individual basis, it is reasonable to encourage parents to avoid exposure of their infant to large numbers of people, and to protect him during the first six months of life from respiratory infections. I concluded in a review article on the subject of SIDS in the *American Heart Journal* in 1977 with a recommendation that my mother, and I think most mothers, understood. Infants thrive on a regular schedule, particularly for sleep. There is a reasonable ground for insisting that babies not be carried around the country, even for so noble a cause as visiting grandparents. If travel is important, let it wait until after six months of life. The danger of sleep fragmentation seems to be less after that, but deep sleep with accompanying prolonged sleep apnea is one consequence of changing the infant's routine by traveling and keeping the infant up late for whatever reason.

Immunization Timing

Considering that almost every infant in this country is immunized, the risk of immunization of any single infant must be extraordinarily low. Yet, the reports of SIDS occurring the night after elective immunization are, if only in the minds of the mother, so closely related as to cause great remorse in that family. It seems reasonable if sleep deprivation or fragmentation are causally related to increased sleep apnea, that the fever, pain, and fretfulness after immunization (Cody et al, 1981) may well produce an increased vulnerability to prolonged apnea and to sudden infant death. Even if the only benefit were to be a reduction in the remorse of a parent, it seems appropriate to reconsider the timing of immunization of infants, by analyzing the benefits and risks of delaying the immunization. For small pox vaccination, it became evident even before the world-wide eradication of the disease, that an infant with eczema was more at risk from the vaccination than from the possibility of becoming infected with the true small pox. As small pox became more rare world-wide, the risk for even a normal individual from the vaccination began to outweigh the risk of contracting the disease. Now, it is an easy matter, since there is *no* risk for small pox, unless one is working in one of the few viral laboratories.

It is quite unlikely that an infant will be exposed to diphtheria or tetanus in most of the United States, and there is no logic to early immunization for those two diseases. Pertussis (whooping cough) is a particularly bad disease to get when quite young, and there is assuredly a benefit of early immunization for that disease, if there is a reasonable chance of infection. However, "herd immunity" is quite strong for most infants, particularly the first-born. It seems extremely unlikely that pertussis can be transmitted through an immune adult or child. Therefore, if the infant's parents and siblings are immunized, and the number of individuals that the infant is exposed to is small, I can find little argument for early immunization against pertussis, and therefore against all of the common infections. I am not suggesting that immunization should be abandoned because, in a short while, the herd immunity would have disappeared, and the overall effect of large numbers of cases of infectious diseases would greatly outweigh the very small risk of immunization. I am rather suggesting that for an infant in a home with few siblings, or siblings that are well protected against infectious diseases, that immunizations be postponed to six months of age, past the vulnerable period to SIDS.

Outreach Maternal and Infant Programs

The work from Sheffield of Carpenter and Emery and their colleagues makes clear the advantages of good prenatal and postnatal care for mother and infant in reducing the infant mortality, not only for SIDS, but for all causes of infant death. One of the other lessons was that the mother who fails to return for follow-up clinic with the infant subjects that infant in one way or another to a much-increased risk of dying. Although the cause of this is not proven, this mortality was reduced by the simple maneuver of a home visit by a nurse, whose chief effects seem to be alerting the mother to a health problem that has previously been unsuspected, and a kind of non-specific "fluffing up" of the mother, encouraging her and complimenting her on her child, simply a human contact with supportive words. It is not enough to simply provide the care in the local clinic or hospital, since a tired and depressed mother will have little initiative, and might not make that contact. It is all well and good to argue that we all should be self-sufficient and take care of our own problems, but the unfortunate cost to those marginal people with so little ability to cope seems to include sudden infant death syndrome as one of the costs of that stern policy. An improved outreach program that follows up on mothers and their infants after they have gone home would not be prohibitively expensive, but would do much good psychologically, and appears to be a preventative for many infant disorders, including SIDS.

Research Priorities

The clamor for directed research funding for SIDS was eventually effective in allocations of substantial sums of money for that purpose. It remains to be seen whether those extra dollars bought genuine advances in our knowledge of SIDS, or how to prevent it. The problem is a familiar one to scientists, beginning with the Kennedy era. When the Russians suddenly showed a superior technology in rocket launching in the Sputnik era, our nation made a major commitment of dollars to land a man on the moon, perhaps more as a statement of our belief in our superior technology than because of the science involved. In any event, it was successful, and a point of justifiable pride. There have been spinoffs to the country out of these expenditures, with miniaturization and utilization of solid state electronics, many of which have wound up in medical care and monitoring. However, this was more of an engineering development than true research of a biological or medical nature, in which the goal is equally clear, but the path to success quite obscure. The space problem was one of engineering and production. With a medical problem such as SIDS or cancer, there are a few facts known from pathology and epidemiology, and a few observations on near-miss and animal experiments, but simply providing a million dollars to a scientist does not automatically generate an hypothesis that can or should be tested as to the cause or treatment of this disorder. As we suggested in the first chapter, many if not all of the major advances that can be selected out of the history of research on SIDS were supported by basic science grants, and on rare occasions, no grant at all; the era following the increased, directed funding for SIDS research has not been nearly as effective, if normalized on a dollar basis. In particular, what appears to be directly related to SIDS is attractive from a political point of view, but there is quickly a point of diminishing returns when one continues to perform routine autopsies by the thousands without a new hypothesis or a new methodology. The same is true for epidemiologic studies. The expenses will be the same or greater, but the chance for a substantial increment of knowledge from a study will be slight, unless there is a substantive hypothesis that is novel, and capable of testing in that modality. Now, we are in the era of studying near-misses. Although my conviction is obvious, that the near-miss is directly related to SIDS, I must apply the same cost-effectiveness test to the studies of the near-miss as I have applied to pathology and epidemiologic studies. Although the studies of the near-miss have not been uniform, they have been performed by several competent centers, and the facts are reasonably clear. Further observations, using the same polygraphic methods with the same variables measured, will be very unlikely to reveal a new insight into this problem. The home monitoring is now well-established for most of us as a rational method of management of the near-miss, and supporting the care of these patients at home out of research dollars is inappropriate, considering that the total number of dollars for medical care is rising astronomically, at the expense of research dollars that are becoming increasingly hard to obtain. This principle of asking health care dollars to pay for care, sparing research dollars, is being observed by the National SIDS Foundation, who are reviewing on a voluntary basis proposals for home monitoring near-misses, but happily avoiding the direct funding of these programs, which could entail vast sums of money. Fortunately, the Boston group with Shannon and Kelly and their co-workers have led the way in convincing health insurance carriers of the excellent bargain of sending a child home on a monitor, as opposed to keeping them in an intensive care unit, where only a few days cost would exceed that of the most expensive monitor.

It is my conviction that continued funding of basic research in all aspects of biology is more likely in the long run to provide a genuine break-through in our ultimate understanding and perhaps defeat of this infant tragedy. For those who doubt, I urge a re-reading of Comroe and Dripps (1977) studies of key cardiovascular advances, tracing their roots back to what was in most cases a discovery of a basic science sort, with no particular thought in mind of an application. That is not to say that physicians should not be encouraged in research about these important subjects; I am arguing for a distribution of funding that will avoid huge data-collecting programs costing millions, which could be summarized in a sentence or two. It is hoped that the physician will, through his clinical experiences, and further stimulated by reading both clinical and basic literature, conceive a new hypothesis that can be tested, and will then be encouraged to test it. There is little doubt in my mind that our return for tax monies invested in research are excellent bargains, for the most part, but a naive insistence on a direct investment of the money in a "disease of the month" will sadly dilute the effectiveness of that research investment.

We have come a long way in understanding sudden infant death syndrome. Humility is in order for our generation, however, based on the careful reading of the earlier reports, dating back a century or more. The current advances seem to help only a small part of the entire syndrome — those few lucky enough to survive their initial episode and emerge as the near-miss. For the others, there is no doubt that our treatment of the survivors is much more humane than the persecution of the mother or wet nurse for overlaying in the last century. We may even be humane enough to tackle effectively the abused child, who number only a very small fraction of the SIDS population, but a very large population of older children. To be able to handle that successfully without excessive punitiveness will be a revealing test of our culture. The single most effective remedy for SIDS that emerges now would appear to be a general improvement of maternal and infant health, a goal that seems to run counter to public antipathy toward government involvement in anything other than the military, but a goal which I believe no civilized and affluent country such as ours can long ignore.

References

Abildskov JA: The prolonged QT interval. *Ann Rev Med* **30**:171, 1979.

Abramson H: Accidental mechanical suffocation in infants. *J Pediat* **25**:404, 1944.

Adelson L: Possible neurological mechanisms responsible for sudden death. *J Forensic Med* **1**:39, 1953.

Adelson L: Slaughter of the innocents. *N Eng J Med* **264**:1345, 1961.

Adelson L, Kinney ER: Sudden and unexpected death in infancy and childhood. *Pediatrics* **17**:663, 1956.

Ader R, Friedman SB: Social factors affecting emotionality and resistance to diseases in animals. V. Early separation from the mother and response to a transplanted tumor in the rat. *Psychosom Med* **27**:119, 1965.

Ader R, Tatum R, Beels CC: Social factors affecting emotionality and resistance to disease in animals: 1. Age of separation from mother and susceptibility to gastric ulcers in rats. *J Comp Physiol Psychol* **53**:446, 1960.

Alimurung MM, Joseph LG, Craige E, Massell BF: The Q-T interval in normal infants and children. *Circulation* **1**:1329, 1950.

Allen RJ, Towsley HA, Wilson JL: Neurogenic stridor in infancy. *Am J Dis Child* **87**:179, 1954.

American Academy of Pediatrics (Committee on Infant and Preschool Child): The sudden infant death syndrome. *Pediatrics* **50**:964, 1972.

American Academy of Pediatrics (Task force on prolonged apnea): Prolonged apnea. *Pediatrics* **61**:651, 1978.

Anderson RH, Bouton J, Burrow CT, Smith A: Sudden death in infancy: a study of cardiac specialized tissue. *Brit Med J* **2**:135, 1974.

Ardran GM, Kemp FH: The nasal and cervical airway in sleep in the neonatal period. *Am J Roentgen Radium Ther Nucl Med* **108**:537, 1970.

Arnon SS, Midura TF, Damas K, Et Al: Intestinal infection and toxin production by Clostridium botulinum as one cause of sudden infant death syndrome. *Lancet* **1**:1273, 1978.

Asch SS: Crib deaths: their possible relationship to postpartum depression and infanticide. *Mt Sinai J Med NY* **35**:214, 1968.

Asher MI: Cot deaths in Southland. *NZ Med J* **82**:369, 1975.

Baker TL, McGinty DJ: Reversal of cardiopulmonary failure during active sleep in hypoxic kittens: Implications for sudden infant death. *Science* **198**:419, 1977.

Bass M: Asphyxial crib death. *N Eng J Med* **296**:555, 1977.

Beck GR, Sulzbacher SI, Kawabori I, Et Al: Conditioned avoidance of hypoxemia in an infant with central hypoventilation. *Behav Res Severe Develop Disabilities* **1**:21, 1980.

Beckwith JB: Observations on the pathologic anatomy of the SIDS, **in** *Sudden Infant Death Syndrome* (Bergman et al, 1970), p 83, 122.

Beckwith JB: Commentary: Sudden infant death syndrome: a new theory. *Pediatrics* **55**:583, 1975.

203

Beckwith JB: *Newsletter*, Washington State Chapter, National SIDS Foundation, June, 1979, p 1.

Beinfield HH: A forgotten cause of infant suffocation. *J Int Coll Surg* **22**:447, 1954.

Bergdahl DM, Stevenson JG, Kawabori I, Guntheroth WG: Prognosis in primary ventricular tachycardia in the pediatric patient. *Circulation* **62**:897, 1980.

Berger D: Child abuse simulating "near-miss" sudden infant death syndrome. *J Pediat* **95**:554, 1979.

Bergman AB: Unexplained sudden infant death (letter). *N Eng J Med* **287**:254, 1972.

Bergman AB, Beckwith JB, Ray CG (Eds): *Sudden Infant Death Syndrome*. Seattle, University of Washington Press, 1970.

Bergman AB, Beckwith JB, Ray CG: The apnea monitor business. *Pediatrics* **56**:1, 1975.

Bergman AB, Ray CG, Pomeroy MA, Et Al: Studies of the sudden infant death syndrome in King County, Washington. III. Epidemiology *Pediatrics* **49**:860, 1972.

Black L, Hersher L, Steinschneider A: Impact of the apnea monitor on family life. *Pediatrics* **62**:681, 1978.

Blumenfeld TA, Mantell CH, Catherman RL, Blanc WA: Postmortem vitreous humor chemistry in sudden infant death syndrome and in other causes of death in childhood. *Am J Clin Path* **71**:219, 1979.

Bowlby J: *Attachment and Loss, Vol. II: Separation*. New York, Basic Books, 1973.

Brady JP, Ariagno RL, Watts JL, Et Al: Apnea, hypoxemia, and aborted sudden infant death syndrome. *Pediatrics* **62**:686, 1978.

Brandt CD: Infectious agents from cases of sudden infant death syndrome and from members of their community, in *Sudden Infant Death Syndrome* (Bergman Et Al, 1970), p 161.

Brouardel P: *La Mort et al Mort Subite*. Bailliere, Paris, 1895. (Quoted in Werne and Garrow, 1953).

Butler SR, Suskind MR, Schanberg SM: Maternal behavior as a regulator of polyamine biosynthesis in brain and heart of developing rat pups. *Science* **199**:445, 1978.

Caddell JL: Magnesium deprivation in sudden unexpected infant death. *Lancet* **2**:258, 1972.

Caddell JL: Exploring the magnesium-deficient weanling rat as an animal model for the sudden infant death syndrome: physical, biochemical, electrocardiographic and gross pathologic changes. *Pediat Res* **12**:1157, 1978.

Campbell CJ, Read DJ: Circulatory and respiratory factors in the experimental production of lung petechiae and their possible significance in the sudden infant death syndrome. *Pathology* **12**:181, 1980.

Camps FE, Carpenter RG (Eds): *Sudden and Unexpected Deaths in Infancy (Cot Deaths)*, Bristol, Wright, 1972.

Canby JP: Choanal atresia and sudden death. *Med Bull US Army*, Europe **19**:57, 1962.

Carpenter RG, Emery JL: Identification and follow-up of infants at risk of sudden death in infancy. *Nature* **250**:729, 1974.

Carpenter RG, Emery JL: Final results of study of infants at risk of sudden death. *Nature* **268**:724, 1977.

Carpenter RG, Gardner A, McWeeny PM, Emery JL: Multistate scoring system for identifying infants at risk of unexpected death. *Arch Dis Child* **52**:606, 1977.

Carpenter RG, Shaddick CW: Role of infection, suffocation and bottle-feeding in cot death. *Brit J Prev Soc Med* **19**:1, 1965.

Chacon MA, Tildon JT: Elevated values of tri-iodothyronine in victims of sudden infant death syndrome. *J Pediat* **99**:758, 1981.

Chavez CJ, Ostrea EM, Stryker JC, Smialek Z: Sudden infant death syndrome among infants of drug-dependent mothers. *J Pediat* **95**:407, 1979.

Chipperfield B, Chipperfield JR: Cot deaths and mineral salts (letter). *Lancet* **1**:220, 1979.

Church SC, Morgan BC, Oliver TK, Guntheroth WG: Cardiac arrhythmias in premature infants: An indication of autonomic immaturity. *J Pediat* **71**:542, 1967.

Cody CL, Baraff LJ, Cherry JD, Et Al: Nature and rates of adverse reactions associated with DTP and DT immunizations in infants and children. *Pediatrics* **68**:650, 1981.

Coe JI, Peterson RDA: Sudden unexpected death in infancy and milk sensitivity. *J Lab Clin Med* **62**:477, 1963.

Cole S, Lindenberg LB, Et Al; Ultrastructural abnormalities of the carotid body in sudden infant death syndrome. *Pediatrics* **63**:13, 1979.

Coleman RW, Provence S: Environmental retardation (hospitalism) in infants living in families. *Pediatrics* **19**:285, 1957.

Committee on Infant and Preschool Child: Home monitoring for sudden infant death. *Pediatrics* **55**:144, 1975.

Comroe JH, Dripps RD: *The top ten clinical advances in cardiovascular-pulmonary medicine and surgery between 1945 and 1975: How they came about*. Pub by National Institutes of Health, Bethesda, 1977.

Cornwell AC: Sudden infant death syndrome: a testable hypothesis and mechanism. *Int J Neurosci* **10**:31, 1979.

Cornwell AC, Weitzman ED, Marmarou A: Ambulatory and in-hospital continuous recording of sleep state and cardiorespiratory parameters in "near-miss" for the sudden infant death syndrome and control infants. *Biotelem* **5**:113, 1978.

Cross KW: Session 3, in *Sudden and Unexpected Deaths in Infancy (Cot Deaths)*, (Camps and Carpenter, 1972), p 57.

Cross KW, Lewis SR: Upper respiratory obstruction and cot death. *Arch Dis Child* **46**:211, 1971.

Cullity GJ, Emery JL: Ulceration and necrosis of vocal cords in hospital and unexpected child deaths. *J Pathol* **115**:27, 1975.

Curran WJ: An enigma wrapped in swaddling clothes: Congress and "Crib Death." *N Eng J Med* **287**:235, 1972.

Cushing H: Concerning a definite regulatory mechanism of the vasomotor center which controls blood pressure during cerebral compression. *Bull Johns Hopkins Hosp* **12**:290, 1901.

Daily WJR, Klaus M, Meyer HBP: Apnea in premature infants: monitoring incidence, heart rate changes, and an effect of environmental temperature. *Pediatrics* **43**:510, 1969.

Dawes GS: *Foetal and Neonatal Physiology.* Chicago, Year Book Medical Pub, 1968, p 213.

Dawes GS: Respiratory reflexes, in *Sudden and Unexpected Deaths in Infancy (Cot Deaths),* (Camps and Carpenter, 1972), p 37.

Dawes GS: Discussion in *SIDS, 1974* (Robinson, 1974) p 251.

Defrain JD, Ernst L: The psychological effects of sudden infant death syndrome on surviving family members. *J Fam Pract* **6**:985, 1978.

Denoroy DL, Kopp N, Gay N, Et Al: Activités des enzymes de synthèse des-catecholamines dans des régions du tronc cérébral au cours de la mort subite du nourrisson. *C R Acad Sc Paris* **291**:245, 1980.

Deuel RK: Polygraphic monitoring of apneic spells. *Arch Neurol* **28**:71, 1973.

Dinsdale F, Emery JL, Gadsdon DR: The carotid body: A quantitative assessment in children. *Histopathology* **1**:179, 1977.

Downing SE, Lee JC: Laryngeal chemosensitivity: A possible mechanism for sudden infant death. *Pediatrics* **55**:640, 1975.

Dulac S, Jobin M: Comparison of plasma disappearance of triiodothyronine and thyroxine in rats. *Proc Canad Fed Biol* Sec 15, Abstract 127, 1972.

Elmer E.: Failure to thrive: role of the mother. *Pediatrics* **25**:717, 1960.

Emery JL: Epidemiology of "sudden, unexpected, or rapid" deaths in children. *Brit Med J* **2**:925, 1959.

Emery JL, Carpenter RG: Clinical aspects of the Sheffield prospective study of children at possibly increased risk, in *SIDS, 1974* (Robinson, 1974), p 97.

Emery JL, Dinsdale F: Structure of periadrenal brown fat in childhood in both expected and cot deaths. *Arch Dis Child* **53**:154, 1978.

Emery JL, Swift PGF, Worthy E: Hypernatremia and uraemia in unexpected death in infancy. *Arch Dis Child* **49**:686, 1974.

Fagenholz SA, O'Connell K, Shannon DC: Chemoreceptor function and sleep state in apnea. *Pediatrics* **58**:31, 1976.

Farber S: Fulminating streptococcus infections in infancy as a cause of sudden death. *N Eng J Med* **211**:154, 1934.

Fearn SW: Two cases of sudden and unexplained death of children during sleep. *Lancet* **1**:246, 1834.

Feldman KW, Simms RJ: Strangulation in childhood: epidemiology and clinical course. *Pediatrics* **65**:1079, 1980.

Ferris JAJ: Hypoxic changes in conducting tissue of the heart in sudden death in infancy syndrome. *Brit Med J* **2**:23, 1973.

Finkle BS, McCloskey KL, Kopjak L, Carroll JM: Toxicological analyses in cases of sudden infant death: a national feasibility study. *J Forensic Sci* **24**:775, 1979.

Fraser GR, Froggatt P: Unexpected cot deaths. *Lancet* **2**:56, 1966.

French JW, Beckwith JB, Graham CB, Guntheroth WG: Lack of postmortem radiographic evidence of nasopharyngeal obstruction in the sudden infant death syndrome. *J Pediat* **81**:1145, 1972.

French JW, Morgan BC, Guntheroth WG: Infant monkeys—a model for crib death. *Am J Dis Child* **123**:480, 1972.

Friedleben A: Die Physiologie der Thymusdruese, in *Gesundheit und Krankheit*, Frankfort, 1858.

Friedman GR, Franciosi RA, Drake RM: The effects of observed sudden infant death syndrome (SIDS) on hospital staff. *Pediatrics* **64**:538, 1979.

Froggatt P: Epidemiologic aspects of the Northern Ireland Study, in *Sudden Infant Death Syndrome* (Bergman et al, 1970), p 32.

Froggatt P: A cardiac cause in cot death: a discarded hypothesis? *J Irish Med Assoc* **70**:408, 1977.

Froggatt P, Adgey AAJ: A case of the cardio-auditory syndrome (long Q-T interval and profound deafness) diagnosed in the perinatal period and kept under surveillance for two years. *Ulster Med J* **47**:115, 1978.

Froggatt P, James TN: Sudden unexpected death in infants. Evidence on a lethal cardiac arrhythmia. *Ulster Med J* **42**:136, 1973.

Froggatt P, Lynas MA, MacKenzie G: Epidemiology of sudden unexpected death in infants ("cot death") in Northern Ireland. *Brit J Prev Soc Med* **25**:119, 1971.

Froggatt P, Lynas MA, Marshall TK: Sudden unexpected death in infants ("cot death") *Ulster Med J* **40**:116, 1971.

Gadsdon DR, Emery JL: Fatty change in the brain in perinatal and unexpected death. *Arch Dis Child* **51**:42, 1976.

Gaensbauer TJ: Anaclitic depression in a three and one-half-month-old child. *Am J Psychiatry* **137**:7, 1980.

Gale CC: Neuroendocrine aspects of thermoregulation. *Ann Rev Physiol* **35**:391, 1973.

Gastaut H, Tassinari CA, Duron B: Etude polygraphique des manifestations épisodiques (hypniques et respiratoires), diurnes et nocturnes, du syndrome de Pickwick. *Rev Neurol* **112**:568, 1965.

Geertinger P: Sudden, unexpected death in infancy: with special reference to the parathyroids. *Pediatrics* **39**:43, 1967.

Gilles FH, Bina M, Sotrel A: Infantile atlantoocipital instability. The potential danger of extreme extension. *Am J Dis Child* **133**:30, 1979.

Gold E, Carver DH, Heineberg H, Et Al: Viral infection. A possible cause of sudden, unexpected death in infants. *N Eng J Med* **264**:53, 1961.

Gold E, Godek G: Antibody to milk in serum of normal infants and infants who died suddenly and unexpectedly. *Am J Dis Child* **102**:542, 1961.

Goldbloom A, Wigglesworth FW: Sudden death in infancy. *Canad Med Assoc J* **38**:119, 1938.

Greenwood M, Woods HM: "Status thymico-lymphaticus" considered in the light of recent work on the thymus. *J Hygiene* **26**:305, 1927.

Gregerman RI, Solomon N: Acceleration of thyroxine and triiodothyronine turnover during bacterial pulmonary infections and fever: implications for the functional state of the thyroid during stress and in senescence. *J Clin Endocr* **27**:93, 1967.

Guilleminault C: Sleep apnea syndromes: impact of sleep and sleep states. *Sleep* **3:**227, 1980.

Guilleminault C, Ariagno RL: Why should we study the infant "near miss for sudden infant death"? *Early Hum Develop* **2:**207, 1978.

Guilleminault C, Ariagno R, Korobkin R, Et Al: Mixed and obstructive sleep apnea and near-miss for sudden infant death syndrome: 2. Comparison of near-miss and normal control infants by age. *Pediatrics* **64:**882, 1979.

Guilleminault C, Ariagno R, Souquet M, Dement WC: Abnormal polygraphic findings in near-miss sudden infant death. *Lancet* **1:**1326, 1976.

Guilleminault C, Dement WC, Monod N: Syndrome "mort subite du nourrisson": apnees au cours du sommeil: nouvelle hypothese. *Nouv Presse Med* **2:**1355, 1973.

Guilleminault C, Eldridge FL, Dement WC: Insomnia with sleep apnea: a new syndrome. *Science* **181:**856, 1973.

Guilleminault C, Korobkin R: Sudden infant death: near-miss events and sleep research. Some recommendations to improve comparability of results among investigators. *Sleep* **1:**423, 1979.

Guilleminault C, Peraita R, Souquet M, Dement WC: Apneas during sleep in infants: possible relationship with SIDS. *Science* **190:**677, 1975.

Gunther M: The neonate's immunity gap, breast feeding and cot death. *Lancet* **1:**441, 1975.

Guntheroth WG: Comments, **in** *Sudden Death in Infants* (Wedgwood and Benditt, 1963), p 6.

Guntheroth WG: Some physiologic considerations in SIDS, **in** *Sudden Infant Death Syndrome* (Bergman et al, 1970) p 199.

Guntheroth WG: The significance of pulmonary petechiae in crib death. *Pediatrics* **52:**601, 1973.

Guntheroth WG: Primary apnea, hypoxic apnea, and gasping **in** *SIDS, 1974* (Robinson, 1974), p 243.

Guntheroth WG: Sudden infant death syndrome (SIDS), **in** *Manual on Critical Care Medicine* (Weil MH and Shubin H, eds) NYC, John Kolen, 1975, p 280.

Guntheroth WG: Sudden infant death syndrome (crib death). *Am Heart J* **93:**784, 1977.

Guntheroth WG: Sleep apnea and Q-T interval prolongation—a particularly lethal combination (letter). *Am Heart J* **98:**674, 1979.

Guntheroth WG: Cardiopulmonary changes in kittens during sleep. *Science* **205:**1040, 1979.

Guntheroth WG, Kawabori I: Hypoxic apnea and gasping. *J Clin Invest* **56:**1371, 1975.

Guntheroth WG, Kawabori I, Breazeale DG, Et Al: The role of respiratory infection in intrathoracic petechiae. *Am J Dis Child* **134:**364, 1980.

Guntheroth WG, Morgan BC, Mullins GL: Physiologic studies of paroxysmal hyperpnea in cyanotic congenital heart disease. *Circulation* **31:**70, 1965.

Guntheroth WG, Motulsky AG: Inherited primary disorders of cardiac rhythm and conduction. *Prog Med Genet*, in press.

Guyton AC: Acute hypertension in dogs with cerebral ischemia. *Am J Physiol* **154**:45, 1948.

Haddad GG, Epstein MAF, Epstein RA, Et Al: The Q-T interval in aborted sudden infant death syndrome infants. *Pediat Res* **13**:136, 1979.

Haddad GG, Leistner HL, Lai TL, Mellins RB: Ventilation and ventilatory pattern during sleep in aborted sudden infant death syndrome. *Pediat Res* **15**:879, 1981.

Handforth CP: Sudden unexpected death in infants. *Canad Med Assoc J* **80**:872, 1959.

Harned HS, Herrington RT, Ferreiro JI: The effects of immersion and temperature on respiration in newborn lambs. *Pediatrics* **45**:598, 1970.

Harper RM, Leake B, Hoppenbrouwers, Et Al: Polygraphic studies of normal infants and infants at risk for the sudden infant death syndrome: heart rate and variability as a function of state. *Pediat Res* **12**:778, 1978.

Harris LS, Adelson L: Spinal injury and sudden infant death: a second look. *Am J Clin Path* **52**:289, 1969.

Hasselmeyer EG, Hunter JC: The sudden infant death syndrome. *Obstet Gynecol Annu* **4**:213, 1975.

Heaney S, McIntire MS: Sudden infant death syndrome and barometric pressure. *J Pediat* **94**:433, 1979.

Helpern M: Medical examiners and infant deaths (letter). *N Eng J Med* **287**:1050, 1972.

Helson GA: House dust mites and possible connection with sudden infant death syndrome. *NZ Med J* **74**:209, 1971.

Herbst JL, Book LS, Bray PF: Gastroesophageal reflux in the "near miss" sudden infant death syndrome. *J Pediat* **92**:73, 1978.

Hillier AP: Thyroxine deiodination during cold exposure in the rat. *J Physiol* **197**:135, 1968.

Hillman LS, Erickson M, Haddad JG: Serum 25-hydroxyvitamin D concentrations in sudden infant death syndrome. *Pediatrics* **65**:1137, 1980.

Hirsch EF: *The Innervation of the Vertebrate Heart*. Springfield, Charles C. Thomas, 1970, p 130.

Hirshman CA, Mc Cullough RE, Weil JV: Normal values for hypoxic and hypercapnic ventilatory drives in man. *J Appl Physiol* **38**:1095, 1975.

Hofer MA: Psychological responses of infant rats to separation from their mothers. *Science* **168**:871, 1970.

Holmes TH, Masuda M: Life change and illness susceptibility, in *Separation and Depression*, JP Scott and EC Senary, eds. Washington, DC, AAAS Public No 94, 1973, p 161.

Hoppenbrouwers T, Hodgman JE, Mc Ginty Et Al: Sudden infant death syndrome: sleep apnea and respiration in subsequent siblings. *Pediatrics* **66**:205, 1980.

Houstek J: Sudden infant death syndrome in Czechoslovakia: Epidemiologic aspects, in *Sudden Infant Death Syndrome* (Bergman Et Al, 1970), p 55.

Hukuhara T, Nakayama S, Yamagami M: On the behavior of the respiratory muscles in gasping. *Jap J Physiol* **9**:125, 1959.

Hunt CE: Abnormal hypercarbic and hypoxic sleep arousal responses in near-miss SIDS infants [sudden infant death syndrome.] *Pediat Res* [in press.] **15:**1462, 1981.

Hunt CE, McCulloch K, Brouillette RT: Diminished hypoxic ventilatory responses in near-miss sudden infant death syndrome. *J Appl Physiol* **50:**1313, 1981.

Ingbar SH, Bass DE: Effects of prolonged exposure to cold on production and degradation of thyroid hormone in man. *J Endocr* **15:**2, 1957.

Ingman JM, Ackerman BD, Kearns MS, Sattler FP: Bradycardia—an early indicator of apnea in premature infants. *J Am Med Assoc* **211:**1622, 1970.

James TN: Sudden death in babies: new observations in the heart. *Am J Cardiol* **22:**479, 1968.

James TN: Sudden death of babies (Editorial). *Circulation* **53:**1, 1976.

Jansen AH, Chernick V: Cardiorespiratory response to central cyanide in fetal sheep. *J Appl Physiol* **37:**18, 1974.

Jeffery HE, Reid I, Rahilly P, Read DJC: Gastro-esophageal reflux in "near-miss" sudden infant death infants in active but not quiet sleep. *Sleep* **3:**393, 1980.

Jervell A, Lange-Nielsen F: Congenital deaf-mutism, functional heart disease with prolongation of the Q-T interval, and sudden death. *Am Heart J* **54:**59, 1957.

Johnson AR, Hood RL, Emery JL: Biotin and the sudden infant death syndrome. *Nature* **285:**159, 1980.

Johnson P: Laryngeal induced apnea, in *SIDS, 1974* (Robinson, 1974), p 231.

Jones RW, Sharp C, Rabb LR, Et Al: 1028 neonatal electrocardiograms. *Arch Dis Child* **54:**427, 1979.

Katona PG, Egbert JR: Cardiac monitoring and sudden infant death syndrome (SIDS). *Proc ACEMB* **6:**303, 1974.

Keeton BR, Southall E, Rutter N, Et Al: Cardiac conduction disorders in six infants with "near-miss" sudden infant deaths. *Brit Med J* **2:**600, 1977.

Kelly DH, Shannon DC: Periodic breathing in infants with near-miss sudden infant death syndrome. *Pediatrics* **63:**355, 1979.

Kelly DH, Shannon DC: Episodic complete airway obstruction in infants. *Pediatrics* **67:**823, 1981.

Kelly DH, Shannon DC, Liberthson RR: The role of the Q-T interval in the sudden infant death syndrome. *Circulation* **55:**633, 1977.

Kelly DH, Shannon DC, O'Connell BS: Care of infants with near-miss sudden infant death syndrome. *Pediatrics* **61:**511, 1978.

Kempe CH: Approaches to preventing child abuse. The Health Visitors Concept. *J Am Med Assoc* **130:**941, 1976.

Kempe CH, Silberman F, Steele B, Et Al: The battered child syndrome. *J Am Med Assoc* **181:**17, 1962.

Kendeel SR, Ferris JAJ: Fibrosis of the conducting tissue in infancy. *J Path* **117:**123, 1975.

Kendeel SR, Ferris JAJ: Apparent hypoxic changes in pulmonary arterioles and small arteries in infancy. *J Clin Path* **30:**481, 1977.

Kety SS, Schildkraut JJ: Biogenic amines and emotion. *Science* **156**:21, 1967.

Klaus MH, Kennel JH: *Maternal-Infant Bonding*. St Louis, CV Mosby, 1976.

Krugman R, Gray J, Kempe CH: Home visit soon after delivery curbs child abuse. Reported in *Pediatric News* November, 1978, p 42.

Kuhn CM, Butler SR, Schanber SM: Selective depression of serum growth hormone during maternal deprivation in rat pups. *Science* **201**:1034, 1978.

Kukolich MK, Telsey A, Ott J, Motulsky AG: Sudden infant death syndrome: normal Q-T interval on ECGs of relatives. *Pediatrics* **60**:51, 1977.

Kukull WA, Peterson DA: Sudden infant death and infanticide. *Am J Epidemiol* **106**:485, 1977.

Kulkarni P, Hall RT, Rhodes PG, Sheehan MB: Postneonatal infant mortality in infants admitted to a neonatal intensive care unit. *Pediatrics* **62**:178, 1978.

Landing BH: Review of the problem, in *Sudden Deaths in Infants* (Wedgwood and Benditt, 1964), p 1.

Lawson EE: Prolonged central respiratory inhibition following reflex-induced apnea. *J Appl Physiol* **50**:874, 1981.

Leape LL, Holder TM, Franklin JD, Et Al; Respiratory arrest in infants secondary to gastroesophageal reflux. *Pediatrics* **60**:924, 1977.

Lee CA: Art XII, On the Thymus Gland: its morbid affections, and the diseases which arise from its abnormal enlargement. *Am J Med Sci* **3**:135, 1842.

Legallois JJC: *Experiences sur le Principe de la Vie*. Paris, D'Hautel, 1812, p 38.

Leistner HL, Haddad GG, Epstein RA Et Al: Heart rate and heart rate variability during sleep in aborted sudden infant death syndrome. *J Pediat* **97**:51, 1980.

Lenard HG, Fest U, Scholz W: Complications of pertussis immunization. *Monatsschr Kinderheil* KD **125**:660, 1977.

Lewak N: Sudden infant death syndrome in a hospitalized infant on an apnea monitor. *Pediatrics* **56**:296, 1975.

Lewis T: Lecture on vasovagal syncope and carotid sinus mechanisms with comments on Gower's and Northnagel's syndromes. *Brit Med J* **1**:873, 1932.

Lie JT, Rosenberg HS, Erickson EE: Histopathology of the conduction system in the sudden infant death syndrome. *Circulation* **53**:3, 1976.

Light RJ: Abused and neglected children in America: a study of alternative policies. *Harvard Ed Rev* **43**:556, 1973.

Lindemann E: Symptomatology and management of acute grief. *Am J Psychiat* **101**:141, 1944.

Lucy JF, Peabody J, Philip A: Recurrent undetected hypoxia and hyperoxia (Abstract) *Pediat Res* **11**:537, 1977.

Lumsden T: Observations on the respiratory centers in the cat. *J Physiol* (Lond) **57**:153, 1923.

Mandell F: Cot death among children of nurses. Observations of breathing patterns. *Arch Dis Child* **56**:312, 1981.

Mandell F, McAnulty E, Reece RM: Observations of paternal response to sudden unanticipated infant death. *Pediatrics* **65:**221, 1980.

Mandell F, Wolfe LC: Sudden infant death syndrome and subsequent pregnancy. *Pediatrics* **56:**774, 1975.

Maresch W: Die Bedeutung von Elektrolytbestimmungen des Herzmuskels zur Klarung plotzlicher Todesfalle in Sauglingsalter. *Wien Klin Wschr* **74:**21, 1962.

Maron BJ, Clark CE, Goldstein RE, Epstein SE: Potential role of Q-T interval prolongation in sudden infant death syndrome. *Circulation* **54:**423, 1976.

Marshall E: Visiting experts find the "mystery disease" of Naples is a common virus. *Science* **203:**980, 1979.

Marshall TK: The Northern Ireland study: Pathology findings, in *Sudden Infant Death Syndrome* (Bergman et al, 1970), p 108.

Marx JL: Botulism in infants: a cause of sudden death? *Science* **201:**799, 1978.

Marx JL: Question marks for SIDS test. *Science* **213:**323, 1981.

Mason JK, Harkness RA, Elton RA, Bartholomew S: Cot deaths in Edinburgh: infant feeding and socioeconomic factors. *J Epidemiol Community Health* **34:**35, 1980.

Mason JM, Mason LH, Jackson M, Et Al: Pulmonary vessels in SIDS (letter). *N Eng J Med* **292:**479, 1975.

McCammon RW: A longitudinal study of electrocardiographic intervals in healthy children. *Acta Paediat Scand* (Uppsala) Suppl 126, 1961.

McGinty DJ, Harper RM: Sleep physiology and SIDS: animal and human studies, in *SIDS, 1974* (Robinson, 1974), p 201.

McWeeny PM, Emery JL: Unexpected postneonatal deaths (cot deaths) due to recognizable disease. *Arch Dis Child* **50:**191, 1975.

Medvedev NIU: Sudden death syndrome in infants. *Arkh Patol* **40:**79, 1978 (English Abstract).

Menking M, Wagnitz JG, Burton RD, Et Al: Rumination—a near-fatal psychiatric disease in infancy. *N Eng J Med* **280:**802, 1969.

Midura TF, Arnon SS: Infant botulism. Identification of Clostridium botulinum and its toxins in faeces. *Lancet* **2:**934, 1976.

Money DF: Cot deaths and deficiency of vitamin E and selenium. *Brit Med J* **4:**559, 1971.

Montague TJ, Bagnell PC, Roy DL, Smith ER: Cardiac rhythm in sudden infant death syndrome (Abstract). *Am J Cardiol* **45:**431, 1980.

Morgan BC, Bloom RS, Guntheroth WG: Cardiac arrhythmias in premature infants. *Pediatrics* **35:**658, 1965.

Moritz AR, Zamcheck N: Sudden and unexpected deaths of young soldiers. Disease responsible for such death during World War II. *Arch Path* **42:**459, 1946.

Moshang T, Chance KH, Kaplan MM, Et Al: Effects of hypoxia on thyroid function tests. *J Pediat* **97:**602, 1980.

Mulvey PM: Cot death survey: anaphylaxis and the house dust mite. *Med J Aust* **2:**1240, 1972.

Naeye RL: Organ and cellular development in congenital heart disease and in alimentary malnutrition. *J Pediat* **67**:447, 1965.

Naeye RL: Pulmonary arterial abnormalities in the sudden infant death syndrome. *N Eng J Med* **289**:1167, 1973.

Naeye RL: Hypoxemia and the sudden infant death syndrome. *Science* **186**:837, 1974.

Naeye RL: Brain-stem and adrenal abnormalities in the sudden infant death syndrome. *Am J Clin Pathol* **66**:526, 1976.

Naeye RL: Placental abnormalities in victims of the sudden infant death syndrome. *Biol Neonate* **32**:189, 1977.

Naeye RL: Causes of the excessive rates of perinatal mortality and prematurity in pregnancies complicated by maternal urinary-tract infections. *N Eng J Med* **300**:819, 1979.

Naeye RL: Sudden infant death. *Sci American* **242**:56, 1980.

Naeye RL, Fisher R, Rubin HR, Demers LM: Selected hormone levels in victims of the sudden infant death syndrome. *Pediatrics* **65**:1134, 1980.

Naeye RL, Fisher R, Ryser M, Whalen P: Carotid body in the sudden infant death syndrome. *Science* **191**:567, 1976.

Naeye RL, Ladis B, Drage JS: Sudden infant death syndrome. A prospective study. *Am J Dis Child* **130**:1207, 1976.

Naeye RL, Messmer J, Specht T, Merrit TA: Sudden infant death syndrome temperament before death. *J Pediat* **88**:511, 1976.

Naeye RL, Whalen P, Ryser M, Fisher R: Cardiac and other abnormalities in the sudden infant death syndrome. *Am J Path* **82**:1, 1976.

Nelson NM: But who shall monitor the monitor? *Pediatrics* **61**:663, 1978.

North JB, Jennett S: Impedance pneumography for the detection of abnormal breathing patterns associated with brain damage. *Lancet* **2**:212, 1972.

Oakley JR, Taware CJ, Stanton AN: Evaluation of the Sheffield system for identifying children at risk from unexpected death in infancy. Results from Birmingham and Newcastle upon Tyne. *Arch Dis Child* **53**:649, 1978.

Oliver TK (Ed): *Neonatal Respiratory Adaptation.* Published by National Institutes of Health, Bethesda Md, 1963:117.

Olsen GD, Lees MH: Ventilatory response to carbon dioxide of infants following chronic prenatal methadone exposure. *J Pediat* **96**:983, 1980.

Orlowski JP, Nodar RH, Lonsdale D: Abnormal brainstem auditory evoked potentials in infants with threatened sudden infant death syndrome. *Cleveland Cl Q* **46**:77, 1979.

Osler W: Diseases of the thymus gland, in *Medicine*, 1905, quoted by Savitt, 1975.

Paltauf A: Ueber die Beziehungen der Thymus zum Plotzlichen Tod. *Wien Klin Wochenschr* **2**:877, 1889.

Park MK, Guntheroth WG: Long Q-T syndrome: a preventable form of sudden death. *J Fam Practice* **7**:945, 1978.

Park MK, Guntheroth WG: *How to Read Pediatric ECGs.* Chicago, Year Book Pub, 1981.

Parrish WE, Barrett AM, Gunther M, Camps FE: Hypersensitivity to milk and sudden death in infancy. *Lancet* **2:**1106, 1960.

Perlstein PH, Edwards NK, Sutherland JM: Apnea in premature infants and incubator-air-temperature changes. *N Eng J Med* **282:**461, 1970.

Peterson DR: Sudden, unexpected death in infants. An epidemiologic study. *Am J Epidemiol* **84:**478, 1966.

Peterson DR: Evolution of the epidemiology of sudden infant death syndrome. *Epidemiol Rev* **2:**97, 1980.

Peterson DR: The sudden infant death syndrome—reassessment of growth retardation in relation to maternal smoking and the hypoxia hypothesis. *Am J Epidemiol* **113:**583, 1981.

Peterson DR, Benson EA, Fisher LD, Et Al: Postnatal growth and the sudden infant death syndrome. *Am J Epidemiol* **99:**389, 1974.

Peterson DR, Chinn NM, Fisher LD: The sudden infant death syndrome: Repetitions in families. *J Pediat* **97:**265, 1980.

Peterson DR, Eklund MW, Chinn NM: The sudden infant death syndrome and infant botulism. *Rev Infect Dis* **1:**630, 1979.

Peterson DR, Labbe RF, Van Belle G, Chinn NM: Erythrocyte transketolase activity and sudden infant death. *Am J Clin Nutr* **34:**65, 1981.

Peterson DR, Van Belle G, Chinn NM: Epidemiologic comparisons of the sudden infant death syndrome, with other major components of infant mortality. *Am J Epidemiol* **110:**699, 1979.

Phillipson EA, Bowes G, Sullivan CE, Woolf GM: The influence of sleep fragmentation on arousal and ventilatory responses to respiratory stimuli. *Sleep* **3:**281, 1980.

Pierson PS, Howard P, Kleber HD: Sudden deaths in infants born to methadone-maintained addicts. *J Am Med Assoc* **220:**1733, 1972.

Polgar G, Kong GP: The nasal resistance of newborn infants. *J Pediat* **67:**557, 1965.

Powell GF, Brasel JA, Blizzard RM: Emotional deprivation and growth retardation simulating idiopathic hypopituitarism. Clinical evaluation of the syndrome. *N Eng J Med* **276:**1271, 1967.

Protestos CD, Carpenter RG, McWeeny PM, Emery JL: Obstetric and perinatal histories of children who died unexpectedly (cot death). *Arch Dis Child* **48:**835, 1973.

Quattrochi JJ, Baba N, Liss L, Adrion W: Sudden infant death syndrome (SIDS): a preliminary study of reticular dendritic spines in infants with SIDS. *Brain Res* **181:**245, 1980.

Ragegowda BK, Kandall SR, Falciglia H: Sudden unexpected death in infants of narcotic-dependent mothers. *Early Hum Dev* **2:**219, 1978.

Raven C: Study of sudden death of infants. *J Am Med Wom Assoc* **22:**319, 1967.

Raven C: Crib deaths, sudden unexpected death in infancy, or the sudden infant death syndrome: a hypersensitivity reaction. *J Am Med Wom Assoc* **32:**148, 1977.

Raven C, Maverakis NH, Eveland WC, Ackermann WW: The sudden infant death syndrome: a possible hypersensitivity reaction determined by distribution of IGG in lungs. *J Forensic Sci* **23:**116, 1978.

Ray CG, Beckwith JB, Hebestreit NM, Bergman AB: Studies of the sudden infant death syndrome in King County, Washington: 1. The role of virus. *J Am Med Assoc* **211**:619, 1970.

Ray CG, Hebestreit NM: Studies of the sudden infant death syndrome in King County, Washington: II. Attempts to demonstrate evidence of viremia. *Pediatrics* **48**:79, 1971.

Read DJ: The aetiology of the sudden infant death syndrome: current ideas on breathing and sleep and possible links to deranged thiamine neurochemistry. *Aust NZ J Med* **8**:322, 1978.

Reisinger RC: Pathogenesis and prevention of infectious diarrhea (scours) of newborn calves. *J Am Vet Med Assoc* **147**:1377, 1965.

Restak RM: Psychosocial dwarfism: the evidence grows, the kids don't. *NY Times* Nov. 18, 1979.

Richards IDG, McIntosh HT: Confidential inquiry into 226 consecutive infant deaths. *Arch Dis Child* **47**:697, 1972.

Roberts J, Lynch MA, Golding J: Postneonatal mortality in children from abusing families. *Brit Med J* **2**:102, 1980.

Robin ED, Whaley RD, Crump CH, Travis DM: Alveolar gas tensions, pulmonary ventilation and blood pH during physiologic sleep in normal subjects. *J Clin Invest* **37**:981, 1958.

Robinson RR (ed): *SIDS, 1974.* Canada, pub by The Canadian Foundation for the Study of Infant Deaths.

Romano C, Gemme G, Pongiglione R: Aritmie cardiache rare dell'eta pediatrica. *Clin Pediatr* **45**:656, 1963.

Russell MA, Opitz JM, Viseskul C, Et Al: Sudden infant death due to congenital adrenal hypoplasia. *Arch Path Lab Med* **101**:168, 1977.

Rutter M: *Maternal Deprivation Reassessed.* Hammondsworth, Penguin, 1972.

Sachis PN, Armstrong DL, Becker LE, Bryan AC: The vagus nerve and sudden infant death syndrome: A morphometric study. *J Pediat* **98**:279, 1981.

Sackett GP: Abnormal behavior in laboratory-reared rhesus monkeys, in WU Fox (ed) *Abnormal Behavior in Animals.* Philadelphia, Saunders, 1968, p. 293.

St John WM, Bartless D: Comparison of phrenic motoneuron activity during eupnea and gasping. *J Appl Physiol* **50**:994, 1981.

St John WM, Knuth KV: A characterization of the respiratory pattern of gasping. *J Appl Physiol* **50**:984, 1981.

Savitt, TL: Smothering and overlaying of Virginia slave children: a suggested mechanism. *Bull Hist Med* **49**:400, 1975.

Savitt, TL: Social and medical history of crib death. *J Fla Med Assoc* **66**:853, 1979.

Schrauzer GN, Rhead WJ, Saltzstein SL: Sudden infant death syndrome: plasma vitamin E levels and dietary factors. *Ann Clin Lab Sci* **5**:31, 1975.

Schwartz PJ: Cardiac sympathetic innervation and the sudden infant death syndrome. *Am J Med* **50**:167, 1976.

Schwartz PJ: The sudden infant death syndrome. *Rev Perinatal Med* **4**:475, 1981.

Schwartz, PJ, Periti M, Malliani A: The long Q-T syndrome. *Am Heart J* **89**:378, 1975.

Severinghaus JW, Mitchell RA: Ondine's curse—failure of respiratory center automaticity while awake. *Clin Res* **10**:122, 1962.

Shannon DC, Kelly DH, O'Connell K: Abnormal regulation of ventilation in infants at risk for SIDS. *N Eng J Med* **297**:747, 1977.

Shaw EB: Sudden unexpected death in infancy syndrome. *Am J Dis Child* **116**:115, 1968.

Shaw EB: Sudden unexpected death in infancy. *Am J Dis Child* **119**:416, 1970.

Shnaps Y, Frand M, Rotem Y, Tirosh M: The chemically abused child. *Pediatrics* **68**:119, 1981.

Short R, Reite M, Seiler C, Et Al: Physiologic changes accompanying 10-day maternal separations in pigtail (M nemestrina) infants. *Am Soc Primatologists*, Abstracts, 1978.

Sieker HO, Heyman A, Birchfield RI: The effects of natural sleep and hypersomnolent states on respiratory function. *Ann Int Med* **52**:500, 1960.

Silver HK, Finkelstein M: Deprivation dwarfism. *Pediatrics* **70**:31, 1967.

Sinclair-Smith C, Dinsdale F, Emery J: Evidence of duration and type of illness in children found unexpectedly dead. *Arch Dis Child* **51**:424, 1976.

Smialek JE, Monforte JR: Toxicology and sudden infant death. *J Forensic Sci* **22**:757, 1977.

Smialek JE, Smialek PZ, Spitz WU: Accidental bed deaths in infants due to unsafe sleeping situations. *Clin Pediat* **16**:1031, 1977.

Smialek Z: Observations on immediate reactions of families to sudden infant death. *Pediatrics* **62**:150, 1978.

Smith TA, Mason JM, Bell JS, Francisco JT: Sleep apnea and Q-T interval prolongation—a particularly lethal combination. *Am Heart J* **97**:505, 1979.

South Australia Committee: *Sudden Infant Death Syndrome in Adelaide, South Australia,* 1976.

Southall DP, Arrowsmith WA, Oakley JR, Et Al: Prolonged Q-T interval and cardiac arrhythmias in two neonates: sudden infant death syndrome in one case. *Arch Dis Child* **54**:776, 1979.

Southall DP, Orrell MJ, Talbot JF, Et Al: Study of cardiac arrhythmias and other forms of conduction abnormality in newborn infants. *Brit Med J* **2**:597, 1977.

Southall DP, Richards J, Brown DJ, Et Al: 24-hour tape recordings of ECG and respiration in the newborn infant with findings related to sudden death and unexplained brain damage in infancy. *Arch Dis Child* **55**:7, 1980.

Southall DP, Vulliamy DG, Davies MJ, Et Al: A new look at the neonatal electrocardiogram. *Brit Med J* **2**:615, 1976.

Spain DM, Bradess VA, Greenblatt IJ: Possible factors in sudden and unexpected death during infancy. *J Am Med Assoc* **156**:246, 1954.

Spain DM, Bradess VA, Mohr C: Coronary atherosclerosis as a cause of unexpected and unexplained death. An autopsy study from 1949-1959. *J Am Med Assoc* **174**:384, 1960.

Spector WG: Session 3 in *Sudden and Unexpected Deaths in Infancy (Cot Deaths)*, (Camps and Carpenter, 1972), p 72.

Speer L: Aborted crib death? (Letter). *J Am Med Assoc* **223**:1512, 1973.

Spiers PS: Estimated rates of concordancy for the sudden infant death syndrome in twins. *Am J Epidemiol* **100**:1, 1974.

Spiers PS, Wang L: Short pregnancy interval, low birthweight, and the sudden infant death syndrome. *Am J Epidemiol* **104**:15, 1976.

Spitz RA: Hospitalism: an inquiry into the genesis of psychiatric conditions in early childhood. *Psychoanal Study Child* **1**:53, 1945.

Stanton AN, Downham MA, Oakley JR, Et Al: Terminal symptoms in children dying suddenly and unexpectedly at home. *Brit Med J* **2**:1249, 1978.

Stanton AN, Scott DJ, Downham MA: Is overheating a factor in some unexpected infant deaths? *Lancet* **1**:1954, 1980.

Steele R: Sudden infant death syndrome in Ontario, Canada, in *Sudden Infant Death Syndrome* (Bergman et al, 1980), p 64.

Steele R; SIDS in Ontario: epidemiologic aspects, in *SIDS 1974* (Robinson, 1974), p 71.

Steele R, Langworth JT: The relationship of antenatal and postnatal factors to sudden unexpected death in infancy. *Canad Med Assoc J* **94**:1165, 1966.

Stein IM, White A, Kennedy JL, Et Al: Apnea recordings of healthy infants at 40, 44, and 52 weeks postconception. *Pediatrics* **63**:724, 1979.

Steinschneider A: Prolonged apnea and the sudden infant death syndrome: clinical and laboratory observations. *Pediatrics* **50**:646, 1972.

Steinschneider A: The concept of sleep apnea as related to SIDS, in *SIDS, 1974* (Robinson, 1974) p 177.

Steinschneider A: A re-examination of the "apnea monitor business". *Pediatrics* **58**:1, 1976.

Steinschneider A: Sudden infant death syndrome and prolongation of the Q-T interval. *Am J Dis Child* **132**:688, 1978.

Stephenson JBP: Two types of febrile seizure: anoxic (syncopal) and epileptic mechanisms differentiated by oculocardiac reflex. *Brit Med J* **2**:726, 1978.

Stevens LH: Sudden unexplained death in infancy. *Am J Dis Child* **110**:243, 1965.

Stone I: Homo sapiens ascorbicus, a biochemically corrected robust human mutant. *Med Hypotheses* **5**:711, 1979.

Stowens D: Sudden unexpected death in infancy. *Am J Dis Child* **94**:674, 1957.

Stowens D, Callahan EL, Clay J: Sudden unexpected death in infancy: a new hypothesis of cause. *Clin Pediat* **5**:243, 1966.

Sturner WQ, Susa JB: Sudden infant death and liver phosophoenolpyruvate carboxykinase analysis. *Forensic Sci* **16**:19, 1980.

Sullivan CE, Henderson-Smart DJ, Read DJC (Eds): Control of breathing during sleep. *Sleep* **3**:221, 1980.

Sullivan CE, Issa FG: Pathophysiological mechanisms in obstructive sleep apnea. *Sleep* **3**:235, 1980.

Sunderland R, Emery JL: Apparent disappearance of hypernatraemic dehydration from infant deaths in Sheffield. *Brit Med J* **2**:575, 1979.

Sunderland R, Emery JL: Febrile convulsions and cot death. *Lancet* **2**:176, 1981.
Swann HE: Occurrence of pulmonary edema in sudden asphyxial deaths. *Arch Path* **69**:557, 1960.
Sweetman L, Surh L, Baker H, Et Al: Clinical and metabolic abnormalities in a boy with dietary deficiency of biotin. *Pediatrics* **68**:553, 1981.
Takashima S, Armstrong D, Becker L, Bryan C: Cerebral hypoperfusion in the sudden infant death syndrome? Brainstem gliosis and vasculature. *Ann Neurol* **4**:257, 1978a.
Takashima S, Armstrong D, Becker LE, Huber J: Cerebral white matter lesions in sudden infant death syndrome. *Pediatrics* **62**:155, 1978b.
Task Force on Prolonged Apnea (American Academy of Pediatrics): Prolonged apnea. *Pediatrics* **61**:651, 1978.
Templeman C: Two hundred and fifty-eight cases of suffocation of infants. *Edinburgh Med J* **38**:322, 1892.
Thach BT, Stark AR: Spontaneous neck flexion and airway obstruction during apneic spells in preterm infants. *J Pediat* **94**:275, 1979.
Theorell K: Clinical value of prolonged polygraphic recordings of high-risk newborn infants. *Neuropaediatrie* **5**:383, 1974.
Thoman EB, Arnold WJ: Effects of incubator rearing with social deprivation on maternal behavior in rats. *J Comp Physiol Psych* **65**:441, 1968.
Thoman EB, Miano VN, Freese MP: The role of respiratory instability in the sudden infant death syndrome. *Develop Med Child Neurol* **19**:729, 1977.
Tilkian AG, Guilleminault C, Schroeder JS, Et Al: Sleep-induced apnea syndrome. *Am J Cardiol* **63**:348, 1977.
Tonkin S: Sudden infant death syndrome: hypothesis of causation. *Pediatrics* **55**:650, 1975.
Towbin A: Sudden infant death (cot death) related to spinal injury. *Lancet* **2**:940, 1967.
Trube-Becker E: Enteral bacterial infection as a possible cause of cot death. *Forensic Sci* **11**:171, 1978.
Turner KJ, Baldo BA, Hilton JM: IGE antibodies to Dermatophagoides pteronyssinus (housedust mite), Aspergillus fumigatus, and beta-lactoglobulin in sudden infant death syndrome. *Brit Med J* **1**:351, 1975.
Valdes-Dapena MA: Serum proteins, viral isolation, antibodies to milk, and epidemiologic factors in sudden death, **in** *Sudden Death in Infants* (Wedgwood and Benditt, 1963, p 81.
Valdes-Dapena MA: Sudden and unexpected death in infancy: a review of the world literature 1954-66. *Pediatrics* **39**:123, 1967.
Valdes-Dapena MA: The changing incidence of sudden death in infancy, **in** *SIDS, 1974* (Robinson, 1974), p 83.
Valdes-Dapena MA: Sudden infant death syndrome: a review of the medical literature 1974-1979. *Pediatrics* **66**:597, 1980.
Valdes-Dapena MA, Eichman MF, Ziskin L: Sudden and unexpected death in infants: I. Gamma globulin levels in the serum. *J Pediat* **63**:290, 1963.

Valdes-Dapena MA, Gillane MM, Cassidy JC, Et Al: Wall thickness of small pulmonary arteries. *Arch Path Lab Med* **104**:621, 1980.

Valdes-Dapena MA, Gillane MM, Catherman R: Brown fat retention in sudden infant death syndrome. *Arch Path Lab Med* **100**:547, 1976.

Valdes-Dapena MA, Gillane MM, Ross D, Catherman R: Extramedullary hematopoiesis in the liver in sudden infant death syndrome. *Arch Path Lab Med* **103**:513, 1979.

Valdes-Dapena MA, Greene M, Basavanand N, Et Al: The myocardial conduction system in sudden death in infancy. *N Eng J Med* **289**:1179, 1973.

Valdes-Dapena MA, Hummeler K: Sudden and unexpected deaths in infants: II. Viral infections as causative factors. *J Pediat* **63**:398, 1963.

Valimaki I: Tape recordings of the electrocardiogram in newborn infants. *Acta Paediat Scand*, Suppl 199, 1969.

Walsh JK, Farrell MK, Keenan WJ, Et Al: Gastroesophageal reflux in infants: relation to apnea. *J Pediat* **99**:197, 1981.

Walsh ZS: Electrocardiographic intervals during first week of life. *Am Heart J* **66**:36, 1963.

Ward OC: New familial cardiac syndrome in children. *J Irish Med Assoc* **54**:103, 1964.

Wedgwood RJ, Benditt EP (Eds): *Sudden Death in Infants*, 1963, USPHS publication No. 1412.

Weiss S: Instantaneous "physiologic" death. *N Eng J Med* **223**:793, 1940.

Welch AS, Welch BL: Isolation, reactivity and aggression: evidence for an involvement of brain catecholamines and serotonin, in *The Physiology of Aggression and Defeat*, BE Eleftherion and JS Scott (Eds). New York, Plenum Press, 1971, p 91.

Werne JJ, Garrow I: Sudden deaths of infants allegedly due to mechanical suffocation. *Am J Pub Health* **37**:675, 1947.

Werne JJ, Garrow I: Sudden apparently unexplained death during infancy. I. Pathologic findings in infants found dead. *Am J Path* **29**:633, 1953.

Williams A, Vawter G, Reid L: Increased muscularity of the pulmonary circulation in victims of sudden infant death syndrome. *Pediatrics* **63**:18, 1979.

Woeber KA: Alterations in thyroid hormone economy during acute infection with Diplococcus pneumoniae in the rhesus monkey. *J Clin Invest* **50**:378, 1971.

Wolf S: Sudden death and the oxygen conserving reflex. *Am Heart J* **71**:840, 1966.

Woolley PV: Mechanical suffocation during infancy. Relation to total problem of sudden death. *J Pediat* **26**:572, 1945.

Wright CF, Medenilla GA, Sommers SC: Causes of perinatal death. *Calif Med* **100**:336, 1964.

Ziegler RF: *Electrocardiographic Studies in Normal Infants and Children*. Springfield, Charles C. Thomas, 1951.

Index

The Horseman's Spanish/English Dictionary

The Horseman's
Spanish / English Dictionary

El diccionario de español / inglés del equitador

MARIA BELKNAP

BOOK HOUSE

N E W   Y O R K

Maxwell Macmillan Canada

TORONTO

Maxwell Macmillan International

NEW YORK • OXFORD • SINGAPORE • SYDNEY

Howell Book House	Maxwell Macmillan Canada, Inc.
Macmillan Publishing Company	1200 Eglinton Avenue East
866 Third Avenue	Suite 200
New York, NY 10022	Don Mills, Ontario M3C 3N1

Macmillan Publishing Company is part of the Maxwell Communication Group of Companies.

Library of Congress Cataloging-in-Publication Data

Belknap, Maria.
    The horseman's Spanish / English dictionary = El diccionario de español / inglés del equitador / Maria Belknap.
        p.   cm.
    Includes indexes.
    ISBN 0-87605-828-4
    1. Horses—Dictionaries. 2. Horsemanship—Dictionaries.
3. Horses—Dictionaries—Spanish. 4. Horsemanship—Dictionaries—
Spanish. 5. English language—Dictionaries—Spanish. 6. Spanish
language—Dictionaries—English. I. Title: Diccionario de
español / inglés del equitador.
SF278.B45 1992   91-40738
798'.03—dc20   CIP

Illustrations by Dan Shewmaker
Book design by Jennifer Dossin

Macmillan books are available at special discounts for bulk purchases for sales promotions, premiums, fund-raising, or educational use. For details, contact:

Special Sales Director
Macmillan Publishing Company
866 Third Avenue
New York, NY 10022

10 9 8 7 6 5 4 3 2 1

Printed in the United States of America

To Sundancer

Contents

2. The Horse and Rider

3. Equine Facility Management

4. Commonly Used Words and Phrases

Los Capítulos

1. El Caballo

2. El Caballo y el Jinete

3. Administración de Instalaciones Ecuestres

4. Palabras y Frases Comunes

Illustrations

Lista de Ilustraciones

I would like to thank Dr. Walter de la Brosse for his friendship and help with the difficult translations, John Hall for all the hours he labored over my text, and Jesse Mendoza, Señor Luis Fernando Sánchez Tena, Señor Pablo Rincon Gallando, Sam Cisneros, Dr. Greg Ugarte, Roxana Molina, Joan Bennet, and D. Wayne Lukas for their special help in the creation of this dictionary.

Foreword

Prefacio

The history of the horse—his strength, his endurance, and his contributions to mankind—is as magnificent as the horse himself. In fact, the history of the horse spans over 55 million years. Man first domesticated the horse a mere 5,000 years ago, and it was only in the 1600s that the Spanish Conquistadores reintroduced him to the American continent.

As old as the story of the horse may seem, it is also—and perhaps surprisingly—a very young one in this respect: it has only been during the last forty years that the worldwide interest in horses for sport has truly exploded. Countless books have been published about breeding, training, and the psychology and the use of the horse, but very little exists that deals with the terms and language unique to the horse world.

Indeed, how can we talk about a subject as diverse and

complex as the horse without a common ground upon which to base our understanding? As a trainer, I know that communicating my goals and attitude to my staff is not just part of the winning formula, it's the key. If you work hard and you're lucky, winning can become a habit. But this is not a popular psychology book about motivational success. It's more basic—and possibly more important.

I have training facilities across the country, and more than 75 percent of my staff is Spanish-speaking. But I do not speak Spanish. Still, we all work as a team to win. To win you've got to set goals and develop a winning attitude. You've got to preach it. You've got to think it. You've got to feel it. And perhaps most importantly, you've got to communicate it. Moreover, in the world of horses, you've got to communicate highly specialized information and instruction.

Not until Maria Belknap compiled this dictionary has such a comprehensive communication resource been available to English- and Spanish-speaking horsemen. This dictionary not only provides equivalent Spanish words and phrases for the terminology and jargon of those who ride, train, and show, but it also gives many of the regional idiomatic expressions found in the Spanish language. Bilingual, labeled illustrations of the anatomy of the horse are a further bonus.

It is not enough to say that this book is the first of its kind. It must be acknowledged as an important and necessary reference for horsemen everywhere. For me, it will become an invaluable and inseparable part of my work, which is my life.

La historia del caballo—su fuerza, su resistencia, y su contribución a la humanidad—es tan magnifica como el mismo caballo. En realidad, la historia del caballo se extiende sobre más de 55 millones de años. El hombre domesticó el caballo tan solo hace 5,000 años, y fue solo en el siglo XVII que los conquistadores españoles lo reintrodujeron al continente americano.

Tan vieja coma la historia del caballo paresca, es también—y tal vez sorprendente—muy joven en este respecto: es solo durante los últimos cuarenta años que el interés mundial por el caballo como deporte ha explotado. Numerosos libros han sido publicados sobre la crianza, el entrenamiento, la sicología y los usos del caballo, pero muy poco existe que trata con los términos y la lenguaje que es único en le mundo del caballo.

En efecto, ¿como podemos hablar sobre un sujeto tan diverso y complejo como el caballo sin tener terreno común en el cual basar nuestro entendimiento? Como entrada, yo sé que comunicar mis objetivos y mi actitud a mis empleados no es solo parte de la formula ganadora, es la llave. Si trabaja duro y tiene suerte, el ganar puede hacerse un hábito. Pero este libro no es sobre éxito motivante. Es más básico que eso—y posiblemente más importante.

Tengo centros hípicos a través de los Estados Unidos, y más del 75% de mis empleados son de habla española. Pero yo no hablo español. Sin embargo, todos trabajamos juntos como un equipo para ganar. Para ganar tenemos que poner metas y desarrollar una actitud ganadora. Tenemos que predicarla, pensarla, y sentirla. Tal vez más importante, tenemos que comunicarla. Además, en el mundo del caballo, tenemos que comunicar información e instrucciones de alta especialidad.

No ha sido disponible un recurso de comunicación tan amplio para el jinete de habla inglés-español, hasta que Maria Belknap compiló este diccionario. Este diccionario no se solo provee palabras y frases en español equivalentes a la terminología y jerga de esos que montan, entrenan, y concursan, pero también da muchas expresiones regionales idiomáticas que se encuentran en el idioma español. Ilustraciones con etiquetas bilingües de la anatomía del caballo es otra prima.

No es suficiente decir que este libro es el primero en su clase. Debe ser reconocido como una referencia importante y necesaria por jinetes en todos los lugares. Para mi, se hará un inestimable e inseparable parte de mi trabajo, que es mi vida.

D. Wayne Lukas

Introduction

Introducción

"The difference between the almost right word and the right word is really a large matter—'tis the difference between the lightning bug and the lightning." MARK TWAIN

I have been riding horses since I was a small child and they still continue to be a vital part of my life. I would like to believe that I've finally begun to understand them, but that I think, shall take a lifetime.

Although man's interest in the horse is universal, the languages spoken by horsemen are not. Despite the shrinking international boundaries, huge language barriers still exist within the world of the horse. Nowhere is this problem felt more than in the management, training and showing of horses by—and with—the Spanish- and English-speaking horsepeople in the United States, and increasingly, around the world.

Over the past ten years, I have been asked so frequently to translate between horse owner, horse trainer, horse rider and those Spanish-speaking people who care for and manage our horses and facilities, that I realized there was a need for a clear, correct and precise communication tool.

Not knowing how to communicate or communicating incorrectly can be very frustrating. Further, I have seen the inability to correctly express oneself jeopardize the safety of the horse, the rider and those around him.

Hence this dictionary.

This translation dictionary contains over 40,000 words,

phrases and sentences. For easy reference, it is divided into four chapters—The Horse, The Horse and Rider, Equine Facility Management, and Commonly Used Words and Phrases —with multiple subsections in each. The entries within each subsection are listed alphabetically. I have included many regional variations to the Spanish translations in this book, the origins of which are identified parenthetically following the entry: Argentina–Arg, Brazil–Br, Chile–Ch, Mexico– Mex, Spain–Sp, Venezuela–Ven and Uruguay–Ur.

Yo e montado a caballo desde muy niña y aun todavía continúan siendo una parte muy vital de mi vida. Mi gustaría creer que al fin los empiezo a comprender, pero eso yo creo, tardará una vida.

Aunque el interés del hombre en el caballo es universal, los lenguajes hablados por los jinetes no los son. A pesar de la disminución internacional de fronteras, todavía existe una gran barrera dentro del mundo del caballo. En ninguna lugar se nota más este problema que en el mantenimiento, el entrenamiento y la enseñanza del caballo por—y con—la gente caballista de habla inglés-español en los Estados Unidos, y cada vez más, alrededor del mundo.

Durante los últimos diez años, me han preguntado con frecuencia que traduzca entre dueño de caballos, entrenador de caballo, jinete, y esas gentes de habla español quienes mantiene y manejan nuestros caballos y instalaciones, fue cuando me di cuenta de la necesidad de un instrumento de comunicación preciso, claro y correcto.

No poderse comunicar o comunicarse incorrectamente puede ser algo frustrante. Además, e visto que la incapacidad de poderse expresar correctamente ha puesto en peligro la seguridad del caballo, el jinete, y todos a su alrededor.

Por lo tanto este diccionario.

Este diccionario de traducción contiene más de 40,000 palabras, frases y oraciones. Para facilitar su uso, este diccionario está divida en cuatro capítulos—El Caballo, El Caballo y Jinete, Administración de Instalación Equestre, y Frases y Palabras Comunes—cada con subdivisiones múltiples. Yo incluido varias variaciones regionales a las traducciones en español de este libro, el origen de cuales están identificadas en paréntesis después de cada entrada: Argentina–Arg, Brazil–Br, Chile–Ch, México–Mex, Spain–Sp, Venezuela–Ven, y Uruguay–Ur.

The Horseman's Spanish/English Dictionary

The Horse

El caballo

horse and pony breeds	razas de caballos y poneys
Akhal-Teké	Turkmeno
Alter-Real	Alter
American Mustang	Mustango Americano, Mesteño Americano
American Saddle Horse	Paso Americano
Andalucian	Andaluz
Appaloosa	Appaloosa
Arab	Caballo Árabe, Árabe
Ardennais	Ardenés, Ardenas
Argentinian Creole	Criollo Argentino
Auxois	Auxoise
Barb	Beréber
Bavarian Warmblood	Media Sangre Bávaro

Beberbeck	Beberbeck
Belgian Ardennes	Ardenés Bélgica
Belgian Draft Horse, Brabant	Caballo de Tiro Belga, Brabanzón
Boulonnais	Bullones
Brazilian Creole	Criollo Brasileño
Breton	Bretón
Burro	burro
Charollais	Charollais
Chilean Creole	Criollo Chileno
Clydesdale	Clydesdale
Cob	jaca
Comtois	Comtoise
Connemara	Connemara
Creole	Criollo
Dole Trotter	Dole, Gundbransdal
Don	Don
Donkey	asno, burro
Dutch Draft Horse	Caballo de Tiro Holandés
Dutch Warmblood	Caballo Holandés de Media Sangre
Einsiedler	Einsiedler
Exmoor	Exmoor
Fell	Fell Poney
Finnish	Finlandesa
Fjord	Caballo de los Fiordos
Frederiksborg	Frederiksborg
French Anglo-Arab	Angloárabe Francés
French Trotter	Caballo Trotón Francés
Freidberger	Freidberger
Frisian	Frisón, Frisia
Furioso	Furious, Furioso
Gelderland	Caballo de Gueldría
Gidran Arabian	Gidranés

Groningen	Caballo de Gróninga
Hackney	Hackney
Haflinger	Raza Aveliñesa, Haflinger
Hanoverian	Hanoverian, Hanover, Hanoveriano
Highland	Poney de Highland
Holsteiner/Holstein	Caballo de Holstein, Holsteiner
Irish Draught	Caballo de Tiro Irlandés
Irish Hunter	Media Sangre Irlandés
Italian Heavy Draft	Tiro Pesado Italiano
Jutland	Jutlandia
Karabardin	Karabarda
Karabair	Karabagh
Kazakh	Kazakh
Kirghiz	Kirguiz
Knabstrup	Knabstrup
Latvian	Lóton
Limousin	Limosino
Lipizzaner	Lipizano
Lusitano	Lusitana
Maremmana	Maremmano
Miniature Horse	Caballo Miniatura, Falabella
Missouri Fox Trotter	Caballo Trote-Zorro de Misuri
Morgan	Morgan
Mule	mula, macho
Mustang	Mustango, Mesteño
New Forest	New Forestal
Nonius	Nonius
Noriker	Norico
North Swedish	Caballo Sueco del Norte
Oldenburg	Oldenburg, Oldenburgo

Orlov	Orloff
Paint	Paint, Caballo Pinto
Palomino	Palomino
Paraguayan Creole	Criollo Paraguayo
Paso Fino	Paso Fino
Percheron	Percherón
Peruvian Paso	Paso Peruano, Caballo Aguililla
Pinto	Pinto
Pleven	Pleven
Poitevin	Poitevin
Pony of the Americas	Poney de las Américas
Quarter Horse	Cuarto de Milla
Rhineland Heavy Draft	Tiro Pesado Renania
Russian Heavy Draft	Tiro Pesado Ruso
Saddlebred	Caballo de Silla Norteamericano
Salerno	Salerno
Schleswig	Schleswig
Selle Français	Silla Francesa
Shagya Arabian	Árabe Shagya
Shetland Pony	Poney de Shetland
Shire	Shire
Spanish Barb	Beréber Español, Árabe Española, Criollo (Arg, Ch, Br)
Spanish Mustang	Mustango Española, Mesteño, Criollo (Arg, Ch, Br)
Standard Bred	Caballo de Trote
Suffolk	Suffolk
Swedish Ardennes	Ardenés Sueco, Ardenas Sueco

Swedish Warmblood	Caballo Sueco de Media Sangre, Caballo Sueco de Sangre Tibia
Tennessee Walking Horse	Caballo de Paso de Tennessee
Thoroughbred	Pura Sangre, Fino
Trakhener	Trakhener, Trakhenen
Venezuelan Creole	Criollo Venezolano
Welsh Pony	Poney Galense
Westfalian	Westfalian
Württemberg	Württemberg

classifications of horses

clasificaciones de caballos

beginner's horse	caballo de entrenamiento, caballo de novicio, caballo de jinete noviciado
breeding horse	caballo de cría, caballo de crianza
carriage horse	caballo de coche, caballo de tiro
cart horse	caballo de carro, calesa
coach horse	caballo de coche
coldblood	caballo de sangre fría
colt	potro, potranco
young colt	potrillo
cutting horse	caballo de apartar
docked horse	caballo rabón
draft horse	caballo frisón, caballo de tiro

driving horse	caballo de tiro
dressage horse	caballo de adiestramiento, caballo de alta escuela
endurance horse	caballo de dureza, caballo de resistencia, caballo de aguante
event horse	caballo de prueba completa, caballo de prueba militar
fast horse	caballo ligero, caballo rápido
filly	potra, potranca
young filly	potrilla
halfbred horse	mestizo
heavy horse	caballo pesado
horse	caballo
hot-blooded horse	caballo de sangre caliente
hunter	cazador, caballo de caza
hackamore horse	caballo de falsa rienda, caballo de jáquima
jumper	saltador/a, caballo de salto
jumping horse	caballo de salto
light horse	caballo liviano
mare	yegua
mature horse	caballo maduro
mount (a)	un caballo
bad mount	mala monta (Mex)
beginner's mount	caballo de jinete novicio
good mount	buena monta (Mex)
poor mount	pobre monta (Mex)
nag	rocino
worn-out nag	rocinante

pacing horse	caballo de paso
pack horse	caballo de carga
pedigree horse	caballo de raza
pleasure horse	caballo de paseo, caballo de placer
polo mount	caballo de polo, jaca de polo
polo pony	poney de polo, jaca de polo
pony	poney, jaca, caballico/ito, pony,
pureblood horse	caballo de pura sangre
race horse	caballo de carrera
registered horse	caballo registrado, caballo inscrito
reining horse	caballo de cala, caballo de riendas, caballo arrendado
riding horse	caballo de silla
roping horse	caballo de lazo
saddle horse	caballo de silla
school horse	caballo de escuela
show horse	caballo de concurso
small horse	jaca
stallion	semental
stock horse	caballo vaquero
three-gaited horse	caballo de tres pasos
trail horse	caballo huellero
trick horse	caballo de circo, caballo de trucos, caballo de astucia
trotter	caballo trotón, caballo de trote
vaulting horse	caballo de circo, caballo de trucos, caballo de astucia

work horse	caballo frisón, caballo de tiro
warmblood	caballo de media sangre, caballo de sangre tibia
western horse	caballo de vaquero

points of the horse   puntos del caballo

abdomen	abdomen
ankle	tobillo
anus	ano
arm	brazo
artery	arteria
back (lower)	lomo
back (upper)	espalda
barrel	costilla
belly	estomago, barriga
body	cuerpo
bone	hueso
breast	pecho
bridge of the nose	puente de la nariz
bridle path	nuca, pasaje de freno
buttock	grupa, nalga
cannon bone	caña
cheek	carrillo, mejilla
chest	pecho
chestnut	ergot, castaña, espejuelo
chin	mentón
chin groove	ranura de mentón
coffin bone	bolillo
coffin joint	articulación del bolillo
coronet	corona, corona del casco, margen superior del casco

crest	cresta, cresta del cuello
croup	grupa, rabadilla
dock	maslo, maslo de cola
ear	oreja
elbow	codo, codillo
elbow joint	articulación del codo
ergot	especie de espolón en las patas
eye	ojo
eyeball	globo del ojo
face	cara
feathers	cernejas
feet	pies, patas
back feet	patas
front feet	manos
fetlock	cerneja, nudo, nudillo
fetlock joint	articulación de la cerneja, menudillo
flank	flanco
foot	pie, pata
back foot	pata
front foot	mano
forearm	antebrazo, brazuelo, brazo
forehead	frente
foreleg	brazo anterior
forelock	copete, chasca, mechón, tupe
gaskin	muslo de la pierna, muslo
girth	cinchera, ruedo
groin	ingle
hair	pelo
haunch	anca
head	cabeza

heel	talón, talón del casco
hind leg	pierna posterior, posterior
hindquarter	cuarto trasero, cuarto
hip	cadera
hip joint	articulación de la cadera
hock	corvejón, garrón, corva, tarso
hocks	corvejos
hoof	casco, pezuña
frog	ranilla, horquilla, corazón del casco
heel	talón
heel bulb	punta del talón
hoof wall	pared del casco
sole	suela, planta
toe of the hoof	punta de pie, uña del casco, uña, dedo, punta
intestine	intestino
large intestine	intestino grueso
small intestine	intestino delgado
jaw	quijada
jawbone	hueso de quijada
joint	articulación, coyuntura
jugular groove	canal yugular
jugular vein	vena yugular
knee	rodilla
leg	pierna
back leg	pierna trasera, pata trasera
front leg	pierna delantera, pata delantera, pierna anterior

ligament	ligamento
limb	pierna, miembro
lip	labio
lower lip	labio inferior
under lip	labio bajo, mentón
upper lip	labio superior
loins	ijadas, lomos
lung	pulmón
mane	tuse/a, crin, crinera, clin
mouth	boca
muscle	músculo
musculature	musculatura
muzzle	hocico, boca
neck	cuello, pescuezo
nerve	nervio
nipple/teat	teta, pezón
nose	nariz
nostril	ollar
organs	órganos
pastern	cuartilla, cuarta
pastern joint	articulación de la cuarta
pelvis	región caudal, pelvis
penis	pene, verga
point of the hip	punta de la cadera
point of the hock	punta del corvejón
point of the shoulder	punta del hombro, punta del pecho
poll	nuca
rib	costilla
scrotum	escroto
sheath	vaina
shoulder	hombro
shoulder joint	articulación del hombro

skeleton	esqueleto
spine	columna vertebral, espina
stifle	babilla
fold of the stifle	pliegue de la babilla
stifle joint	articulación de la babilla
stomach	estómago
tail	cola, rabo
tail hair	cerda
teeth	dientes
canine teeth	dientes caninos, caninos
changing teeth	dientes cambiantes, dientes de cambio, incisivos cambiantes
Galvayne's groove	canal de Galvayne
grinding surface	superficie moledora
incisor	incisivo
central incisor	incisivos central, incisivo
corner incisor	incisivo del borde
lateral incisor	incisivo lateral
milk teeth	dientes de leche
molar	molar
permanent teeth	dientes permanentes
wolf teeth	dientes de lobo
tendon	tendón
testicle	teste, testículo, huevos
thigh	muslo
thorax	tórax
throat	garganta
throatlatch	fiador, ahogador
tooth	diente
trunk	tronco
udder	ubre
vagina	vagina

vein	vena
vertebra	vertebra
vulva	vulva
windpipe	traquea
withers	cruz

colors of the horse   colores del caballo

albino	albino, zarco
bay	bayo, colorado
bay with black points	bayo cabos negros
blood bay	zaino colorado
brown bay	bayo oscuro, zaino negro
chestnut bay	bayo castaño
cream bay with white mane and tail	bayo ruano
dapple bay	tordo rodado
dark bay	colorado requemado
light bay	bayo dorado, bayo blanco, pangaré
mealy bay	zaino pangaré
red and white flecked bay	bayo rosillo
red bay	zaino colorado
yellow bay	bayo amarillo
black	oscuro, tordillo (Mex), negro (Arg)
black points	carbos negros, puntos negros
black with white legs and face	picazo
shiny black	caballo retino
brown	marrón

dark brown	zaino negro, café oscuro
light brown	doradillo, café claro
buckskin	gateado
chestnut-striped dun	gateado naranjado
red-striped dun	gateado rubio
striped dun	gateado claro
striped light bay	gateado pangaré
chestnut	castaño, alazán
chestnut with black mane and tail	raya de mula, raya cruzada
chestnut with white mane and tail	ruano
dark chestnut	castaño oscuro, tostado
light chestnut	castaño claro
cream	crema
dun	perlino
blue dun	lobuno
red dun	rosado
yellow dun	amarillo
grey	gris, tordillo
black grey	tordillo negro
dapple grey	rucio rodado, tordillo rodado
flea-bitten grey	pardo, tordillo mosqueado
flecked grey	tordillo
silver grey	tordillo plateado
smoke grey	tiznado
steel grey	tordillo carbonero
white grey	tordillo blanco
white-striped grey	yaguane
grulla	grulla, barroso
leopard	leopardo
mouse-colored	cebruno

overo	overo
bay and white	zaino overo
black and white	overo negro
chestnut and white	alazán overo
dark chestnut and white	tostado overo
odd-colored dun and white	bayo overo
odd-colored blue dun and white	lobuno overo
odd-colored chestnut with white	overo rosado
odd-colored mouse and white	cebruno overo
odd-colored with blue and white	azulejo overo
red and white	manchado
palomino	palomino, ruano
piebald	picazo/a, tobiano negro, overo negro
pinto	pinto
red	colorado
common red	colorado corriente
red and white spot	overo
roan	rodado, roano, rosillo
blue roan	rosillo moro, moro
chestnut roan	rosillo rubio
light roan	rosillo blanco
red roan	rosillo colorado
striped roan	rosillo gateado
skewbald	pío, tobiano colorado
sorrel	alazán, alazán claro
brown sorrel	alazán tostado
dapple sorrel	alazán rodado
golden sorrel	alazán dorado

tobiano	tobiano
white	caballo blanco
flea-bitten white	blanco mosqueado
porcelain white	blanco porcelana
red-speckled white	blanco sabino
rose-flecked white	blanco procelana rosado
silver white	blanco plateado
snow white	tapado, nevado
speckled white	caballo rubicán
white with black eyes	blanco con ojos negros, blancas anteojeras negras
What color is the horse?	¿De qué color es el caballo? ¿Cómo está pintado?

colors of the mane and tail

colores de la crin y la cola

black	negro
flaxen	rubio
silver	plateado
silver tail	rabicano
white	blanco

markings of the horse

marcas del caballo

body marks	marcas del cuerpo
dorsal stripe	marcas de la espina dorsal
saddle marks	marcas en el lomo, fajados
speckled belly	lagarto
spotted	manchado

striped	atigrado, barcino, cebrado
white around the back and cinch	fajado
face marks	marcas de la cara
bald	malacara, calbo, pampa
blaze	lista
lip marks	marcas en el labio
snip	mancha, pico blanco
star	estrella, frontino
large star	lucero
small star	estrella/ita
star-and-stripe	estrella y cordón
star, stripe, and snip	estella, cordón y mancha
stripe	cara blanca, cordón, lista
wall eye	ojo azul, zarco
leg marks	marcas de las piernas
ankle mark	tobillo manchado, tobillo marcado, tobillo pintado
coronet marks	manchas de la corona, cornillas
distal spots	marcas distales
half pastern marks	pintas de media cuartilla
half stocking	medio calzado
pastern marks	pintas de la cuartilla
socks	albas
one white sock	una alba, uno blanco
one white sock in front, and one behind	una alba anterior y una alba posterior
two white socks	dos albas, dos blancos
two white socks behind	dos albas de atrás, dos albas posteriores, maneado de atrás

two white socks in front	dos albas adelante, dos albas anteriores, dos blancos adelante, maneado de adelante
three white socks	tres albas, tres blancos
four white socks	cuatro albas, cuatro calzados de blancos, cuatro blancos
stockings	caldos, medidas
horse with black stockings	caballo calzado de negro
horse with white stockings	caballo calzado de blanco
white heels	talones blancos
white inside heel	talón blanco adentro
white outside heel	talón blanco afuera
white marks or spots	pintas, manchas, marcas blancas
white on the right back leg	argel (Arg, Urg, Br)

measuring the horse   ## midiendo el caballo

bone circumference	circunferencia del hueso, ruedo del hueso
centimeter	centímetro
girth circumference	ruedo de la cincha
hand (4 inches/10.16 cm)	diez punto dieciséis centímetros, mano = cuatro pulgadas o 10.16 cm

The horse is 16 hands tall.

El caballo tiene dieciséis manos.

The horse is 17 hands tall.

El caballo tiene diecisiete manos.

height at the withers

altura a la cruz

measuring stick

metro

tape measure

métrica

weight of the horse

peso del caballo

How tall is your horse?

¿Cuánto mide su caballo?
¿Cuantos centímetros tiene su caballo? ¿Cuántas manos tiene su caballo? ¿Qué altura tiene su caballo?

identifying the horse

identificación del caballo

age of the horse
How old is the horse?

edad del caballo
¿Cuántos años tiene el caballo?

blood type

grupo sanguíneo, tipo de sangre

brand (the)
to have a brand

el hierro, la marca
tener marca

brand (to)

marcar, herrar

branded (to be)

estar marcado

branding

marcando

branding iron

hierro de marcar

cold brand (the)

marca fría

electrical implants

injertos eléctricos

fingerprinting of horse chestnuts	huellas de los espejuelos
freeze brand (to)	marcar a congelación, marcar al frío
hide brand (to)	marcar en la piel
hot brand (to)	marcar a fuego
lip tattoo (the)	tatuaje del labio superior
lip tattoo (to)	tatuar el labio superior
natural markings	marcas naturales, señales

blemishes of the horse   defectos del caballo

bog spavin	esparaván falso
bone spavin	esparaván óseo
bowed tendon	tendinitis, curva en el tendón
bucked shins	periostitis de los huesos metacarpianos, sobre huesos en la caña
capped elbow	capalete (Sp, Arg), bursitis del codo
capped hock	bursitis corvejón
crooked tail	cola chueca, rabo chueco
curb	corva, corvaza
firing marks	puntas de fuego
mouth deformity	boca deformada
quarter crack	cuarto rajado, fisura de cuarto
ring bone	sobrehueso, sobrehueso de la cuartilla, sobre-hueso de la corona

rope burns	quemaduras de lazo, quemaduras de reata
saddle sores	mataduras, pasmudos
scars	cicatrices
scar on the face	cicatriz en la cara
scar on the leg	cicatriz en la pierna
seedy toe	separación del casco, hormiguillo
side bones	endurecimiento de los cartílagos de las patas
skin conditions	condiciones del cuero, condiciones de la piel
splints (without lameness)	sobrehuesos
thoroughpin	hinchazón tarsal
toe crack	fisura de la uña
wind gall (without arthritis)	inflamación de la bursa, distensiones sinoviales de la cerneja
wire cut	corte de alambre

conformation of the horse

conformación del caballo

back (lower)	lomo
back (upper)	espalda
hollow/sunken back	espalda hueca
long back	espalda larga
roached back	espalda corvada, espalda curcuncha (Ch, Arg)

round back	espalda redonda
short back	espalda corta
straight back	espalda derecha, espalda recta
strong back	espalda fuerte
swaybacked	espalda panda, sillón
weak back	espalda débil
belly	estómago, barriga
big belly	barrigudo, barrigón
cow-bellied	barriga de vaca
herring gut/narrow-bellied	barriga de pescado, barriga de anguilla
potbellied	barrigón
body	cuerpo
balanced body	cuerpo balanceado
body width	amplitud del cuerpo
close-coupled body	cuerpo compacto, cuerpo apretado
compact body	cuerpo bien hecho, cuerpo compacto
depth to the body	cuerpo profundo
lacking depth	cuerpo sin profundidad
proportioned body	cuerpo proporcionado
round lines	cuerpo con líneas redondas
short-coupled body	cuerpo apretado, cuerpo en junto
stocky body	cuerpo rechoncho, cuerpo robusto
sturdy body	cuerpo fuerte
body build	conformación del cuerpo
body structure	estructura del cuerpo

chest
  narrow chest
  pigeon chest
  thick chest
  wide chest
croup
  broad croup
  flat croup
  goose-rumped

  long croup
  narrow croup
  oval croup
  short croup
ears
  lop ears
  mule ears

eyes
  blindness
  cataracts
  cloudy eye
  moon blindness
  pig eyes
  small eyes
  wall eye
  wide eyed/big eyed
feet
  broken-back foot

  broken-forward foot

pecho
  pecho angosto
  pecho de pichón
  pecho grueso
  pecho ancho
grupa, rabadilla
  grupa espesa, grupa ancha
  grupa plana
  grupa de ganso, grupa de
    pollo
  grupa larga
  grupa angosta
  grupa ovalada
  grupa corta
orejas
  orejas caídas
  orejas de mula, orejas de
    macho
ojos
  ceguera
  cataratas
  nube en el ojo, nublado
  ceguera, nocturna
  ojos puercos
  ojos pequeños
  zarco
  ojón
pies, patas
  inclinación excesiva
    hacia atrás
  inclinación excesiva
    hacia adelante

clubfoot	pie zopo
clubfooted	de pie zopo
mule foot	pata de mula
no heel	destalonado
forearms	antebrazos, brazuelos
flat forearms	antebrazos planos
long forearms	antebrazos largos
narrow forearms	antebrazos angostos
short forearms	antebrazos cortos
weak forearms	antebrazos débiles
wide forearms	antebrazos anchos
frame	marco, esqueleto
head	cabeza
big head	cabeza grande
dish face	hundida
fine head	cabeza fina
heavy head	cabeza corriente, cabeza ordinaria, cabeza pesada
noble head	cabeza noble
poor head	cabeza pobre
Roman nose	nariz acarnerada, nariz romana
small head	cabeza chica
straight head	cabeza recta
hindquarters	cuartos posteriores, piernas, piernas traseras
weak hindquarters	cuartos posteriores débiles
hip	cadera
pointed hip	cadera puntuda
prominent hip	cadera saliente, cadera prominente

legs	piernas
cannon bone	caña
defined cannon bone	caña definida
long cannon bone	caña larga
short cannon bone	caña corta
weak cannon bone	caña débil
wide cannon bone	caña ancha
elbow	codo
loose elbows	codos sueltos
turned-in elbow	codo hacia adentro
turned-out elbow	codo hacia afuera
fetlock lump	hinchazón en la cerneja, hinchazón en el nudo
front legs	piernas anteriores
bowlegged	curvada, rodilla arqueada
camped out	plantado adelante
camped under/under in front	remitido adelante
closed in front	cerrado adelante
crooked legs	piernas chuecas
open in front	abierto adelante
pigeon-toed	pie de paloma
stand close (to)	pararse cerrado
stands close	se para cerrado
stand wide (to)	pararse abierto
stands wide	se para abierto
toes out	patizambo
gaskin	muslo de la pierna
defined gaskin	muslo de la pierna definido
long gaskin	muslo de la pierna largo

short gaskin	muslo de la pierna corto
strong gaskin	muslo de la pierna fuerte
tied-in gaskin	muslo de la pierna amarrado
weak gaskin	muslo de la pierna débil
well-muscled gaskin	muslo de la pierna bien definido, muslo de la pierna musculoso
hind legs	piernas posteriores, piernas traseras
bowlegged	piernas arquedas de atrás
camped out	plantado de atrás
camped under	remitido de atrás, pata de sable
closed behind	piernas cerradas de atrás, cerrado de atrás
long hind legs	piernas largas posteriores
narrow hind legs	piernas angostas de atrás
open behind	piernas abiertas de atrás
sloping hind legs	piernas anguladas posteriores
well-muscled hind legs	piernas posteriores bien musculosas
wide-set hind legs	piernas abiertas de atrás
hocks	corvejos, corvas

bent/sickle hocks	patas de sable
bog spavin	corvejo con esparaván falso
bone spavin	corvejo con esparaván oseo
bowed hocks	corvejos arqueados
cow hocks	patizambo, corvas de vaca
hocks close to the ground	corvejón cerca de la tierra
large hocks	corvejos grandes
lean hocks	corvejos secos, corvejos enjutos
long hocks	corvejos largos
open hocks	corvejos abiertos
spongy hocks	corvejos esponjosos
straight hocks	corvejos derechos, corvejos erguidos
well-defined hocks	corvejos bien definidos
wide hocks	corvejos anchos
knees	rodillas
buck knees	sobre las rodillas, rodillas de pichón
calf knees	rodillas de buey
flat knees	rodillas planas
hollow knees	rodillas trascortas, rodillas huecas
knock-kneed	patizambo
large knees	rodillas grandes
long knees	rodillas largas
open knees	rodillas abiertas
over at the knee	sobre la rodilla
rounded knees	rodillas redondas

sprung knee	transcorto
well-defined knees	rodillas definidas
wide knees	rodillas anchas
pastern	cuartilla
long pastern	cuartilla larga, larga de cuartilla
short pastern	cuartilla corta, corta de cuartilla
sloping pastern	cuartilla angulada
stumpy pastern	corto de cuartilla
too long pastern	cuartilla muy larga
upright pastern	cuartilla erguida, pie de mula
weak pastern	cuartilla débil
stifle	babilla
large stifle	babilla grande
lean stifle	babilla seca
open stifle	babilla abierta
loins	ijadas, lomos
level loins	ijadas planas
long loins	ijadas largas
narrow loins	ijadas angostas
short loins	ijadas cortas
strong loins	ijadas fuertes
sunken loins	ijadas caídas
weak loins	ijadas débiles
wide loins	ijadas anchas
mouth	boca
monkey mouth	boca de mono
mule mouth	boca de mula
parrot mouth (overshot jaw)	boca de loro
sow mouth (undershot jaw)	boca de chancho, boca de arda

neck
  bowed neck
  bull neck
  elegant neck
  ewe neck

  heavy neck
  high-set neck
  long neck
  low-set neck
  poorly proportioned neck
  proportioned neck
  short neck
  straight neck
  swan neck
  thick neck
  well-muscled neck
  well-proportioned neck

shoulder
  long shoulder
  pronounced shoulder
  short shoulder
  sloping shoulder
  straight shoulder
  weak shoulder
tail
  broken tail
  broom/bang tail
  deep-set tail
  docked tail

  full tail

cuello, pescuezo
  cuello arqueado
  cuello de toro
  cuello elegante
  cuello hundido, cuello
     invertido
  cuello grueso
  cuello insertado alto
  cuello largo
  cuello insertado bajo
  cuello mal proporcionado
  cuello proporcionado
  cuello corto
  cuello derecho
  cuello de cisne
  cuello grueso
  cuello bien musculoso
  cuello bien proporcio-
     nado

hombro
  hombro largo
  hombro pronunciado
  hombro corto
  hombro angulado
  hombro derecho
  hombro débil
cola
  cola quebrada
  cola de escoba
  cola insertada profunda
  cola mochada, cola
     mocha
  cola llena

high-set tail	cola insertada alta, cola de origen alto
long tail	cola larga
low-set tail	cola insertada baja, cola de origen bajo
rat tail	cola de rata, rabón
tail attached too high	cola insertada muy alta
tail attached too low	cola insertada muy baja
thin tail	cola delgada
topline/profile of a horse	perfil, el perfil de un caballo
trueness to breed	fiel a la raza, estirpe
withers	cruz
bony withers	cruz huesuda
high withers	cruz alta, cruz definida
long withers	cruz larga
narrow withers	cruz angosta
pronounced withers	cruz pronunciada
short withers	cruz corta
wide withers	cruz ancha

vices of the horse

vicios del caballo

aggressive (to be)	ser agresivo
bite (to)	morder
bolt food (to)	desbocar comidas
buck (to)	corcovear, reparar
charge (to)	embestir, atacar
chew wood (to)	morder la madera, masticar la madera
chewing wood	masticador de madera
chew the feeder (to)	masticar los comederos
chewing the feeder	mordisquero de los comederos
crib (to)	chupar aire, tragar aire

crowd (to)	amontonar, empujar
eat dirt (to)	comer tierra, ingestar tierra
eating dirt	comiendo tierra, ingestión de tierra
eat feces (to)	comer las heces, ingestar heces, comer excrementos
fight (to)	pelear
hang out the tongue (to)	arrastrar la lengua, sacar la lengua
kick (to)	dar coces, patear
mouthy (to be)	ser mordedor
mouthy horse	mordelón
nasty (to be)	ser necio, de mal temperamento
nipper	mordelón
nipper (to be a)	ser mordedor
nod the head (to)	cabecear
nodding the head	cabeceo
obstinate (to be)	ser obstinado
obstinate horse	caballo obstinado
paw (to)	piafar
pull back (to)	echarse atrás, repropriarse atrás
pull the halter (to)	echarse atrás, repropriarse atrás
rear (to)	empinar
shy (to)	espantarse
stall walk (to)	caminar
stall walker	caminador en el establo, caminador de establo
strike (to)	tirar una patada, manotar

tail rub (to)	frotar la cola, refregar la cola
tail rubbing	frotado de la cola
weave (to)	zigzaguear
weaving	zigzagueo

temperament of the horse

temperamento del caballo

aggressive horse	caballo agresivo
angry horse	caballo enojado
balky horse	caballo repropio
calm horse	caballo calmado, caballo tranquilo
disobedient horse	caballo desobediente
fresh horse	caballo fresco
frisky horse	caballo juguetón
gentle horse	caballo manso, caballo gentil
handy horse	caballo suave
high-spirited horse	caballo fogoso, caballo brioso
high-strung horse	caballo difícil, caballo tenso
hot horse	caballo caliente
mean horse	caballo malo
nasty horse	caballo necio
obedient horse	caballo obediente
quiet horse	caballo tranquilo, caballo calmado
relaxed horse	caballo relajado, caballo tranquilo

scared horse	caballo asustado, caballo asustadizo, caballo espantadizo
skittish horse	caballo espantadizo, caballo medroso
spooky horse	caballo asustado, asustón
stubborn horse	caballo terco
tense horse	caballo nervioso
timid horse	caballo tímido, caballo miedoso
weak horse	caballo débil
wild horse	caballo salvaje, caballo feral

breeding the horse

crianza del caballo

ancestry	ascendencia, descendencia
artificial insemination	inseminación artificial
barren mare	yegua seca, yegua abierta, yegua infecunda
bloodline	línea de procedencia
What is the bloodline?	¿Cuál es la línea de procedencia?
bloodstock	caballos de pura sangre
breed (the)	raza
breed (to)	reproducir, inseminar, dar servicio
breed classifications	clasificaciones de raza
cross breed	cruzado
half breed	mestizo
in-bred	procreado en consan-guinidad

mixed breed	mezcla
pedigree horse	caballo de raza
pure breed/pure blood	caballo de pura sangre
registered horse	caballo registrado
breed registry	registro de raza
breed stock	animales para reproducción
breeding	cría, crianza
cross breeding	crianza de cruzamiento
horse breeding	cría de caballos
inbreeding	procreación en consanguinidad
incestuous breeding	procreación incestuosa
breeding ailments	enfermedades de crianza
abortion	aborto
agalactia	agalactia
congenital defect	defecto congénito
cystic mare	ovario quístico en la yegua, yegua enquistada
dry mare/empty mare	yegua infecunda, yegua seca
in-born defect	defecto innato
infertile	infecundo/a, infértil
infertile mare	yegua seca
infertile stallion	semental vano
infertility	infecundidad, esterilidad
mastitis	mastitis
stallion infertility	semental infértil, semental infecundo, vano, infertilidad
sterile	estéril
sterility	esterilidad
tipped vulva	vulva empuntada

breeding animal	reproductor/a
breeding contract	contrato de servicio
breeding equipment	equipo de cría
hobble	traba, manea
hobble strap	tira de la manea, manea
kicking boots	pateadoras
neck guard	manta de cuello, protección, protector
rigging	equipo de inseminar, equipo
teasing boards/rails	barda de calentamiento, riel de calentamiento
twitch	naricera
breeding farm	rancho de criador, criadero, yeguada
breeding methods	métodos de servicio
breeding period	período de cría
breeding record	registro de cría de caballos
breeding season	tiempo de la reproducción
breeding soundness evaluation	evaluación del potencial reproductor
breeding soundness evaluation of the male	examen de las condiciones reproductoras del macho
broodmare	yegua de vientre
castrate (to)	castrar, emascular
colt/foal	potranco, potro
young colt	potrillo
colostrum	calostro
cover (to)	inseminar, cubrir
crossbreed (to)	cruzar, mestizar

cut (to castrate)	emascular, castrar
cut horse	caballo castrado, caballo capado
dam	yegua madre
embryo transfer	transferencia de embriones
fertile	fértil
fertile mare	yegua fértil
fertile stallion	semental fértil
fetus	feto
filly	potranca, potra
young filly	potrilla
foal (the)	potro/a
foal (to)	parir
foal certificate registration	certificado de nacimiento de caballo
geld (to)	capar, castrar, emascular
gelding	caballo capado, caballo castrado, caballo emasculado
gestation	gestación
gestation period	período de gestación
period of gestation	tiempo de gestación
half brother	medio hermano
half sister	media hermana
heat (in)	en calor, en celo
out of heat	fuera de calor, fuera de celo
hereditary	hereditario/ria
heredity	herencia
hobble (to)	trabar, manear
inbreed (to)	procrear en consanguinidad
in foal (to be)	estar en cinta, estar preñada

in season	en calor, en celo
When is the mare in season?	¿Cuándo está la yegua en celo?
inherit (to)	heredar
inseminate (to)	inseminar
labor	parto
in labor (to be)	estar en parto
lactate (to)	lactar
lactating mare	yegua lactante
lineage/line	línea
mare	yegua
mare at foot	yegua con potrillo, yegua parida
mare's milk	leche de yegua
mate (to)	acoplar, aparear, montar
miscarry (to)	abortar
mount/jump (to)	dar servicio, montar
The stud mounts the mare.	El semental monta la yegua.
nine-day heat	calor de nueve días, celo de nueve días
nurse/suckle (to)	lactar, mamar
offspring	procedentes, descendientes
ovulate (to)	ovular
ovulation	ovulación
papered (to be)	tener papeles
papered horse	caballo con papeles
papers	papeles
parturition	parición, parto, parturición
induced parturition	parto inducido
premature parturition	parto prematuro
pedigree	pedigree, pedigrí
What is the pedigree?	¿Cuál es el pedigrí?

performance test	prueba de actuación, prueba de habilidad
potency	potencia, fuerza
pregnancy	preñez
pregnant	preñada, encinta
pregnant (to be)	estar preñada, estar encinta
puberty	pubertad
registration	registro, registración
reproductive cycle	el ciclo de reproducción
reproductive track	sistema reproductivo
semen collection	recolección de semen
semen evaluation	evaluación de semen
served mare	yegua servida, yegua inseminada
service (to give)	dar servicio, servir
sire (the)	padre, semental, garañón
great-grandsire	bisabuelo
grandsire	abuelo
This horse had a good sire.	Este caballo tuvo buena línea.
sire (to)	engendrar, producir
stallion	semental
stud (at)	al servicio
stud	semental
stud book	registro genealógico de caballos
stud farm	yeguada
stud fee	precio del servicio, maquila
stud horse	caballo semental, caballo padre
suck (to)	mamar
tease (to)	calentar
teaser	calentador

throw (to)	producir
throwback (a)	retroceso
throw back (to)	retroceder
true to type	tira al tipo, tira a la raza, representa a su raza
not true to type	no tira al tipo, no tira a la raza, no representa a su raza
udder	ubre
wax (to)	producir cera en las tetas
wean a foal (to)	destetar
weanling	potrillo/a, animal recién destetado
young stock	potrillada

symptoms of the sick horse
síntomas del caballo enfermo

chronic	crónico
distended abdomen	abdomen distendido, abdomen hinchado
emaciation	emaciación, adelgazamiento
exudate	exudado
pale membranes in the nose and mouth	membranas claras en la nariz y la boca
rapid pulse	pulso rápido
rough coat	piel seca
stunted growth	crecimiento canijo
temperature (normal: 99.5°–101.5°F)	temperatura (normal: 37°–38°C)
What is the body temperature (of the horse)?	¿Cuál es la temperatura (del caballo)?, ¿Qué temperatura tiene el caballo?

tucked-up flanks	flancos chupados, contracción en los flancos
unthrifty	despilfarrador
weakness	debilidad

ailments/diseases of the horse

enfermedades del caballo

abort (to)	abortar
abortion	aborto
abscess	absceso
adhesion	adhesión
aerophagia	aerofagia
African horse sickness	enfermedad equina africana
allergy	alergia
dust allergy	alergia de polvo
anemia	anemia
anthrax	ántrax
arthritis	artritis
arthritis of the shoulder joint	artritis en la articulación del hombro
ataxia	ataxia
atrophy	atrofia
avulsion	avulsión
azoturia	azoturia
back sores	úlceras, heridas en la espalda
bacteria	bacteria
bean	esmegma, piedra de esmegma
bee sting	picazón de abeja
bicipital bursitis	bursitis bicipital
birth defect	defecto congénito
bladder infection	infección de la vejiga

bleeder	epistaxis equina, sangrador
bleeding	sangrando
bleeding horse	caballo sangrante
bloody (to be)	estar sangrando, sangriento
bone chip	esquirla, chip, pedacito de hueso
bone spur	espolón, calcificación
botulism	botulismo
bowed tendon	tendinitis, tendón botado (Arg, Ch, Ven), tendón arqueado
break out (to sweat)	sudar
brittle hoofs	cascos quebradizos
broken leg	hueso roto, pierna rota
broken wind	pulmón dañado, corto de resuello
bronchitis	bronquitis
bruised sole	contusión de la suela, planta contusa
bucked shins	periostitis de los huesos metacarpianos
burn	quemadura
friction burn	quemadura fricción, rozadura
rope burn	quemadura de lazo, quemadura de reata
sunburn	quemadura de sol
bursitis	bursitis
calking	empacamiento
cancer	cáncer
canker	ulceración
capped elbow (shoe-boil)	capelet (Sp, Arg), higroma del codo, bursitis del codo

capped hock	higroma del corvejón, bursitis del corvejón
carcinoma	carcinoma
carpal hygroma	higroma carpiano
carpitis (capped knee)	carpitis, rodilla dislocada
cast	atorado, atroba
cast horse	caballo atorado
cataract	catarata
choke (to)	atragantarse, ahogarse
choking	atragantamiento
chronic alveolar emphysema	enfisema alveolar crónica
chronic obstructive pulmonary disease	enfermedad pulmonar obstructiva crónica
cinch sores	úlceras de cincha
cold (to have a)	estar resfriado
colic	cólico
colic in foals	cólico en potrillos
obstructive colic	cólico obstructivo
sand colic	cólico de arena
verminous colic	cólico verminoso
colicky	cólico
colitis	colitis
coma	coma
concussion	conmoción cerebral
conjunctivitis	conjuntivitis
constipation	estreñimiento, constipación (Arg)
contagious disease	enfermedad contagiosa
contracted heels	talones encogidos, talones contraídos (Arg)
contracted tendon	tendón encogido, tendón contraído (Arg)

contusion	contusión
corns	callos
cough (to)	toser
cough (to have a)	tener tos
coughing	tosiendo
coxitis	coxitis
cracked heels	talones rajados
cracked hoof	casco rajado, vaso partido, fisura del casco
toe crack	fisura de la uña
quarter crack	fisura del cuarto
sand crack	fisura del casco
crib (to)	chupar aire
cryptorchid	cryptorchidio, criptórquido
cryptorchism	cryptorchidismo, criptorquidia
curb	corva, corvaza
cut (to be)	estar cortado, estar lacerado
cut horse	caballo lacerado
cyst	quiste
cystic mare	ovario quístico en la yegua, yegua enquistada
cystitis	cistitis
damaged back	espalda lesionada, espalda dañada
dead (to be)	estar muerto
defect	defecto
depraved appetite	mal apetito, apetito depravado
dehydrated	deshidratado
diarrhea	diarrea
chronic diarrhea	diarrea crónica

chronic diarrhea in horses	diarrea crónica en los caballos
dislocated joint	luxación
dislocation of the hip	dislocación de la cadera
distemper	moquillo
drool (to)	babear
dropped sole	suela caída
dry coat	pelo seco
dysentery	disentería
dysphagia	disfagia
dysuria	disuria
dysuric horse	caballo disúrico
edema	edema
embolism	embolia
emphysema	enfisema
empyema	empiema
encephalomyelitis	encefalomielitis
enteric diseases in foals	enfermedades entéricas de los potrillos
enteritis	enteritis
entropion	entropión
epidemic	epidemia
epilepsy	epilepsia
epiphysitis	epífisitis
epistaxis	epistaxis equina
equine abortion	aborto equino
equine infectious anemia	anemia infecciosa equina
equine influenza	gripe, influenza equina
equine Potomac fever	fiebre equina del Potomac
equine viral arteritis	arteritis viral equina
equine viral rhinopneu-monitis	rinoneumonitis equina viral
exotosis	exotosis equina

fever	fiebre, calentura
fever (to have)	tener fiebre
fever in the feet	fiebre de los cascos, laminitis
high fever	fiebre alta, fiebre elevada
mud fever	fiebre de lodo
slight fever	poco de fiebre, fiebre moderada
feverish	febril
fistula	fístula
fistular	fistular
fistulous withers	cruz fistulosa, fistulada, mal de cruz (Arg)
foal septicemia	septicemia, septicemia en los potrillos
founder/laminitis	aguado, laminitis, infosurado
grain founder	aguado de grano
foundered horse	caballo aguado, caballo infosurado
fracture (to)	fracturar
fracture (a)	fractura
compound fracture	fractura complicada
fracture of the elbow	fractura del codo
fracture of the navicular bone	fractura del hueso navicular
fracture of the pedal bone	fractura del hueso podal
fracture of the shoulder	fractura del hombro
pelvic fracture	fractura pélvica
saucer fracture	fractura en platillo
sesamoid fracture	fractura sesamoidea
frostbite	congelación
gangrene	gangrena

gastritis	gastritis
glanders	muermo
glaucoma	glaucoma
goiter	bocio
gonitis	gonitis
granulation	granulación
gravel	arenilla
greasy heel	talón graso
heat cramps	calambres por calor
heat exhaustion	agotamiento por calor
heaves (pulmonary emphy- sema)	huélfago, hemiplejía laríngea, enfisema, alveolar crónico
heaves (to have)	estar enfisematoso, tener enfisema
hematoma	hematoma
hemophilia	hemofilia
hemorrhage	hemorragia
hepatitis	hepatitis
hernia	hernia
horse pox	viruela equina
hunter's bumps	chinchón de cazador
hurt withers	matado en la cruz
hyperlipemia	hiperlipemia
hyperthermia	hipertermia
hypothermia	hipotermia
illness	enfermedad
immobile	inmóvil
impaction	impactación
impaction of the colon	impactación del colón
impaction of the intes- tine	impactación del intes- tino, impactación de la tripa

infected	infectado/a, infecto/a
infected wound	herida infectada
infection	infección
infectious	infeccioso
inflammation	inflamación
acute inflammation	inflamación grave
chronic inflammation	inflamación crónica
inflammation of the fetlock	inflamación del nudo
inflammation of the hock	inflamación del corvejón
inflammation of the stifle	inflamación de la babilla
injury	daño, herida
jaundice	ictericia
keratoma	queratoma
kidney failure	falla de los riñones
lame	cojo/a
lame in the foot	cojo en el pie, cojo en la pata, manco (Arg)
lame in the leg	cojo en la pierna, rengo (Arg)
laminitis	laminitis
laryngeal hemiplegia	hemiplejía laríngea
laryngitis	laringitis
lethargic horse	caballo letárgo, caballo aletargado
lethargy	letargia
limp (to)	cojear
limping	está cojeando
lipoma	lipoma
lockjaw	trismo
lose the appetite (to)	perder el apetito
lose the hair (to)	perder el pelo
loss of appetite	pérdida de apetito

loss of hair	pérdida de pelo
lymphangitis	linfangitis ulcerante equina
meningitis	meningitis
motion sickness	mareo, enfermedad de movimiento, enfermedad de moción
muscle spasm	espasmo de músculo
muscle tear	desgarro del músculo
muscle tremor	temblor de músculo
narcosis	narcosis
nasal discharge	moquillo
navicular disease	enfermedad navicular, navicular
obesity	obesidad del caballo, gordura
off (to be)	estar coja
off behind	está coja en el trasero
off in the left hind leg	está coja en la pierna izquierda trasera
off in the right hind leg	está coja en la pierna derecha trasera
off in front	está coja en la delantera
off in the left front leg	está coja en la pierna izquierda delantera
off in the right front leg	está coja en la pierna derecha delantera
osselets	huesecillos, osteítis
osteitis	osteítis
osteomyelitis	osteomielitis
paralysis	parálisis
parasites (external)	parásitos externos
flies	moscas
black fly	mosca negra

deer fly	mosca de ciervo
fly bite	picadura de mosca
horse fly	tabáno
stable fly	mosca de establo
lice	piojo
maggots	cresas, gusanos
mites	aradores
ear mites	aradores de las orejas
mange mites	aradores de sarna
mosquito	mosquito
mosquito bite	picadura de mosquito
screwworm	lombriz de heridas abiertas
ticks	garrapatas
ear ticks	garrapatas en las orejas
warbles	habronemiasis, reznos
parasites (internal)	parásitos internos
ascarids (parascaris)	ascáridos
parascaris infection	infección de parascaris
bots (gasterophilus)	gastrophilus, gastrófilo
gasterophilus infection	infección de gastrophilus, infección de gastrófilo
equine piroplasmosis	piroplasmosis del caballo
large strongyles	estróngilos grandes
large-stongyles infection	infección de estróngilos grandes
lung worm	lombriz del pulmón
pinworm (oxyuris)	oxiuria
oxyuris infection	infección de oxiuria
small stomach worm (trichostrongylus)	tricostróngilo

trichostrongylus infection	infección por tricoróngilo
small strongyles	estróngilos pequeños
small-strongyles infection	infección de estróngilos pequeños
stomach worm (habronema)	habronema
habronema infection	infección de habronema
strongyloides	estrongiloides
strongyloides infection	infección de estrongiloides
tapeworm	lombriz solitaria, tenia
tapeworm infection	infección de tenias
worms	lombrices
patellar luxation	luxación de la patela
pedal osteitis	osteítis podal
periodic ophthalmia (moon blindness)	ceguera, nocturna
peritonitis	peritonitis
pleurisy	plueresía
pneumonia	pulmonia, neumonia
poll evil	úlcera de la nuca
poisoned (to be)	estar envenenado
poisoning	envenenamiento
blood poisoning	envenenamiento de la sangre
chemical poisoning	envenenamiento químico
digestive poisoning	envenenamiento digestivo
lead poisoning	saturnismo

plant poisoning	envenenamiento por plantas
proud flesh	mejido granulado
pulmonary hemorrhage—exercise-induced	hemorragia pulmonar inducida por esfuerzo
pumiced hoof	casco pómez
pyramidal disease	enfermedad piramidal
quittor	gabarro
rabies	rabia, hidrofobia
rhinopneumonitis	rinoneumonitis equina viral
ring bone	sobrehueso, sobrehueso de la cuartilla, sobrehueso de la corona
roaring	huélfago, roncando
rupture	ruptura, hernia
saddle sores	mataduras
salmonellosis	salmonelosis
scab (the)	costra
scab (to)	costrar
scours	diarrea
scratches	rasguños, raspaduras
seedy toe	separación del casco, separación de la punta del casco, hormiguillo, separación de la uña
sesamoiditis	sesamoiditis
sheared heels	asimetría del talón
shock	choque
sick	enfermo/a
sick horse	caballo enfermo

side bones	endurecimiento de los cartílagos laterales de las patas
skin condition	dermatitis
dermatitis	dermatitis, dermitis
eczema	eccema
fungus	fungo, fungus
hives	urticaria
mange	roña, sarna
mangy	sarnoso/a
rash	sarpullido
ringworm	tiña
scabies	sarna
summer sores	lastimados de verano, ulceraciones de verano
wart	verruga, excrecencia cutánea
skin disease	dermatosis, enfermedad de la piel
snake bite	mordedura de serpiente
sore	lastimado, úlcera
sore back	espalda dolorida
sore knee	rodilla dolorida
sore muscles	músculos lastimados, músculos doloridos
sore shins	tibias doloridas
spavin	esparaván
blood spavin	esparaván venosa
bog spavin	esparaván falso
bone spavin	esparaván óseo
occult spavin	esparaván oculto

splint	sobrehueso
spondylitis	espondilitis
sprain (a)	torcedura, esfuerzo
sprain (to)	torcer
spur wound	espoleadura
starvation	inanición
starve to death (to)	hacer morir de hambre
starving to death	haciendo morir de hambre
stifled	desviación de la patela
stiff	anquilosada
stiffen (to)	anquilosar
stock up (to)	hinchar
stocking up	hinchando
stone bruise	contusión de piedra
stones	cálculos, piedras
strain	esfuerzo
strangles/distemper	papera equina
stringhalt	mioclonia de las patas traseras
sunstroke	insolación
sweeny	atrofia de los músculos del hombro
swell (to)	hinchar
swelling	hinchazón
swollen	hinchado/a
temperature (to have)	tener fiebre, tener temperatura, tener calentura
tender (to be)	tener dolorido/a
tenosynovitis	tenosinovitis
tetanus	tétano
tetanus toxoid	tétano toxoide

thoroughpin	hinchazón tarsal
thrush	afta, enfermedad del pie del caballo con descarga fétida
tie up (to)	engarrotar, envarar (Arg)
torn	desgarrado, roto
torn ear	oreja abierta, oreja lesionada
torn ligament	ligamiento roto
torn muscle	músculo roto
tumor	tumor
benign tumor	tumor benigno
malignant tumor	tumor maligno
sarcoid (skin) tumor	tumor epidérmico
twist (a)	torsión
twist (to)	tocer
twisted gut	torsión del intestino
tying up	envardura, síndrome de paralización
unsound	insaludable, mal de salud
vesticular stomatitis	stomatitis vesticular
villonodular synovitis	sinovitis villonodular
viral arteritis	arteritis viral
virus	virus
vomit (to)	vomitar
vomiting	vómito, vomitando
weak	débil
weave (to)	zigzaguear
whirlbone lameness	cojera de rótula
whistling	chiflando
wind gall	distensiones sinoviales de la cerneja
wind puffs	bolsas de aire

wind suck	chupar aire
wire cut	corte de alambre
wobbles	potranco/a tambaleante
wound	herida
abrasion	abrasión
bruised wound	herida con contusión
clean cut	herida limpia
contusion (bruise)	contusión
cut (a)	una herida, incisión, corte
gall	matado, bilis
saddle gall	lastimado por la silla, desolado
galled horse	caballo matado
laceration	laceración
lesion	lesión
puncture wound	herida de punción
puncture wound of the foot	herida podal por pinchazo
torn cut	herida desgarrada
ulcers	úlceras

veterinary equipment — equipo veterinario

bucket	cubeta, balde, bote, cubo
catheter	cáteter
first-aid kit	botiquín de urgencia, botiquín de emergencia
hoof tester	pinza de casco probante del casco
laser	láser
cold laser	láser frío
needles	agujas

rubber gloves	guantes de goma, guantes quirúrgicos
sphygmometer	esfigmómetro
stethoscope	estetoscopio
syringe	jeringa
tape	cinta adhesiva, cinta
thermometer	termómetro
tooth rasp	raspadura de dientes, escarpelo de dientes
ultrasound	ultrasonido

veterinary treatments — tratamientos veterinarios

acupressure	acupresión
acupuncture	acupuntura
aspirate (to)	aspirar
ausculate (to)	auscultar
autopsy (to)	autopsiar
bathe the wound (to)	regar la herida
blister (the)	ampolla, blistera
blister (to)	levantar ampollas en la pierna, producir ampollas en la pierna, ampollar
call the vet (to)	llamar al veterinario/a
cast (the)	vendaje enyesado
cast (to)	enyesar
castrate (to)	castrar, emascular
catheterize (to)	cateterizar
cauterize (to)	cauterizar
check (to)	examinar
check the breathing (to)	examinar la respiración

check the respiration (to)	examinar la respiración
chiropractics	quiroprácticos
clean (to)	limpiar
clean the sheath (to)	limpiar la vaina
clean the wound (to)	limpiar la herida
clip the hair (to)	trasquilar el pelo
cold hose the legs (to)	regar las piernas con agua fría
cut (a)	una incisión, un corte
cut (to)	cortar
cut (to castrate)	castrar, emascular
destroy a horse (to)	eliminar el caballo, destruir el caballo
deworm (to)	quitar las lombrices, desparasitar
diagnose (to)	diagnosticar
diagnosis	diagnóstico
disinfect (to)	desinfectar
dress a wound (to)	vendar
drug (to)	drogar
drug test (the)	examen de drogas
drug test (to)	examinar para droga
dry the wound (to)	secar la herida
enema (to give an)	dar un enema
examination	examen
examine (to)	examinar
exercise, no	no ejercicio
float the teeth (to)	raspar los dientes, igualar los dientes
hand walk (to)	pasear a mano
hand walk the horse (to)	pasear el caballo a mano
hand walk for five minutes a day (to)	pasear a mano por cinco minutos un día

heal (to)	sanar
healing	sanando
The wound is healing.	La herida está sanando.
heat therapy	terapia caliente
immobilize (to)	inmovilizar
incise (to)	cortar
incision	incisión
injection (to give an)	dar inyección, inyectar
intramuscular injection	inyección intramuscular
intravenous injection	inyección intravenosa
subcutaneous injection	inyección subcutánea
inoculate (to)	inocular
inoperable (to be)	ser inoperable, ser impracticable
internal blister	ampolla profunda, blistera profunda (Mex)
kill the germs (to)	matar los germenes
massage (to)	dar masajes
nerve (to)	cortar los nervios
nerve block (to)	obstruir los nervios
operate (to)	operar
pack (to)	rellenar
pack the hoof (to)	rellenar el casco
palpate (to)	palpitar
percussion	percusión
physical examination	reconocimiento médico
pin-fire (to)	poner puntas de fuego
plaster cast	vendaje enyesado
poultice (to apply a)	aplicar un emplasto
prepurchase exam	examen antes de compra
prescribe (to)	recetar
pulse (to take the)	tomar el pulso
digital pulse	pulso digital

lateral pulse	pulso lateral
normal pulse (32–44 beats per minute)	pulso normal (32–44 latidos del corazón por minuto)
pulse point	punto del pulso
quarantine (the)	cuarentena
quarantine the horse (to)	poner el caballo en cuarentena
rehabilitate (to)	rehabilitar
rest the horse (to)	descansar el caballo
salve, put on the wound (to)	aplicar ungüento a la herida
sanitize (to)	sanear
shave the hair (to)	rasurar el pelo
shot (a)	inyección
give a shot (to)	dar inyección
receive a shot (to)	recibir inyección
soak (to)	remojar
soak the hoof (to)	remojar el casco, remojar la pata
stall rest the horse (to)	descansar el caballo en el establo
sterilization	esterilización
sterilize (to)	esterilizar
stitch (to)	tomar puntada
stop the bleeding (to)	parar la sangre
surgery	cirugía
suture (to)	suturar
sweat the legs (to)	sudar las piernas
temperature (to take the horse's)	tomar la temperatura del caballo
test (to)	examinar
therapeutic	terapéutica
therapy	terapia

tourniquet	torniquete
tracheotomy	traqueotomía
traction	tracción
tranquilize (to)	tranquilizar
treat the horse (to)	curar el caballo, tratar el caballo
undress a wound (to)	quitar el vendaje, desvendar
unsanitary	antihigiénico
vaccinate (to)	vacunar
vaccination (to give a)	dar una vacuna
vet check (the)	la revisada veterinaira, el examen del veterinario
vet check (to)	revisar por veterinario, examinar por veterinario
vet clean (to)	revisar sanamente, pasar el examen de veterinario limpio
vet out (to)	revisar sanamente, pasar el examen de veterinario
The horse did vet out.	El caballo pasó el examen del veterinario.
The horse did not vet out.	El caballo no pasó el examen del veterinario.
veterinary medicine	medicina veterinaria
vital functions (to check)	examinar las funciones vitales
X-ray (to)	radiografiar
X ray (to take an)	examinar con rayos x, radiografiar
X rays	radiografías

veterinary medications

medicaciones veterinarias

ace	promazin
adjuvant	auxiliar
analgesic	analgésico
anesthesia	anestesia
local anesthesia	anestesia local
topical anesthesia	anestesia topical
anesthetic	anestésico
anthelmintic	antihelmíntico
antibiotic	antibiótico
antihistamine	antihistamínico
anti-inflammatory drugs	drogas anti-inflamatorias
antiphlogistic drugs	drogas antiflogísticas
antiseptic	antiséptico
antispasmodic	antiespasmódico
antitetanus serum	suero antitétano
antitoxin	antitoxina
bactericidal	bactericida
brace	linimento
cortisone	cortisona
counterirritant	revulsivo
dimethasulphoxide (DMSO)	dimetisulfoxide
disinfectant	desinfectante
diuretic	diurético
dose	dosis
packet	paquete
tablespoon	cucharada
tablet	pastilla
drug	medicamento, medicina, droga
laxative	laxante

leg brace	linimento
liniment	linimento
medication	medicación
medicine	medicina
muscle relaxant	relajante de músculos
narcotic	narcótico
ointment	crema
penicillin	penicilina
phenylbutazone (Bute)	butazolidan
poultice	emplasto
salve	ungüento, remedio
sedative	sedativo
serum	suero
steroids	esteroide
stimulant	estimulante
tetanus antitoxin	suero antitetánico
tranquilizer	tranquilizante
turpentine	terpentina
vaccine	vacuna
venice turpentine	terpentina denecia

feeding the horse

alimentando el caballo

bale	fardo, paca
bag/sack	saco, bolsa, costal
bolt food (to)	desbocar comidas
fat horse	caballo gordo
feed (the)	comida, forraje, alimento
feed (to)	alimentar, dar de comer forrajear, mantener

Do not feed the horse.　　Favor de, no alimenta el caballo.

feed bag	cebadera morral
feed bucket	cubo, balde forrajero, cubeta de comida
feed cubes (to)	alimentar cubos
do not feed cubes	favor de, no alimentar cubos
feeding	alimentación
flake/section	sección, escama
fodder/forage	forraje
good keeper	bien tenido
graze (to)	pastar
graze the horse (to)	pastar el caballo
hand graze the horse (to)	pastar el caballo a mano
hay net	red para heno
hungry horse	caballo hambriento
nutritional content of the feed	contenido nutritivo de la comida
poor keeper	mal tenido
put the feed away (to)	guardar la comida
rate of feeding	ritmo de alimentación
cut the feed (to)	reducir la comida
double feed	doble comida
double the feed (to)	doblar la comida
extra feed	más comida, comida extra
half feed	mitad de comida
half feed (to give)	dar media comida
increase the feed (to)	aumentar la comida
lack of feed	falta de comida
no feed	no comida
overfeed (to)	sobrealimentar, comer demasiado
ration	ración
daily ration	ración diaria

full ration

todo de racíon, ración
llena, ración completa

half ration

mitad de ración,
semiración

working ration

ración para trabajo,
comida para trabajo

reduce the feed (to)

reducir la comida

self feed (to)

auto alimentar

too little feed

muy poca comida

too much feed

mucha comida, dema-
siada comida

skinny horse

caballo flaco

thin horse

caballo delgado

thirsty horse

caballo sediento

turn out to grass (to)

solar al potrero, soltar al
pastizal

water (to)

darle agua

water the horses (to)

abrevar los caballos, darle
agua a los caballos

The horse has a depraved
appetite.

El caballo tiene un mal
apetito; El caballo
tiene un apetito de-
pravado.

The horse is not eating.

El caballo no está
comiendo.

The horse is sick, do not
feed him.

El caballo está enfermo, no
alimenta por favor.

types of feed

tipos de comidas

commercial feed

comida comercial, alimento
comercial

concentrates

concentrados

grains
  barley
    rolled barley
  bran
    bran mash
    make bran mash (to)

    wheat bran
  corn
    cracked corn
  cottonseed meal

  cracked/rolled

  linseed
    linseed meal
  mixed feed

  oats
    rolled oats
  sorghum grain
  soybean meal
  sweet feed
  wheat
grasses/forages
  alfalfa
    alfalfa cubes
  clover
  grass
  hay
    first-cut hay

granos
  cebada
    cebada aplastada
  salvado afrecho, salvado
    amasijo de salvado
    remojar el afrecho, hacer el amasijo de salvado
    salvado de trigo
  maíz
    maíz aplastado
  harina de semilla de algodón
  molido, aplastado, quebrado, triturado
  avena aplastada
  linaza
    harina de linaza
  granos compuestos, granos
  avena
    avena aplastado
  grano de sorgo
  harina de soja
  comida dulce, melaza
  trigo
hierbas
  alfalfa
    cubos de alfalfa
  trébol
  hierba, pasto
  heno, pasto seco, paja
    heno de primer corte

haystack	almiar, pajar
meadow hay	prado, pastizal
oat hay	heno de avena
second-cut hay	heno de segundo corte
seed hay	heno se semilla de pasto
pasture	pasto, pastizal
pellets	bolitas
alfalfa pellets	bolitas de alfalfa, cubos de alfalfa
roughage	forraje
silage	ensilaje
straw	paja
timothy	heno de fleo
innutritious feed	comida poco nutritiva
succulent feed	comida suculento
supplementary feed	comida suplementaria
supplements	suplementos
amino acids	aminoacidos
apple	manzana
carbohydrates	carbohidratos
carrot	zanahoria
citrus pulp	pulpa cítrica
electrolytes	electrólitos
fats	grasas
flax seed	linaza
limestone	caliza
minerals	minerales
calcium	calcio
chlorine	cloro
cobalt	cobalto
copper	cobre
fluorene	flúor, fluoreno
iodine	yodo

iron	hierro
magnesium	magnesio
manganese	manganeso
molybdenum	molibdeno
phosphorus	fósforo
potassium	potasio
selenium	selenio
sodium	sodio
sulfur	azufre
zinc	zinc, cinc
molasses	melaza
cane molasses	melaza de caña
oil	aceite
corn oil	aceite de maíz
linseed oil	aceite de linaza, aceite de lino
soybean oil	aceite de soja
wheatgerm oil	aceite de trigo
protein	proteína
high protein	alta proteína
salt	sal
mineral salt	sal mineral
rock salt	sal de roca
salt block	bloque de sal
salt lick	lamedura, salegar
starch	almidón
sugar	azúcar
have sugar cubes (to)	tener azúcar en cubos, tener cubos de azúcar
sugar cube	cubo de azúcar
sugar beets	remolachas, betarragas
sugar beet pulp	pulpa de betarragas, pulpa de remolachas

urea	úrea
vegetables	vegetales
vitamins	vitaminas
ascorbic acid	acido ascórbico
biotin	biotina
carotene	caróteno
folacin	folacina
niacin	niacina
pathothenic acid	acido pantoténico
riboflavin	riboflavina
thiamine	tiamina
vitamin A	vitamina A
vitamin B_{12}	vitamina B_{12}
vitamin D	vitamina D
vitamin E	vitamina E
vitamin K	vitamina K
water	agua
clean water	agua limpia
fresh water	agua dulce, agua fresca
yucca	yuca

shoeing the horse   herrando el caballo

barefoot	descalzo/a, sin herradura
borium	borio
calk	ramplón
clenches	remaches
clips	agarraderas
quarter clips	agarraderas de cuartos
toe clips	agarraderas de punta
farrier	herrero/a

My farrier is . . .	Mi herrero se llama . . . , Mi herrero es . . .
Where is the farrier?	¿Dónde está el herrero?
forge (to)	forjar
horse shoes	herraduras de caballo, herraduras
aluminum shoes/plates	herraduras de aluminio
bar shoes	herraduras de barras
cold shoes (ready-made)	herraduras hechas, herraduras de fábrica
corrective shoes	herraduras correctivas
hot shoes	herraduras calientes
pads	cojines, protectoras de plantas
put pads on the front feet (to)	poner protectores en los pies delanteros
plain shoes	herraduras simples
poultice shoe	herradura con lodo, herradura con emplasto
racing plates	herraduras de carrera
rim shoes	herraduras de reborde, herraduras de canto
steel shoes	herraduras de acero
training plates	herraduras de entrenamientos
hoof	casco
frog	ranilla, hendidura del talón de caballo
heel	talón
heel bulbs	punto de talón
hoof wall	uña, pared
sole	suela, planta
toe	punta de pie, uña del casco, punto

hoof dressing (to apply)	aplicar crema para el casco
horse shoeing tools	herramientas de herraje
clinch	apretador de clavos
forge	forja
hammer	martillo
hoof knife	cuchillo herrero
nail	clavo
rasp	lima, escofino
loose shoe	herradura suelta
This horse has a loose shoe.	Este caballo tiene una herradura suelta.
lose a shoe (to)	perder una herradura
lose a back shoe (to)	perder una herradura trasera, perder una herradura de una pata
lose a front shoe (to)	perder una herradura delantera, perder una herradura de una mano
pack the foot (to)	rellenar el casco
pricked	pinchado
pull the shoes (to)	desherrar, sacar las herraduras
reset the shoe (to)	reaplicar la herradura
shod	herrado
shoe (the)	la herradura
Does this horse need shoes?	¿Necesita este caballo herraduras?
shoe (to)	herrar
cold shoe (to)	herrar en frío
hot shoe (to)	herrar caliente

shoe the back feet only (to)	herrar solamente las patas
shoe the front feet only (to)	herrar solamente las manos
shoe the front only (to)	herrar solamente el frente
shoe the horse (to)	herrar el caballo
shoe the horse every . . . weeks (to)	herrar el caballo cada . . . semanas
How many horses need shoeing?	¿Cuántos caballos necesitan herraduras?
stud kit	equipo para remachar
studs	remaches
screw-in studs	remaches atornillados
take this horse to the farrier (to)	llevar este caballo al herrero
throw a shoe (to)	perder una herradura
The horse threw a shoe.	El caballo perdió una herradura.
Do you have the shoe the horse threw?	¿Tiene Ud. la herradura el caballo perdió?
trim the foot (to)	recortar el casco
trim the hoof (to)	recortar el casco
What barn does this horse come from?	¿Qué cuál quadril viene este caballo?
What is the name of this horse?	¿Cómo se llama Ud. este caballo?
Who is the owner of this horse?	¿Quién es el dueño de este caballo?

clipping and trimming the horse

rasurando y recortando el caballo

braid (the)	trenza

dressage braid	trenza para adiestramiento
hunter braid	trenza para salto, trenza para cacería
stallion braid	trenza para potro, trenza para padrillo
braid (to)	trenzar
braid the forelock (to)	trenzar el copete
braid the mane and forelock with tape (to)	trenzar la crin y el copete con cinta
braid the mane and forelock with yarn (to)	trenzar la crin y el copete con lana de tejer
braid the mane and tail (to)	trenzar la crin y la cola
hunter braid the tail (to)	trenzar la cola para cacería
clip the horse (to)	rasurar el caballo
blanket clip (to)	rasurar las piernas
body clip (to)	rasurar completo, trasquilar
full clip (to)	rasurar todo, rasurar completo
hunter clip (to)	rasurar para cacería
saddle-patch clip (to)	rasurar bajo la montura
trace clip (to)	rasurar pizca
clipper (person)	trasquilador
clipping and trimming equipment	equipo de recorte
clipper blade	hoja de rastrillo, navaja de rasurar
change the blade (to)	cambiar la navaja de rasurar
clippers	máquina de rasurar, maquinilla

body clippers	máquina para rasurar el cuerpo
electric clipper	rasurador eléctrico
face clippers	máquina para rasurar la cara
comb (a)	peine, peineta
elastic/rubber band	banda elástica, banda de goma, liguillas
scissors	tijeras
tape	cinta, huincha
thinning shears	tijeras raleadoras
yarn	lana de tejer
comb (to)	peinar
cut (to)	cortar
cut the mane (to)	cortar la crinera
dressage cut the tail (to)	cortar la cola de adiestramiento
dock (to)	descolar
dock the tail (to)	descolar, recortar la cola
grow a coat (to)	dejarse pelo, crecer pelo
grow a heavy coat (to)	dejarse pelo espeso
grow a second coat (to)	dejarse pelo segundo
grow a winter coat (to)	dejarse pelo de invierno
plait (to)	trenzar
plait the mane (to)	trenzar la crin
plait the tail (to)	trenzar la cola
plaited tail	cola trenzada
pull the mane (to)	jalar crin, igualar crin, entresacar
roach the mane (to)	rozar la crin
shed the coat (to)	mudar el pelo
shed a summer coat (to)	mudar a pelo de verano
thin the mane (to)	entresacar la crin

trim (to)	emparejar, recortar, atusar
trim the bridle path (to)	atusar la nuca
trim the ears (to)	atusar las orejas
trim the feathers (to)	atusar las cernejas
trim the muzzle (to)	atusar el hocico
trim the tail (to)	atusar la cola

grooming the horse   aseando el caballo

bath (to give a)	dar un baño
bathe (to)	bañar
bathe the horse (to)	bañar el caballo
bathe with medicated shampoo (to)	bañar con champú medicinal
bathe with shampoo (to)	bañar con champú
bathe with warm water (to)	bañar con agua tibia
bathing	bañando
blanket (to)	cubrir con manta, cobijar, encamisar (Mex), mantear
blanket the horse every night (to)	cobijar el caballo cada noche
blanketing	cobijado, encamisado, manteando
brush (to)	almohazar, cepillar
brush the horse (to)	almohazar el caballo
check the feet (to)	revisar las patas
clean the feet (to)	limpiar las patas
comb (to)	peinar
comb the mane and tail (to)	peinar la crin y la cola
condition the mane and tail (to)	condicione la crin y la cola

curry (to)	almohazar, rasquetear
groom (to)	asear cuidar, curar, almohazar, limpiar el caballo
groom the horse (to)	asear el caballo
grooming	cuidado
hose off the horse (to)	bañar el caballo, regar el caballo con agua
hose off the legs (to)	bañar las piernas, regar las piernas con agua
oil the hooves (to)	aceitar los cascos
paint the hooves (to)	pintar los cascos
pick out the hooves (to)	limpiar los cascos
put the horse away when he is dry (to)	encerrar el caballo cuando está seco
put the horse in the cross-ties (to)	poner el caballo en los amarraderos
put the horse on the hot walker (to)	poner el caballo en mecánica para pasear, poner el caballo al caminante
rub down the horse (to)	dar masajes al caballo, sober el caballo
rub the legs with liniment (to)	dar masajes a las piernas con linimento
scrub the face with soap (to)	limpiar la cara con jabón
sponge bath	baño de esponja
give a sponge bath (to)	bañar con esponja
sweat the neck (to)	sudar el pescuezo, sudar el cogote
unblanket (to)	descobijar
unblanket the horse (to)	descobijar el caballo

unblanket the horse every morning (to)	descobijar el caballo cada mañana
unwrap the legs (to)	desvendar las piernas
vacuum the horse (to)	limpiar el caballo con la aspiradora, aspirar el caballo
walk the horse until it is dry (to)	caminar el caballo hasta que se seque, caminar el caballo sudado
wash the mane and tail with soap (to)	lavar la crin y la cola con jabón
wash the wraps (to)	lavar las vendas
wipe off the horse (to)	limpiar el caballo
wrap all four legs (to)	vendar las cuatro piernas
wrap the back legs (to)	vendar las piernas traseras
wrap the front legs (to)	vendar las piernas delanteras
wrap the legs in standing wraps (to)	vendar las piernas con vendas de descansa
Do not stand behind this horse.	No se para detrás de este caballo.
Do not tie this horse in the wash rack.	No amarre el caballo en el lavadero.
This horse will not tie.	Este caballo no se puede amarrar.

The Horse and Rider
El caballo y el jinete

training the horse	**entrenando el caballo**
bit up (to)	enfrenar
blindfold (to)	vendar los ojos
break (to)	amansar, domar
busy colt	potrillo inquisitivo, potranca inquisitiva
cavaletti	caballetes
cavaletti work at a walk	trabajando caballetes al paso
cavaletti work at a trot	trabajando caballetes al trote
collection in hand	colección a mano
degree of training	grado de doma, grado de entrenamiento
broke to lead	manso de tiro, respecta la cabeza
bronco	bronco

green horse	caballo crudo, caballo redomón
green-broke horse	caballo recién amansado
halter broke	manso de tiro, respecta la cabeza
halter horse	caballo de pose
made horse	caballo hecho, caballo bien domado, caballo de bien rienda
obedient horse	caballo obediente
push-button horse	caballo hecho
ridable horse	un caballo que se puede montar
schooled horse	caballo bien riendado, caballo enseñado, caballo bien hecho
spoiled horse	caballo mañoso, caballo malogrado
submissive horse	caballo obediente
trained horse	caballo hecho, caballo entrenado
untrained horse	caballo sin entrenamiento, caballo sin trabajo, caballo crudo
well-made horse	caballo bien hecho
well-schooled horse	caballo de escuela, caballo bien trabajado, caballo bien riendado
well-trained horse	caballo bien entrenado, caballo bien trabajado

wild horse	caballo salvaje, caballo ladino
easy to tie (to be)	ser fácil de amarrar
ground drive (to)	andar entre las líneas
ground work	trabajo a la mano
gymnastic work	trabajo gimnástico
horse at intense work	caballo con trabajo pesado
horse at light work	caballo con trabajo ligero
horse at moderate work	caballo con trabajo moderado
hung up (to be)	estar colgado
jumping without a rider	salto libre, salto sin jinete
leave in a bitting rig (to)	dejar en apero de embridar
line drive (to)	andar por las líneas, andar entre las líneas
long rein (to)	trabajar con riendas largas
longe over cavaletti (to)	trabajar a la cuerda por caballetes, darle cuerda por caballetes
longe the horse (to)	trabajar a la cuerda, darle cuerda
loose jumping	salto de manera suelta
overwork (to)	aplastar
overwork the horse (to)	aplastar el caballo
sack out (to)	enmantar
school (to)	trabajar
school the horse (to)	trabajar el caballo, darle escuela
tie to a patience post (to)	atar a poste de paciencia
train the horse (to)	entrenar el caballo, domar el caballo

training	entrenamiento, doma, adiestramiento
trotting poles	postes de trote, caballetes
work from the ground (to)	trabajar a la mano
work in a bitting rig (to)	trabajar con apero de embridar
work in long reins (to)	trabajar con riendas largas
work in the round pen (to)	trabajar en pista cerrada
work in the pillars (to)	trabajar en los pilares

condition of the horse   condición del caballo

exhausted horse	caballo exhausto, caballo agotado
fit horse	caballo en buena condición
lazy horse	caballo perezoso, caballo poltrón, caballo heuvón
overworked horse	caballo aplasto
stiff horse	caballo tieso
strong horse	caballo fuerte
supple horse	caballo flexible
tired horse	caballo cansado
unfit horse	caballo fuera de condición

gaits and movements of the horse   aires y movimientos del caballo

airs above the ground	aires sobre el piso, aires arriba de la tierra
amble (to)	amblar
back (to)	retroceder, andar atrás, recular

ballotade	balotada
beat (the)	tiempo
four beat	cuatro tiempos
three beat	tres tiempos
two beat	dos tiempos
canter (the)	galope
canter depart	salida al galope, partida al galope, rompe al galope, empieza a galope
canter simple change	cambio de galope simple
collected canter	galope reunido
counter canter	galope en falso, contra galope
cross canter	galope cruzado
disjointed canter	galope desunido
extended canter	galope largo
false canter	galope falso
medium canter	galope medio
true canter	galope, galope verdadero
working canter	galope ordinario
canter (to)	galopar
capriole	cabriola
change lead (to)	cambiar de la mano, cambiar del pie
circle (to)	dar la vuelta, dar vueltas, circular
counter change of hand	contracambio de mano
curvet	corveta
figure eight	figura ocho
flying change	cambio de pie en el aire
flying change of leg	cambio de pie en el aire, volapié

single flying change	cambio de pie simple
gallop (to)	galopar
gallop through	pasa la rienda
gallop (the)	galope
at a full gallop	a toda brida, a todo galope, a galope tendido
at a gallop	a galope
full gallop	galope tendido, todo galope, galope de toda brida
hand gallop	galope sostenido, medio galope, galope a mano
hunting gallop	correr
racing gallop	correr
good gait (a)	un buen aire, un buen paso
halt (the)	la parada, alto
half halt	media parada
half turn	media vuelta
half turn reverse	media vuelta reversa
irregular gait	paso irregular
irregular steps	pasos irregulares
jig (to)	trotinar
jog (the)	paso lento
jog (to)	trotinar, andar a trote corto
lead change	cambio de la mano
levade	lanzada
movements	movimientos
high school movements	movimientos de alta escuela
lateral movements	moviemientos laterales
half-pass (to)	apoyar

haunches in (pesade)	grupa a fuera, grupa al muro
leg-yield	cesión a las piernas
renvers	grupa adentro
shoulder-in	espaldas adentro
travers	cabeza afuera, cabeza al muro
school movements	movimientos escuelas
pace (the)	paso, aire
free and regular paces	aires regulares y libres
irregular paces	pasos irregulares
pace (to)	pasear
pacing	paseando
passage	pasage
piaffe (the)	piaf
piaffe (to)	piafar
pirouette (the)	hacer pirueta, hacer cabriola
canter pirouette	pirueta al galope
half pirouette	media pirueta
walk pirouette	pirueta al paso
pirouette (to)	pirueta
prance (the)	cabriola
prance (to)	hacer cabriolas, encabritarse
run (to)	correr
run at full speed (to)	correr a rienda suelta
school figures	figuras escuelas
serpentine	serpentina
three-loop serpentine	serpentina de tres círculos
four-loop serpentine	serpentina de cuatro círculos

simple change of leg	cambio de pie simple, cambio sencillo de pierna
stop in time (the)	la parada a tiempo
stride (the)	la pisada
tempi changes	cambios a tiempos
transition	transición
downward transition	transición por abajo
upward transition	transición por arriba
trot (the)	trote
at an easy or slow trot	a trote corto
at the trot	al trote
break into a trot (to)	empezar a trotar, comenzar el trote
collected trot	trote reunido
extended trot	trote largo, trote extenso
medium trot	trote medio
working trot	trote ordinario
trot (to)	trotar
turn (the)	la vuelta
turn on the forehand (the)	la vuelta sobre el anterior, vuelta en las manos
turn on the haunches (the)	la vuelta sobre el posterior, vuelta sobre la grupa
turn (to)	dar vuelta
turn on the forehand (to)	dar vuelta sobre el anterior
turn on the haunches (to)	dar vuelta sobre el posterior
volte	volte, vuelta (seis metros)
half-volte	media volte
increase the volte (to)	aumentar el volte

walk (the)	el paso
collected walk	paso reunido
extended walk	paso largo, paso extendido
free walk	paso libre
medium walk	paso medio
working walk	paso ordinario
walk (to)	caminar, andar

reactions of the ridden horse

reacciones del caballo montado

above the bit	sobre la brida
above the bit (to be)	estar sobre la brida, elevar la cabeza
accept the bit (to)	aceptar el freno, aceptar la brida, aceptar el filete
action (to have)	tener movimiento, tener acción
active hocks (to have)	tener corvas activas, tener corvejos activos
active quarters (to have)	tener cuartos activos
airy movement (to have)	tener movimiento airoso, tener airosidad
balance	equilibrio, balance
balance (to have)	tener equilibrio, tener balance
balanced (to be)	equilibrar, balancear
behind the bit	detrás de la brida, detrás de la mano, detrás del freno

behind the bit (to be)	estar detrás de la brida, estar detrás de la mano, estar detrás del freno
bend (the)	curva, pliegue, doblez
bend (to)	curvar, plegar, doblar
bend at the poll (the)	flexión en la nuca
bend at the poll (to)	ceder la nuca
bob the head (to)	subir y bajar la cabeza
bolt (to)	desbocar
bolter	desbocado/a
bolting	desbocamiento
bolting horse	caballo desbocado
brush/knock (to)	rozar, tocar
buck (the)	corcovo
buck (to)	corcovear, desmontar, reparar, derribar
buck off (to)	desmontar de un corcovo
cadence	cadencia, ritmo medido
champ at the bit (to)	masticar el freno
change leads (to)	cambiar las manos
collected (to be)	estar reunido
over collected (to be)	estar reunido excesivamente, estar colectado excesivamente
collection (to have)	tener reunión
contact	contacto
contact (to have)	tener contacto
no contact	sin contacto
crow hop (to)	reparar
disobedient (to be)	ser desobediente

drag the feet (to)	arrastrar los pies
draw up the tongue (to)	levantar la lengua, hacer bola con la lengua
drop the back (to)	botar la espalda
drop the shoulder (to)	bajar el hombro, botar el hombro
elevated steps (to have)	tener pasos elevados, tener pasos erguidos
engage (to)	reunir, plegar, emplear
engage the haunches (to)	entrar el posterior, reunir el posterior
fear of water (to have)	tener miedo del agua
fight himself (to)	pelearse
flex the neck (to)	encorvar el pescuezo, encorvar la nuca
foam (to)	espumar
foaming	espumante
good hock action (to have)	tener buena acción del garrón
grind the teeth (to)	rechinar las dientes
hang out the tongue (to)	arrastrar la lengua
have tempo (to)	tener ritmo
head in front of the verticle	cabeza adelante de la vertical, cabeza frente de la vertical
head set (the)	la cabeza en posición
head shy (to be)	tener miedo de la cabeza
hold the bit (to)	mantener el freno, mantener el filete
hollow back (to have a)	tener una espalda hueca, tener una espalda hundida

hollow the back (to)	hundir la espalda, hundir el lomo, botar la espalda
impulsion (to have)	tener impulsión
in front of the bit	frente del freno, delante del freno
in front of the bit (to be)	estar frente del freno
inactive hind legs	pereza de las traseras
inactive hind legs (to have)	tener piernas traseras inactivas, tener traseras perezosas
jump (to)	saltar
kick (to)	dar una coz a, patear, dar una patada
lean (to)	apoyar
lean on the bit (to)	apoyar en el freno
light in the forehand (to be)	estar liviano de anteriores
motionless (to be)	permanecer inmóvil, estar quieto
mouth (a good)	una buena boca
fresh mouth	boca fresca, boca nueva
hard mouth	boca dura
sensitive mouth	boca sensitiva
soft mouth	boca suave, boca dulce
wet mouth	boca húmeda, boca mojada
move forward (to)	mover adelante, avanzar, adelantar
move with impulsion (to)	mover con impulsión
movement	movimiento
collected movement	movimiento reunido, movimiento colectivo
elastic movement	movimiento elástico

fluid movement	movimiento fluido
free movement	movimiento libre
obedient (to be)	ser obediente
obedient to the aids (to be)	ser obediente a las ayudas, ser obediente a las señales
on the bit (to be)	estar en la mano, estar en frenado
on the forehand (to be)	estar sobre las manos
over the bit (to be)	estar sobre el freno
overreach (to)	alcanzar, sobrepasar
play with the bit (to)	jugar con el freno
power (to have)	tener la fuerza, tener potencia
powerful (to be)	ser poderoso, ser fuerte, ser airoso
pull or bore (to)	jalar, timonear
pulling horse	caballo jalando a mano, caballo tirando de mano, caballo con tirón de mano
put the tongue out (to)	sacar la lengua
put the tongue over the bit (to)	poner la lengua sobre el freno
raise the head (to)	levantar la cabeza, engallarse
rear (to)	encabritar
refuse (to)	rehusar, parar
refuse the bit (to)	rehusar el freno
resist (to)	resistir
resist the action of the hand (to)	resistir la acción de la mano
resistance	resistencia
responsive (to be)	ser sensible, ser responsivo

responsive to the aids (to be)	ser sensible a las ayudas
rhythm (to have)	tener ritmo
round back (to have a)	tener espalda redonda, tener lomo redondo
run away with (to)	desbocar
runaway horse	caballo desbocado
shake the head (to)	sacudir la cabeza
shy (to)	espantarse
stand still (to)	parar
stiff back (to have a)	tener una espalda inflexible, tener una espalda tiesa
stubborn (to be)	ser terco/a
stumble (to)	tropezar
submit to the aids (to)	someterse a las ayudas
supple (to be)	estar flexible
supple back (to have)	tener espalda flexible
supple horse	caballo flexible
suspension (to have)	tener suspensión
switch leads (to)	cambiar de pie, cambiar la mano
switch the tail (to)	menear la cola
switched the tail	meneó la cola
take the bit (to)	tomar el freno
tempo (to have)	tener ritmo
throw the rider (to)	tirar el jinete, derribar el caballista, derribar el jinete
track (to)	andar en las huellas
unbalanced (to be)	estar desequilibrado
untrack (to)	quitar del bilateral
work on two tracks (to)	trabajar a dos pistas, pasar de costado
yield (to)	dar, ceder

riding technique	técnica de montar
aids	ayudas, señales
back aids	ayudas de espalda
body aids	ayudas de todo el cuerpo, ayudas de cuerpo, ayudas de peso del cuerpo
driving aids	ayudas de impulso
leg aids	ayudas de las piernas
rein aids	ayudas con la rienda, ayudas con la mano
simple aids	ayudas simples
voice aids	ayudas con la voz
click (to)	chasquear
cluck (to)	chascar
apply the aids (to)	usar las ayudas, aplicar las ayudas
bend the horse (to)	plegar el caballo, doblar el caballo
bend the horse around the leg (to)	doblar el caballo sobre la pierna
bend the horse to the inside (to)	doblar el caballo hacia adentro
bend the horse to the outside (to)	doblar el caballo hacia afuera
bend the horse uniformly (to)	doblar el caballo con uniformidad
brace with your back (to)	afirmar la espalda
calm the horse (to)	calmar el caballo, sosegar el caballo
canter the horse (to)	galopar el caballo
change diagonal (to)	cambiar diagonal
change direction (to)	cambiar de dirección

change leads (to)	cambiar de pies
collect the horse (to)	reunir el caballo
cool out the horse (to)	enfriar el caballo, normalizar el caballo
cool the horse down (to)	enfriar el caballo, normalizar el caballo
cross the stirrups (to)	cruzar los estribos
decrease the circle (to)	disminuir el círculo
decrease the pace (to)	disminuir el paso, reducir el paso
dismount (to)	desmontar
drive forward (to)	impulsar, empujar
engage the haunches (to)	emplear el posterior, emplear las ancas
exercise the horse (to)	trabajar el caballo
fall from the horse (to)	caerse del caballo
fell from the horse (he/she)	se cayó del caballo
feel the horse (to)	sentir el caballo, simpatizar con el caballo
flex to the left (to)	encorvar a la izquierda, requerir flexión a la izquierda
flex to the right (to)	encorvar a la derecha, requerir flexión a la derecha
gallop the horse (to)	galopar el caballo
give (to)	dar
good hands (to have)	tener buenas manos
hack (to)	pasear, montar
hack the horse (to)	pasear el caballo, montar el caballo
hacking out	pasear a campo abierto
hold in the haunches (to)	sostener el posterior, mantener el posterior

hold the horse between the hands and legs (to)	mantener el caballo entre las manos y las piernas
in harmony with the horse (to be)	estar en armonía con el caballo
increase the circle (to)	aumenter el círculo
increase the pace (to)	aumentar el aire, acelerar el aire
jump (to)	saltar
lack of control (to have)	estar sin control, faltarle el control
leg (to use the)	usar la pierna
active leg	pierna activa
bending leg	pierna plegada
driving leg	pierna impulsada
inside leg	pierna interior, pierna interna, pierna de adentro
leg contact	contacto de la pierna
leg contact (to have)	tener contacto con las piernas
leg position	posición de la pierna
leg up (to give a)	dar una mano para montar, hacer estribo con las manos
lengthen the leg (to)	alargar la pierna
move off the leg (to)	impulsar con las piernas
outside leg	pierna externa, pierna de afuera
passive leg	pierna pasiva
quiet leg	pierna tranquila, pierna relajada
use your leg	usar su pierna
lengthen the stride (to)	alargar el paso
maintain impulsion (to)	mantener la impulsión

mount the horse (to)	montar el caballo, montar
mounted	a caballo, montado a caballo, montado
move the horse at an angle (to)	mover el caballo a ángulo, mover el caballo hacia un ángulo
overwork the horse (to)	aplastar el caballo
pat the horse (to)	acariciar el caballo
post (to)	levantar al trote
post the trot (to)	levantar al trote
posting trot (the)	trote levantado
punish the horse (to)	castigar el caballo
quiet hands (to have)	tener manos suaves, tener manos quietas
react quickly (to)	responder rápido
reactions of the rider	responde del jinete, reacciones del jinete
rein (the)	rienda
active rein	rienda activa
bearing rein	rienda de una mano
direct rein	rienda directa
firm rein	manos firmes, rienda firme
inside rein	rienda interna, rienda de adentro
indirect rein	rienda indirecta
indirect rein behind the withers	rienda indirecta detrás de la cruz
indirect rein in front of the withers	rienda indirecta delante de la cruz
loose rein	rienda suelta
neck rein	rienda de una mano
open rein	rienda suelta, rienda abierta

outside rein	rienda exterior
passive rein	rienda pasiva
plow rein	rienda de conducción
rein (to)	enfrenar
adjust the reins (to)	ajustar las riendas
bridge the reins (to)	hacer puente con las riendas
change rein (to)	cambiar de mano, cambiar de rienda
give the reins (to)	aflojar las riendas, soltar las riendas, dejarla pasar
hold the reins (to)	llevar las riendas, tomar las riendas
lengthen the reins (to)	soltar las riendas, aflojar las riendas
long rein (to give a)	dar rienda larga
loosen the reins (to)	dar las manos, dar las riendas
play with the inside rein (to)	tentar con la rienda de adentro, jugar con la rienda de adentro
rein back	rienda de paso atrás
rein in (to)	refrenar
rein in sharply (to)	sofrenar
seesaw the reins (to)	aserruchar las riendas
shake the reins (to)	agitar las riendas, vibrar las riendas
shorten the reins (to)	cortar las riendas, tomar las riendas
support with the outside rein (to)	soportar con la rienda de afuera

remount the horse (to)	remontar, remontar el caballo
reward the horse (to)	premiar el caballo
ride (to)	montar, cabalgar
ride astride (to)	montar a horcajadas
ride back (to)	volver a caballo, regresar a caballo
ride bareback (to)	montar a pelo
ride by (to)	pasar a caballo
ride double (to)	montar en ancas
ride in (to)	llegar a caballo
ride off (to)	irse a caballo
ride on (to)	seguir adelante, montar adelante
ride on horseback (to)	montar a caballo
ride out (to)	salir a caballo
ride sidesaddle (to)	montar a la amazona, montar a mujeriegas
ride the transition (to)	montar la transición
ride to death (to)	montar hasta muerto
ride up (to)	llegar a caballo
ride without stirrups (to)	montar sin estribos
riding position	posición de monta
chin up	quijada arriba
elbows and arms close to the body	brazos y codos adentro, brazos y codos junto al cuerpo
eyes down	ojos bajos
eyes forward	ojos delante
hands high	manos altas
hands low	manos bajas, manos abajo
hands together	manos juntas

head up	cabeza arriba
heels down	talones abajo
lean over (to)	inclinarse
look down (to)	mirar abajo
perch (to)	encaramarse
pinched knee	rodilla adentro
steady legs and thighs (to have)	tener piernas y muslos tranquilos, tener piernas y muslos firmes
stretch the legs (to)	estirar las piernas
supple hips (to have)	tener caderas flexibles
three point	pararse en el estribo, posición de salto
toes out	talones adentro, pie afuera
two point	monta de rodilla
well balanced	buen equilibrio, buen balance
rising trot	trote levantado
run the horse at full speed (to)	correr el caballo a rienda suelta
seat	asiento
correct seat (to have a)	tener un asiento correcto
deep seat (to have a)	tener un asiento sólido, tener un asiento firme, tener un asiento profundo
dressage seat	asiento de adiestramiento
forward seat	asiento para saltar, posición de salto

independent seat (to have an)	tener un asiento independiente
jockey seat	asiento de carrera, asiento para correr
stiff seat (to have a)	tener un asiento rígido, tener un asiento tieso, tener un asiento inflexible
supple seat (to have a)	tener un asiento flexible
set the head (to)	fijar la cabeza
shift the weight (to)	mudar el peso, influenciar con el peso, cambiar el peso
sit the trot (to)	sentar el trote
sitting trot	trote sentado
spur the horse (to)	espolear el caballo, picar el caballo con las espuelas, usar las espuelas
prod with a spur	espolada
spurring the horse	espoleo del caballo
straighten the horse (to)	enderezar el caballo
stretch the neck (to)	estirar el cuello, alargar el cuello, estirar el pescuezo
supple the horse (to)	soltar al caballo, ablandar al caballo
suppling exercises	ejercicios de soltamiento
thrown from the horse (to be)	perder los estribos, ser tirado del caballo
trot the horse (to)	trotar el caballo
turn the horse (to)	voltear el caballo, dar vueltas al caballo

walk the horse (to)	caminar el caballo, andar el caballo
warm down the horse (to)	enfriar el caballo
warm-up (the)	el calentamiento, ejercicios de calentamiento, ejercicios de preparación
warm up (to)	calentar
warm up the horse (to)	calentar el caballo
whip (to)	azotar, fustigar, dar latigazos
whip on (to)	dar latigazos
whip the horse (to)	fustigar el caballo, azotar el caballo, dar latigazos al caballo
work (the)	el trabajo
fast work	trabajo rápido
flat work	trabajo de picadero, trabajo plano
work on two tracks (to)	trabajar en dos pistas
work the horse (to)	trabajar el caballo, usar el caballo

dressage — adiestramiento

(See also **gaits and movements of the horse**)	(Vea también **aires y movimientos del caballo**)
center line	linea central, centro del picadero
change of rein	cambio de rienda
change of rein down the center line	cambio de rienda por la línea central

change of rein from circle to circle	cambio de rienda de círculo a círculo
change of rein on the diagonal across half the arena	cambio de rienda por el diagonal atravesando por la mitad del cuadrángulo
change of rein on the diagonal across the whole arena	cambio de rienda por el diagonal atrevesando el cuandrángulo entero
change of rein through the circle	cambio de rienda dentro del círculo
circle	círculo
8-meter circle	círculo de ocho metros
10-meter circle	círculo de diez metros
15-meter circle	círculo de quince metros
20-meter circle	círculo de veinte metros
collective marks	notas colectivas
diagonal (the)	el diagonal
diagonal (to be on the)	estar en el diagonal
down the center line	por la línea central
dressage horse	caballo de adiestramiento, caballo de alta escuela
dressage test	lección de adiestramiento, prueba de adiestramiento
Haute Ecole	Alta Escuela
high school	alta escuela
manege	arena, ring de equitación
markers	señales, letras, marcas
middle line	línea central
pas de deux	pas de deux
quadrille	cuadrilla

quarter line	línea cuarta
ride along the rail (to)	montar al riel
ride along the wall (to)	montar por la pared
ride down the center line (to)	montar por la línea central
tests	lecciones
first level	primer nivel
second level	segundo nivel
third level	tercer nivel
fourth level	cuarto nivel
Grand Prix	Grand Prix
intermediate	intermedia
Prix St. George	premio San Jorge
training level	nivel de entrenamiento

eventing   prueba militar

competitions	pruebas, competencias
cross-country phase	fase de cross, fase de campo abierto
dressage phase	fase de adiestramiento
roads and tracks	caminos y pistas
show-jumping phase	fase de salto, fase de concurso de salto
speed and endurance phase	fase de velocidad y resistencia
steeplechase phase	fase de steeplechase
event horse	caballo de prueba completa, caballo de prueba militar
event rider	jinete de prueba completa, jinete de prueba militar
eventing	prueba completa, prueba militar

one-day event	prueba de un día
three-day event	prueba de tres días
faults	faltas, errores
circle at the same obstacle	círculo antes del obstáculo, círculo al mismo obstáculo
enter or leave the penalty zone without addressing the obstacle (to)	entrar o salir al área de penalidad sin tomar el obstáculo, entrar o salir de la zona sin intentar el obstáculo
exceed the time limit (to)	exceder el tiempo, exceder al límite de tiempo
fall of horse	caída del caballo
fall of rider	caída del jinete
foot in the water	pie en el agua
jump an obstacle in the wrong order (to)	saltar un obstáculo fuera de orden, saltar un obstáculo fuera de secuencia
knockdown	botada, tirada
refusal	rehusada
retake an obstacle (to)	retomar un obstáculo, repetir un obstáculo
run out	evasión, salida de cancha
fences/obstacles	vallas, obstáculos
banks and steps uphill	taludes y peldaños arriba
combinations	combinaciones
cross-country	campo abierto
jump-through fences	saltos de pasada
spread fences	saltos anchos
steps down and drop fences	peldaños abajo y saltos botados

uprights	verticales
water fences	saltos de agua
halfway	media cancha, medio ca-mino
jumping derby	derby de salto
levels of competition	niveles de competición
novice	novicio
intermediate	intermedio
advanced	avanzado
veterinary check	examen veterinario
veterinary inspection	inspección veterinaria

hunting   cazando

at bay	acosado, a la tierra
bitch/gyp	perra
brush	matorral
capping fee	tarifa de caza
couple	pareja, un par
cross-crountry (to ride)	montar a campo traviesa, montar a campo libre, montar a campo abierto
cub hunt (to)	cazar por cachorro
cubbing	zorrilando
cunning	astuto
ditch	zanja
dogs	perros
drag hunt (to)	cazar por arrastre
field (the)	el campo
fox	zorro
fox hole	zorrera
fox hound	perro raposero

fox hunt (to)	cazar por zorros
fox tail	cola de zorro
hedge	seto
hounds	perros de caza, mastines
hunt (to)	cazar
hunt an area for foxes (to)	recorrer una región en busca de zorros, cazar una región de zorros
hunt cap	trago
hunt trials	pruebas de caza
hunter (horse)	caballo de caza
hunter (person)	cazador/a, montera
hunting	caza, cacería, montería
cub hunting	caza de cachorro
drag hunting	caza de arrastre
fox hunting	caza de zorros
stag hunting	caza de ciervo
hunting dogs	perros de caza
hunting dress	traje de caza
hunting field	terreno de caza, terreno de cacería, campo de caza
hunting horn	cuerno de caza
hunting manners	modales de caza, etiqueta de caza
huntsman	cazador
kennel	perrera
kennel huntsman	cazador de perrera
kill (the)	muerte
kill (to)	matar
kill the fox (to)	matar el zorro
master of the hounds	maestro de los perros

master of the hunt	maestro de la caza
pack (the)	perrada, jauría, perrería
pick up the scent (to)	encontrar el rastro, ollar el rastro
quarry	presa
ride cross-country (to)	montar a campo traviesa, montar a campo libre, montar a campo abierto
ride the hounds (to)	cazar con jauría
scent	rastro, olfato
second horse	segundo caballo
stag hunt (to)	cazar de ciervo
trophy	trofeo
whelp	cachorro
whipper-in	montero

jumping — saltando

(See also **gaits and movements of the horse**)	(Vea tabmién **aires y movimientos del caballo**)
a lot of jump (to have)	tener mucho salto
angle of the approach	ángulo del aproche, enfoque
approach the fence (to)	aproximarse el obstáculo, acercarse el obstáculo
bent line	línea chueca
bring down a fence (to)	botar un obstáculo, bajar el salto
brush (to)	rozar, tocar
bury the horse (to)	hundir el caballo
center of the jump	centro del salto

Chef d'équipe	jefe de equipo
chip (to)	astillar
clear the fence (to)	saltar limpio
competitions	concursos
calcutta	calcuta
Grand Prix jumping	salto de gran premio, salto de Grand Prix
open jumping	salto abierto
puissance	salto de potencia
show jumping	concurso hípico, concurso de saltos
speed jumping	salto de velocidad
team jumping	salto por equipos
count the strides of the horse (to)	contar las pisadas del caballo
course plan	plano del recorrido, plano por el curso
cups (the)	soportes
bounce in the cups (to)	saltar en los soportes
deep cups	soportes profundos
flat cups	soportes planos
shallow cups	soportes llanos, soportes poco profundos
cut the corner (to)	cortar la esquina, abreviar la esquina
distance between the fences	distancia entre los saltos
estimate (to)	estimar, calcular
estimate the distance (to)	estimar la distancia
fall (the)	la caída
fall (to)	caer
faults	errores, faltas
circling	rodeando, circulando
disobedience	desobediencia

exceed the time allowed (to)	exceder el tiempo permitido
fall of horse	caída del caballo
fall of rider	caída del jinete
foot in the water	pie en el agua, pisar agua
knock down a fence (to)	botar un obstáculo, derribar
land on tape (to)	pisar la cinta, tocar la cinta
loss of gait	pierde el aire, pierde el paso
off course	fuera del recorrido
refusal	rehusada
run out	salida de cancha, evasión
unauthorized assistance	ayuda externa, ayuda sin autorización
fences/obstacles	saltos, obstáculos, vallas
banks, slopes and ramps	banquetas, cuestas y rampas
brush box	muro de ramas
closed obstacle	salto cerrado
combination fence	combinación, salto compuesto
double fence	salto doble
fixed fence	salto fijo
gates	puertas
hog's back	salto de lomo de chancho
in and out	dentro y fuera
jump stands	postes, verticales
liverpool	liverpool
multiple obstacles	saltos múltiples
natural obstacle	salto natural

open ditch	zanja abierta
oxer	oxer
ramped oxer	oxer de rampa, oxer oblicuo
Swedish oxer	oxer sueco
roll top	rodón
spread fence	salto ancho
standards	postes, verticales
straight fence	salto recto, salto derecha
trebles	triples
triple bar	barra triple
triple combination	combinación triple
uprights	verticales
wall	pared, muro, muralla
water jump	salto de agua
ground line	cuerda
How many strides?	¿Cuántas pisadas?
jump (the)	salto
jump (to)	saltar
jump the horse over the fence (to)	hacer saltar el caballo sobre el salto
jump off (the)	desempate
first jump off	primer desempate
jump off (to)	desempatar
jumper	caballo de salto
Grand Prix jumper	caballo de salto de gran premio, caballo de salto de Grand Prix
intermediate jumper	caballo de salto intermedio
open jumper	caballo de salto abierto
preliminary jumper	caballo de salto preliminario
speed/modified jumper	caballo de salto modificado

jumping ability	habilidad de salto, talento de salto
knock down (to)	derribar, botar
knock down a fence (to)	derribar un salto
knock over (to)	botar, tirar
know the course (to)	conocer el curso
land (to)	llegar
landing	llegada
line	línea
miss the spot (to)	errar la distancia, faltar la distancia
pole/bar	vara, barreta, caña
rap pole	caña
tack pole	caña con clavos
Prix de Nations	Premio de Naciones, Prix de Nations
rail (the)	riel, reja
back rail	riel de atrás
front rail	riel de adelante, riel de frente
ground rail	riel de tierra
side rail	riel de lado, riel cerca
rap (to)	rozar
refuse a fence (to)	rehusar un salto
release (the)	aflojamiento
neck release	rienda a la crin
secondary release	afloja secundaria
release (to)	dar las riendas, aflojar las riendas
review the course (to)	revisar el curso
ride a turn (to)	hacer un recorrido, montar la vuelta
roll a bar (to)	voltear la vara, rollar un riel
rub (to)	tocar

school on the flat (to)	trabajar sin saltos, trabajar en picadero, ensayar movimientos planos
see a spot (to)	ver un lugar, conocer el punto
straight line	línea recta
stride (to)	pasar
take off	punto de picar, punto de saltar
turn (the)	la vuelta
short turn	vuelta corta
wide turn	vuelta abierta, vuelta ancha
turn (to)	volver
turn quickly (to)	volver rápidamente
turn wide (to)	volver ancho
walk the course (to)	caminar la cancha, caminar el curso
walk off the stride (to)	caminar las batidas, pisar distancia
weight requirement	peso reglamentario, peso requerido
work over fences (to)	calentar sobre saltos, trabajar sobre saltos

polo   polo

arena polo	polo de arena
back the ball	tiro para atrás
chukka	chukka, entrada
free hit from center	tiro libre del centro
free hit from a spot	tiro libre del lugar
goal	gol, tanto, meta
high goal	juego de polo alta categoría
low goal	juego de polo baja categoría

medium goal	juego de polo mediana categoría
handicap	valor en goles de cada jugador, handicap, desventaja
collective handicap	handicap colectivo, suma de valores individuales
team handicap	handicap de equipo, suma de los cuatro goles
hit out from behind	saque
hook (to)	enganchar
hooking	enganche con el mazo
infringement	infracción, violación
match	juego
offside, forehand stroke	golpe por la derecha
penalty	castigo
penalty 3	castigo 3
penalty 4	castigo 4
penalty 5a (30-yard hit)	castigo 5a (tiro de 30 yardas)
penalty 5b (40-yard hit)	castigo 5b (tiro de 40 yardas)
penalty 6 (60-yard hit with defenders)	castigo 6 (tiro de 60 yardas con defensores, tiro de 60 yardas con poder intercepción)
penalty 7a (another hit)	castigo 7a (otro tiro)
penalty 7b (hit in by a defender)	castigo 7b (tiro de un defensor)
penalty 7c (hit in from the 30-yard line)	castigo 7c (tiro de 30 yardas, gol abierto)
penalty 7d (unnecessary delay)	castigo 7d (retraso innecesario de juego, espera innecessaria)

penalty 8 (player to retire)	castigo 8 (jugador expulsado)
penalty 9a (pony disqualified)	castigo 9a (caballo descalificado, poney descalificado)
penalty 9b (pony ordered off)	castigo 9b (caballo que se autoriza a cambiar)
penalty 9c (player ordered off)	castigo 9c (jugador que se autoriza a cambiar)
penalty 10 (player excluded)	castigo 10 (jugador excluido)
penalty goal	gol de castigo, gol abierto
penalty hit	tiro de castigo
period	tiempo
play (to)	jugar
play polo (to)	jugar polo
player	jugador
8-goal player	jugador de ocho goles
10-goal player	jugador de diez goles
19-goal player	jugador de diecinueve goles
playing field	campo de jugando polo
polo club	club de polo
polo field	campo para polo
polo lessons	lecciones de polo
polo pitch	campo de polo
polo player	jugador de polo, polista
polo pony	poney de polo, caballo de polo
polo pony market	mercado del poney de polo
polo strokes	golpes
polo team	equipo de polo

position	posición
ones	uno delantero
twos	dos delantero
threes	tres delantero
team captain	capitan del equipo
forward	delantero
professional polo	polo de profesión
ride off (the)	caballazo, carga
safety zone	contra cancha, zona de seguridad
score a goal (to)	marcar un gol
throw in (the)	bola puesta en juego por árbitro o juez
umpire	árbitro, árbitro de polo
How much time is left to play?	¿Cuándo tiempo queda de juega?

racing   carreras

added	extra para ganador
added-money races	carreras de extra dinero
all-ages sale	venta de todas las edades
also eligible	elegibles
backstretch	estero de atrás
bad ride (to have a)	tener mala montura
bear out	se tira para afuera
bet (to)	apostar
bet (the)	apuesta
off-track betting	apuestas afuera del hipódromo
place a bet (to)	apostar

Where can I place a bet?	¿Dónde está la ventanilla de apuestas?
betting window	ventana de apuestas
break post (to)	empezar la carrera
break the maiden (to)	correr la primera vez
breakage	quebrada
Breeder's Cup	Copa de Criadores
breeding-stock sale	venta de criadores
breeze (the)	galope ligero
breeze (to)	galopar ligero
carry weight (to)	cargar peso
chute	cajón
claimer	caballo de reclamo
claiming price	precio de reclamo
classic	clásico
come in first (to)	llegar primero
coupled	acoplado/a
crowd (to)	empujar
dead heat	empate
disqualification	descalificación
dope (to)	endrogar, drogar
draw the race (to)	seleccionar los caballos en la carrera
drug (to)	endrogar, drogar
entry	entrada, apunte
exacta	exactamente
excluded	fuera de la carrera
favorite	favorito
field (the)	el grupo de los caballos en la carrera
tough field	el grupo difícil de los caballos en la carrera
field horse	el caballo en la carrera

film patrol	patrulla cinematográfica, patrulla de filmación
finish (the)	el final
finish (to)	finalizar
finish strong (to)	finalizar fuerte
finish line	línea de final
first running	primera vez, corriendo primero
foul	falta
front stretch	el derecho de atrás, recta inicial
furlong	estadio, medida de dos cientos uno metros
futurity	carrera del futuro
gamble (to)	apostar, jugar
gate (the)	la gatera
to the gates/post	a la gatera
go to the inside (to)	correr hacia adentro
go to the outside (to)	correr hacia afuera
go to the races (to)	ir a las carreras
good ride (to have a)	tener buena montura
grade one race	carrera a grado uno
grade two race	carrera a grado dos
grade three race	carrera a grado tres
graded stakes	carreras de grados
grass horse	caballo carrera en la pista de pasto
guaranteed	garantizado
handicap	desventaja, handicap
hold the position (to)	mantener la posición
horse race	carrera de caballos
horse race (as sport)	hipismo
horse racing	carreras

hurdle races	carreras de salto
infield	el medio de la pista
in the body	adentro de la carrera
inquiry	averigua
jockey	jinete, jockey, vaquerillo (Mex)
apprentice jockey	aprendiz de jockey
jockey fees	sueldo del jinete
jockey valet	mozo, mozo de jockey
jump races	carreras de salto
leading money earner (the horse)	el caballo ganador de más dinero
leading money earner (the rider)	el jinete ganador de más dinero
length (a)	un cuerpo, echada
one length	un cuerpo
listed races	carreras listadas, carreras anunciadas
long shot (to be a)	tener poca oportunidad de ganar, tener poca chance de ganar
maiden horse	caballo sin ganancia
match race	carrera al pelo
minimum weight	peso mínimo
mixed meeting	pura sangre y cuarto de milla
move along the inside (to)	mover por adentro, mover hacia adentro
move along the outside (to)	mover por afuera, mover hacia afuera
nomination	nominación
nomination fee	paga de nominación, paga para nominación

nomination form	forma de nominación
nonqualified, added-money races	no cualificado, carreras de dinero extra
outrider	jinete para ayudar
owner	dueño
pace (the)	el paso
partnership	un conjunto de dueños
pay (to)	pagar
perfecta	perfectamente
photo finish	final de carrera muy reñido
place (to)	llegar en segundo lugar
play the horses (to)	apostar en las carreras de caballos
post position	posición para arancar
purse (the)	el premio
Q race	carreras de más de treinta mil dolares
race	carrera
allowance race	carrera de allowance
claiming race	carrera reclamación
combination race	carrera de combinación, carrera combinada
flat race	carrera plana
maiden allowance race	carrera de allowance para no ganadores
maiden race	carrera de no ganadores
selling race	carrera de reclamación
stakes race	carrera de premio mayor
race (to)	correr
race a horse (to)	correr un caballo
race card	programa de carreras, corta de carreras
racecourse	pista

race goer	aficionado a las carreras de caballos
race horse	caballo de carrera
race program	programa de carreras
race steward	juez de carreras
racer	corredor
races	carreras
racetrack (facility)	hipódromo
racetrack (the track)	pista de carreras
racing	carreras
harness racing	carreras de los trotones, carreras de trote, carreras de trotadores
pacer racing	carreras de caballos de paso
quarter horse racing	carreras de cuarto de milla
standardbred racing	carreras de sangre estándard
thoroughbred racing	carreras de pura sangre
trotter racing	carreras de trote
racing age	edades de carreras
racing commission	comisión hípica, comisión de carreras
racing committee	comité de carreras
racing office	oficina de carreras
racing official	oficial de carreras, funcionario hípico
racing schedule	programa de carreras
racing silks	colores
restricted races	carreras restringidas
save ground (to)	ganar terreno

scratch (to)	retirarse
second running	segunda vez, segunda corrida
set down (the)	suspensión
set down (to be)	estar suspendido
show (to)	tercer lugar, llegar en tercer lugar
shut off (to be)	estar cerrado
silks	colores
sprint (to)	sprinter, correr
sprinter	sprinter, corredor
stakes book	libro de premio mayor
stakes winner	ganador de premio mayor
start (to)	empezar
starter's orders	orden para empezar
starting gate	gatera, barrera, en línea de salida
starting time	tiempo de carrera
stayer	caballo de larga distancia
steeplechase	carrera de obstáculos
take down the number (to)	descualificar el número, descalificar
take position (to)	tomar posición
test (the)	la prueba
drug test	prueba para drogas, prueba de drogas
saliva test	prueba de saliva
urine test	prueba de orina
test the horse (to)	examinar el caballo, hacer un análisis de caballo
throw the jockey (to)	derribar al jinete
The horse threw the jockey.	El caballo derribó al jinete.

ticket	boleto
ticket window	taquilla
Where is the ticket window?	¿Dónde está la taquilla?
track	pista
dirt track	pista de tierra
fast track	pista rápida, pista veloz
grass track	pista de pasto
main track	pista de carreras
major track	pista mayor
muddy track	pista lodosa, pista fangosa
off track	pista mala
racetrack	pista de carreras
sloppy track	pista resvalosa
slow track	pista despacio
training track	pista de entrenamiento
wet track	pista mojada
track steward	juez de la pista
turf	hipódromo
turf course	pista de grama, pista de sacate, pista de pasto
turn (the)	curva
turn (to)	volver
weigh in (to)	pesar
weight allowance	autorización de peso
weight cloth	faldón de pesas
win (to)	ganar
win by a length (to)	ganar por un cuerpo
win by a neck (to)	ganar por un cuello
win by a nose (to)	ganar por una nariz
win by half a length (to)	ganar por un medio cuerpo
winner's circle	círculo de ganadores

winner's picture	fotografía de ganador
yearling sale	venta de potrillos de un año

western	**vaquero**
barrel racing	carrera de barril
bowline knot	nudo de rosa
calf roping	piales
cutting	cortando
cutting horse	caballo de aparta, caballo para cortar
dally (to)	afirmar la reata
dally rope (to)	dar la vuelta, enlazar a reata suelta
dodge (to)	esquivar
duck (to)	agachar, esquivar agachando la cabeza
gaucho life	vida gauchesca, vida de gaucho
give enough rope (to)	darle suficiente cuerda
ground tie (to)	amarrar al piso, amarrar en tierra
gymkhana	gymkhana
hackamore horse	caballo de falsa rienda, caballo de jáquima
have enough cow (to)	saber vaquera
header (to be a)	enlazador de cabeza
heeler (to be a)	enlazador de patas, pillador
heel loop	pial
hitch a horse to a tree (to)	atar un caballo a un árbol
lasso (to)	coger con el lazo, lazar
neck rein	reinda de una mano, rienda sobre el cuello

picket (to)	atar al poste
pleasure horse	caballo de paseo, caballo de placer
rein hand	mano de rienda
reiner	calador
reiner (to be a)	estar arrendado, ser calador
reining horse	caballo arrendado, caballo bien riendado
ride barrels (to)	correr barriles
rodeo	rodeo
roll back (the)	volapié
rope (to)	enlazar
roper	enlazador, de lazo, lazador
roping	enlazando, lazando
roping horse	caballo de lazo
round up (to)	rodear
set and turn	sentado y volapié
sliding stop	sentada enalgada
wild sliding stop	sentada enalgada descontrolada, sentada enalgada fuera de control
stock horse	caballo vaquero
team pen (to)	acorralar por equipos
trail horse	caballo hullero

transporting the horse   transportando el caballo

air transport	transporte aéreo
clean the trailer (to)	limpiar el acoplado, limpiar el trailer, limpiar el remolque
haul (to)	transportar

hitch the trailer to the truck (to)	enganchar el remolque al camión
horse passport	pasaporte de caballo
horse trailer	acoplado, remolque, trailer
horse van	furgón para el transporte de los caballos
horse wagon (train)	vagón para transportar caballos
load (to)	cargar
load the horses (to)	cargar los caballos
quarantine	cuarentena
quarantine regulations	reglamentos de cuarentena
ramp	rampa
trailer (the)	acoplado, remolque, trailer
gooseneck trailer	acoplado de quinta rueda
horse trailer	acoplado para caballos, trailer (Mex), remolque para caballos
two-horse trailer	acoplado para dos caballos
trailer (to)	transportar
truck (the)	el camión
truck (to)	transportar los caballos por camión
unload (to)	descargar
unload the horses (to)	descargar los caballos
van (the)	el camioneta
van (to)	transportar por camioneta

showing the horse   concursando el caballo

announcer	anunciador, locutor
bell (the)	timbre, la campana

clear round	recorrido sin faltas
competition	concurso, competición
competitor	concursante
course	curso
off course	fuera de recorrido, fuera de curso
on course	en recorrido, en curso
set the course (to)	afilar el curso
course designer	deseñador
disqualification	descalificación
disqualified (to be)	ser descalificado/a
eliminate (to)	eliminar
elimination	eliminación
enter the ring (to)	entrar a la cancha, entrar a la arena
entry	inscripción, entrada
entry fee	costo de la inscripción
error	error
error of the course	error de recorrido
error of the test	error en la lección
event (an)	un concurso, un evento
Federation (FEI) rules	reglamento de la Federación Internacional Ecuestre, reglas de la Federación
finish (the)	llegada
finish (to)	llegar, terminar
flags	banderas
red flag	bandera roja
white flag	bandera blanca
in gate	puerta de entrada
judge (the)	juez
judge (to)	juzgar

judge's sheets	planillas
judge's stand	caseta del jurado
judging	juzgando
leave the ring (to)	abandonar la cancha, salir de la cancha
nomination fees	costos de nominación
opening ceremony	comienzo de la ceremonia
out gate	puerta de salida
penalty	falta, penalidad, pena
penalty points	penalidades, puntos penales
penalty seconds	penalidades, segundos de penalidad
percentage	porcentaje
performance	actuación
place (the)	lugar
first place	primer lugar
second place	segundo lugar
third place	tercer lugar
fourth place	cuarto lugar
fifth place	quinto lugar
place (to)	premiar
present the horse (to)	presentar el caballo
prize	premio
regulations	reglamentos
ribbon	tirón
riding accident	accidente de montar
riding time	tiempo del recorrido, tiempo de la lección, tiempo acordado
ring steward	juez de cancha
rules	reglas
salute (the)	saludo

salute (to)	saludar
salute the judge (to)	saludar al juez
scoring	resultados
scratch (to)	retirarse
show (the)	concurso
away show	concurso afuera, concurso distante
indoor show	concurso adentro
show (to)	concursar
show circuit	circuito
showing	concursando
showmanship	talento
sound the bell (to)	tocar el timbre, tocar la campana, sonar la campana
speed	velocidad
time	tiempo
interrupted time	tiempo interrumpido
time allowed	tiempo permitido, tiempo reglamentario, límite de tiempo
time on the clock	tiempo en el reloj de reglamento
time clock	cronómetro, reloj registrador
time limit	tiempo limitado, límite de tiempo
time of resistance	tiempo de resistencia
time penalty	falta por tiempo, falta de tiempo, pena de tiempo
turned out (to be)	estar bien presentado
turned out horse	caballo bien presentado, caballo bien aseado

turned out rider	jinete bien presentado
vaccination certificate	certificado de vacuna, historia de vacunación
vaccination records	registro de vacuna
win (to)	ganar
win a ribbon (to)	ganar una cinta, ganar un tirón
withdraw (to)	retirar

grooming equipment   equipo de aseo

brush	cepillo
body brush	cepillo de cuerpo
face brush	cepillo de cara
natural-bristle brush	cepillo natural
synthetic-bristle brush	cepillo sintético
water brush	cepillo de agua
bucket	balde, bote, cubo, cubeta
water bucket	balde de agua
clipper blade	hoja de rastrillo, navaja de rasurar
clippers	máquina de rasurar, maquinilla
body clippers	máquina de rasurar para el cuerpo
face clippers	máquina de rasurar para la cara, máquina pequeña
comb	peine
curry comb	almohaza, rasqueta
mane comb	peine para la crin
metal curry comb	almohaza de metal
pulling comb	peine de entresacada, peine para jalar crin

rubber curry comb	almohaza de hule, almohaza de goma
tail comb	peine para la cola
conditioner	condicionante
fly spray	espray para moscas, rociador para moscas
grooming box	caja de útiles de limpieza, caja de aseo
grooming glove	guante de limpieza, guante de aseo
hole punch	sacabocado
hoof dressing	crema para el casco
hoof oil	aceite para el casco
hoof paint	pintura para el casco
hoof pick	piquete para el casco
horse vacuum	aspiradora de caballo
oil	aceite
pocketknife	navaja
rag	trapo
scissors	tijeras
shampoo	champú
soap	jabón
sponge	esponja
big sponge	esponja grande
small sponge	esponja pequeña
spray bottle	botella de rociar
tack hook	gancho para el equipo, gancho
tape	cinta, huincha
towel	toalla
twitch	twitch, naricera, torcedura de labio
water/sweat scraper	raspador para secar

riding habit	traje de montar, ropa de montar, artículos de los vaqueros y charros
back protector	protector de la espalda
belt	cinto, cinturón
blouse	blusa
body protector	protector del cuerpo
boots, general	botas, generalmente
clean the boots (to)	limpiar las botas
dust off my boots (to)	limpiar el polvo de mis botas, quitar el polvo a mis botas, sacudir mis botas
polish my boots (to)	brillar mis botas, dar grasa a mis botas, lustrar mis botas
pull on boots (to)	ponerse las botas
shine the boots (to)	sacar brillo a las botas
take off the boots (to)	quitarse las botas, sacarse las botas
boots	botas
ankle boots	botas al tobillo, botas cortas
cowboy boots	botas vaqueras
cuff-lined boot	botas media forradas
custom boots	botas hechas a la medida
dressage boots	botas para adiestramiento
field boots	botas camperas, botas de campo
hunt boots	botas para caza
jodhpur/paddock boots	botín

lined boot	bota forrada
polo boots	botas para polo
racing boots	botas para jockey
rubber riding boots	botas de goma para montar
stiff boots	botas duras, botas rígidas
top boots	botas altas
unlined boots	botas sin forro
boot bag	bolsa para bota
boot brush	cepillo para bota
boot hook	tirabotas, gancho para botas, gancho
bootjack	sacabotas
boot lace	cordón
boot legs	piernas de botas
boot polish	betún, grasa
boot rubbers	galochas
bootstraps	orejas, orejas de mulo
boot tree	horma de bota
breeches	pantalones de montar
bombachas	bombachas
cotton breeches	pantalones de algodón para montar
full-seat breeches	pantalones de montar con asiento completo
half-seat breeches	pantalones de montar con medio asiento
jeans	pantalones de mezclilla, jeans
western-cut jeans	pantalones corte de vaquero
jodhpurs	jodhpurs
riding breeches	pantalones de montar

synthetic breeches	pantalones sintéticos de montar
tailor-made breeches	pantalones hechos a la medida
breeches leather	remonta
change clothes (to)	cambiar las ropas
chaps	chaparreras, zajones (Sp)
custom chaps	chaparreras a la medida
English chaps	chaparreras inglesas
half chaps	chaparreras a la mitad
western chaps	chaparreras de vaquero
clothes bag	bolsa de ropa
coat	saco, chaqueta
black coat	saco negro
dressage coat	saco de adiestramiento, saco de dressage, saco de vestir
hunt coat	saco de caza
melton hunt coat	saco de paño para caza
overcoat	abrigo
pink coat	saco rojo
racing colors	colores
raincoat	saco impermeable
riding coat	saco de montar
shadbelly	frac
tailcoat	frac
tailor-made coat	saco hecho a la medida
tuxedo coat	saco de smoking
waistcoat	chaleco
dress (to)	vestir
face guard	máscara protectora
garter	liga
gloves	guantes

hairnet	redecilla
hairpin	horquilla
hat	sombrero
bowler	bombín, sombrero hongo
cowboy hat	sombrero vaquero, sombrero de cowboy
helmet	casco
hunt cap	casco
hunt derby	tongo, hongo
jockey cap	casco
top hat	sombrero de copa, chistera
silk top hat	sombrero de copa, sombrero de seda
hatbox	sombrerera
hat guard	guarda para sombrero
helmet cover	cubierto para casco
helmet harness	harness de casco
hunt-cap cover	cubierto para casco
hunt crop	fuete de caza, látigo de caza
hunt flask	frasco, licorera
hunt thongs	traíllas
hunt vest	chaleco de caza
jewelry	joyería, joyas
shirt studs	gemelos, colleras
stock pin	alfiler
tie bar	barra
jodhpur knee straps	ligas
leather kneepad	rodillera
leggings	polainas
long underwear	ropa interior larga
neckwear	corbata
bow tie	corbata de lazo
choker tie	corbata ahogadera

kerchief	pañuelo
rat catcher	corbata a la inglesa
silk scarf	pañuelo de seda
stock tie	corbata
pant clips	clips de pantalón
poncho	poncho
racing silks	colores
rain pants	pantalones de lluvia
rain suit	traje de lluvia
rat catcher (blouse)	blusa a la inglesa
riding habit	traje de montar
riding skirt	pollera de montar, falda para montar
safety pin	alfiler, gancho, alfiler de broche, imperdible
shirt	camisa
spur straps	correas para espuela, cintos para espuela
spurs	espuelas
children's spurs	espuelas de niños
dummy spurs	espuelas falsas
men's spurs	espuelas de hombres
rowel spurs	espuelas rodaja
sharp spurs	espuelas puntadas, espuelas con punta
women's spurs	espeulas de mujer
undress (to)	desnudar
wear a size . . . (to)	usar una talla . . .
whip	fusta, látigo
bat	fusta, fuete, plano
crop	fuete, fusta
dressage whip	fuete de adiestramiento, fuete de dressage, fusta de dressage

driving whip	fuete de tiro
longe whip	látigo largo
quirt	cuarta
racing whip	fuete de carreras

tack   equipo

bandages	vendas
anti-inflammatory bandage	venda anti-inflamatoria
cast bandage	venda de enyesar, venda de yeso
exercise bandage	venda de ejercicio
fetlock bandage	venda de cuartilla
hock bandage	venda de garrón
knee bandage	venda de rodilla
poultice bandage	venda de cataplasma
pressure bandage	venda de presión
running bandage	venda de carrera
shipping bandage	venda de transporte, venda de embarque
spider web bandage	venda de telaraña
standing bandage	venda de descanso
support bandage	venda de descanso, venda de soporte
sweat bandage	venda de sudar
tail-wrap bandage	venda de la cola
wound bandage	venda de herida
bib	babero
billet straps	correas de barriguera, látigos
bit	freno
bridoon	bridón

bridoon with cheeks	bridón con patas
egg-butt bridoon	bridón ovalado, filete ovalado
ordinary bridoon	bridón ordinario, filete ordinario
two-jointed bridoon	bridón con doble articulación
curb	freno de palanca, freno de curva
jointed curb	freno de palanca con bocado accionado
straight curb	freno de palanca con bocado recto
double-twisted wire	filete doble de alambre torcido
Dr. Bristol bit	freno Bristol
elevator bit	freno de elevador, levantador
English bit	filete
full-cheek bit	freno con patas
full-cheek snaffle	filete con patas
gag bit	ahogador, filete para ahogador
German-made bit	freno hecho en Alemania
generic bit	freno
kimberwicke bit	freno kimberwick, freno de palanca corta
leverage bit	freno
loose-ring snaffle	filete de anillos sueltos
pelham bit	freno para dos riendas, pollero, pelham
pony bit	freno de poney, filete de poney

rubber bit	freno de goma
silver bit	freno de plata
snaffle bit	filete
spade bit	freno de cuchara
sweet-steel bit	freno de fierro dulce
training bit	freno de trabajo, freno de entrenamiento
western bit	freno de vaquero
Weymouth bit	bocado doble, bocado completo, freno y filete
bit burr	guarda cepillada
bit guard	guarda de freno
bit parts	partes de freno
mouthpiece	bocado
port	portalón
rings	anillos, argollas
bitting harness	arnés de embridar, arreos de embridar, jaez
bitting rig	apero de embridar
blanket	manta, manta para caballos (Sp), camisa (Mex), cobija, frazada
cooler	manta para enfriar
day sheet	manta para día
fly sheet	manta para proteger de moscas
light blanket	manta ligera
quarter sheet	manta grupera
turnout rug	manta de potrero
waterproof blanket	manta impermeable
blanket hood	capucha de la manta
blindfold	venda
blinkers	mascarillas, anteojeras

boots	botas, protectores, zapatillas
back boots	botas traseras, botas de atrás
bell/coronet boots	campanas de hule, botas de goma cubrecascos
brushing boots	rozadoras
easy boot	zapatilla para cascos
fetlock ring	anillo de nudo
front boots	botas delanteras
galloping boots	galopadoras, botas para galope
hind boots	botas traseras
hock boots	garroneras
kicking boots	pateadoras
knee boots	rodilleras
leather boots	botas de cuero
open-front boots	botas frente abierto
overreach boots	alcanzadoras
polo boots	botas de polo
poultice boot	bota de medicación
rubber rings	anillos de goma
service boots	botas de servicio
sheepskin boots	botas de piel de oveja
shin boots	botas de huesos
shipping boots	botas de embarque, botas de transporte, cañeras de viaje
shoe-boil boot	bota para bursitis del codo, bota de descanso
splint boots	cañeras, botas contra sobrehueso
treatment boots	botas para tratamiento

breastplate	pechera, pretal
bridle	brida
double bridle	brida doble
full bridle	brida completa
hackamore	jáquima
racing bridle	brida de carreras
snaffle	brida de filete
split-ear bridle	brida de oreja partida
bridle cover	cubierta de la brida
bridle parts	partes de la brida
bit	freno, filete
browband	frontalera
buckles	hebillas
cheek pieces	mejilleras, piezas para mejillas
crown piece	nuquera, corona
curb chain	cadena
keepers	pasadores
headstall	cabezada
holes	huecos
hooks	ganchos
lip strap	correa labial
mouthpiece	bocado
throatlatch	fiador
bridle rack	gancho para la brida, gancho para la cavesada
bucket heater	calentador
carriage	coche
hackney carriage	coche de alquiler
cart	carretilla, carreta
two-wheeled cart	calesa, carreta de dos ruedas
cavesson	cavesada, cabezón (Sp)

longeing cavesson	cavesada de torneo, cavesada de trabajo a cuerda
chain	cadena
curb chain	cadena para la brida
stud chain	cadena de caballo semental
chambon	chambón
collar	collar
cribbing strap	collar para el chupador
crupper	grupera
driving crupper	grupera para tiro
riding crupper	grupera para montar
feed bag	morral
girth	cincha
breastgirth	pechara
elastic girth	cincha elástica
foregirth	cincha delantera
leather girth	cincha de cuero
nylon girth	cincha de nilón
overgirth	sobrecincha
regular girth	cincha regular
three-folded girth	cincha de tres partes
girth cover	cubierta de la cincha
girth extender	alargador de la cincha
girth tube	cubierta de la cincha
halter	cabestro, ronzal, almartigón, cavesada
adjustable halter	almartigón ajustable
grooming halter	almartigón de aseo
horse halter	almartigón del caballo, almartigón

leather halter	almartigón de cuero
nylon halter	almartigón de nilón
pony halter	almartigón del poney
show halter	almartigón de concurso
halter tube	tubo de almartigón
harness	arreo, arnés, jaez
racing harness	arnés de carrera
head bumper	protectora para la cabeza
hobbles	maneas
hobble strap	tira de la manea
irons	estribos
kicking chains	cadenas de patear, cadenas de cocear
lasso	lazo
lead rope	cuerda
lead shank	cadena
leather oil	aciete para cuero
leather punch	puzón para hacer agujeros
longe line	cuerda larga
longe whip	látigo largo, huasca larga
martingale	martingala
DeGogue martingale	martingala DeGogue
German martingale	martingala alemana
running martingale	martingala de anillos
standing martingale	martingala de bajador
muzzle	bozal
neck cradle	collar de la cuna
neck guard	manta del cuello, protector
neck sweat	sudador del pescuezo
nose bag	morral
noseband	bozal, bozalillo, cavesada, muserola
drop noseband	muserola

figure-eight noseband	cavesada de ocho
flash noseband	cavesada doble, cavesada alemana
lever noseband	cavesada de plancha
padded noseband	cavesada acolchada
overcheck	rienda engalladura
polo mallet	martillo para polo
reins	riendas
bridoon reins	riendas de bridón
double reins	riendas dobles
draw reins	riendas de plancha
driving reins	riendas de tiro
hackamore reins	riendas falsas, mecate
hair reins	riendas de pelo, riendas de crin
leather reins	riendas de cuero
braided reins	riendas trenzadas
laced reins	riendas pasadas
plain reins	riendas comunes
plaited reins	riendas trenzadas
long reins	riendas largas, riendas de cuerda
longeing reins	riendas a la cuerda
roping reins	riendas de lazo
rubber reins	riendas de goma
side reins	riendas de atar
split reins	riendas divididas
web reins	riendas de tela, riendas de lona
rein stops	topes
riata	reata
roller	rodillos
anticast roller	aparato contra atorado

body roller	rodillo de cuerpo
longeing roller	rodillo de trabajo a cuerda
padded roller	rodillo acolchado
training roller	rodillo de entrenamiento
rope	lazo, cuerda
rubber stops	topes de hule (Mex), topes de goma
saddle	silla de montar, montura, albardón
dressage saddle	silla adiestramiento, silla de dressage
endurance saddle	silla de resistencia
English saddle	silla inglesa
flat saddle	silla plana, silla inglesa
forward-seat saddle	silla de salto
hunt saddle	silla de cacería, silla de cazamiento
jumping saddle	silla de salto
pack saddle	albarda, basto, enjalma de carga
polo saddle	silla de polo
race saddle	silla de carrera
saddle with a deep seat	silla con asiento profundo
saddle with a flat seat	silla con asiento plano
saddle with a hard seat	silla con asiento duro
saddle with a long flap	silla con falda larga
saddle with a narrow tree	silla con fuste angosto
saddle with a padded seat	silla con asiento acolchado
saddle with a regular tree	silla con fuste normal, silla con fuste regular

saddle with a wide tree	silla con fuste ancho
sidesaddle	silla de amazona, silla de lado
small riding saddle	sillín
stock saddle	silla, montura vaquera, montura australiana
synthetic saddle	silla sintética
western saddle	silla, montura vaquera
saddlebag	alforja, cantinas
saddlecloth	pelero, sudadero, corona (Mex)
saddle cover	cubierta de la silla
saddle pad	sudadero, mantilla, manta, frazada, pelero
all-purpose pad	sudadero
bareback pad	sudadero con cincha
close-contact pad	sudadero de silla de salto
contour pad	sudadero conformado
cotton pad	sudadero de algodón
dressage pad	sudadero para silla de adiestramiento
fleece pad	sudadero de vellón
foam pad	sudadero de espuma de coma
half pad	medio sudadero
harness pad	almohadilla
lift-back pad	sudadero acolchado de atrás, pelero levantador
numnah	sudadero
partial pad	sudadero parcial
pommel pad	sudadero de arzón, sudadero de la cabecilla

quilted pad	sudadero acolchado
square pad	sudadero cuadrado
thick pad	sudadero grueso, sudadero espeso
thin pad	sudadero delgado
western pad	sudadero vaquero
withers pad	sudadero para la cruz
saddle-pad cover	cubierta del sudadero
saddle-pad liner	forro del sudadero
saddle parts, English saddle	partes de la silla inglesa
cantle	cantileja, borren
girth	cincha
knee roll	rollo
leathers (stirrup leathers)	arciones
pommel	cabecilla
saddle flap	falda
seat	asiento
skirt	falda
stirrup	estribo
stirrup bar	barra de estribo
tree	fuste
twist/waist	angostura, cintura
saddle parts, stock saddle	partes de silla, partes de la montura vaquera
back jockey	sobrefalda
breastgirth	pechera
cantle	borren, teja (Mex), copa (Ch, Arg), cantileja
fender	falda, arción
flank cinch	barriguera
front jockey	sobrefalda

hobble strap	porta manea, porta cuarta, tiro de la manea
horn	cacho cabeza, cuerno
horn neck	cuello de cacho
saddle strings	correas
seat	asiento
side jockey	sobrefalda
skirt	falda
stirrup	estribo
stirrup leather	arción
stirrup tread	piso del estribo
swell	borren, delantero, hombro
saddle rack	portasilla
saddle size	numero de la silla
15.5-inch seat	asiento de 15.5 pulgados o 39.7 centimetros
16-inch seat	asiento de 16 pulgados o 41.03 centimetros
16.5-inch seat	asiento de 16.5 pulgados o 42.31 centimetros
17-inch seat	asiento de 17 pulgados o 43.59 centimetros
17.5-inch seat	asiento de 17.5 pulgados o 44.87 centimetros
18-inch seat	asiento de 18 pulgados o 46.15 centimetros
saddle soap	glicerina, jabón de calabasa (Mex)
saddle stand	caballete
saddlery	herraje de sillero
shadow roll	rollo de sombra
snap	cierre

stall guard	guarda de la puerta
stirrup	estribo
aluminum stirrup	estribo de aluminio
stirrup leathers	arciones, aciones
lined leathers	arciones forrados
synthetic leathers	arciones sintéticos
stirrup pads	colchoneta de los estribos
surcingle	sobrecincha
training surcingle	sobrecincha de escuela
vaulting surcingle	sobrecincha de acrobacia
tack trunk	caja para equipo
tail wrap	venda para la cola
tie-down	bajador
trace	tirante
tug	tirante
wash the wraps (to)	lavar las vendas
whipcracker	tronador
wraps	vendas
jumping wraps	vendas de salto
polo wraps	vendas de polo
race wraps	vendas de carrera
standing wraps	vendas de medicación, vendas de descanso, vendas de reposo

tacking the horse

ensillando el caballo

bit up the horse (to)	embocar del caballo
adjust the bit (to)	ajustar el freno
the bit hangs too low	el freno está muy bajo
the bit is too big	el freno está demasiado grande
the bit is too small	el freno está demasiado chico

use this bit (to)	usar este freno
bridle (to)	embridar, poner la brida
adjust the bridle (to)	ajustar la brida
use this bridle (to)	usar esta brida
buckle the girth (to)	abrochar la cincha
check the girth (to)	revisar la cincha
cinch-bound horse	cinchonado, caballo sensitivo de barril
cinchy (to be)	estar sensitivo de barril
cinchy horse (a)	caballo está sensitivo de barril
The horse is cinchy.	El caballo está sensitivo de barril.
fit the saddle to the horse (to)	acomodar la silla al caballo
give a leg up (to)	dar una mano para montar, hacer estribo con las manos
halter the horse (to)	poner el almartigón al caballo, encabestrar
hand me (to)	darme
hand me my crop (to)	darme mi fuete
hand me my gloves (to)	darme mis guantes
hand me my hat (to)	darme mi casco
harness the horse (to)	aparejar el caballo
have the horse ready (to)	tener el caballo listo
have the horse ready at . . . (to)	tener el caballo listo a . . .
hitch the horses to the cart (to)	enganchar los caballos al carro
hitch up the horses (to)	enganchar los caballos
hobble (to)	manear
hold the horse when I mount (to)	sostener el caballo mientras monto

lead the horse (to)	conducir el caballo
loosen the girth (to)	soltar la cincha
pack a horse (to)	albardar
put a pack saddle on (to)	enalbardar
put the boots on (to)	poner las botas
put the back boots on (to)	poner las botas de atrás
put the front boots on (to)	poner las botas delanteras
run the stirrups to the top of the leathers (to)	poner los estribos hasta arriba de los arciones, subir los estribos
run up the stirrups (to)	poner los estribos arriba, subir los estribos
saddle the horse (to)	ensillar
tack up (to)	ensillar
tack up my other horse (to)	ensillar mi otro caballo
tack up the horse (to)	ensillar el caballo
tie (to)	amarrar, atar
tie up the horse (to)	atar el caballo
tighten the cavesson (to)	apretar la cavesada, apretar el bosal
tighten the girth (to)	apretar la cincha, cinchar
unbridle (to)	desembridar
unharness the horse (to)	desaparejar el caballo
unhitch (to)	desenganchar
unhitch the horse (to)	desenganchar el caballo
unhitching	desenganche
unsaddle (to)	desensillar
unsaddle the horse (to)	desensillar el caballo
untie the horse (to)	desamarrar el caballo, soltar el caballo
unwrap the legs (to)	desvendar las piernas

use a foam pad (to)	usar el pelero de espuma de goma
use a lift-back pad (to)	usar el pelero acolchado atrás
wrap the legs (to)	vendar las piernas
wrap the front legs (to)	vendar las piernas de lanternas
wrap all the legs with polo wraps (to)	vendar todas las piernas con vendas de polo

equine personnel · personal ecuestre

amateur rider	caballista amateur
apprentice	aprendiz
apprentice jockey	jockey aprendiz
assistant trainer	asistente, asistente de entrenador
beginning rider	jinete en entrenamiento, jinete novicio
boot maker	zapatero, botero
braider	trenzador
breeches maker	pantalonero
buckaroo	vaquero
cart driver	calesero
circus rider	jinete de circo
clipper	trasquilador
coach driver	conductor de carruaje
competitor	concursante
course builder	constructor del curso
course designer	diseñador
cowboy	vaquero
equestrian	ecuestre, caballista, jinete
equestrienne	amazona, caballista

farrier	herrero/a
feeder	alimentador de caballos
foreman	supervisor, mayordomo
gaucho	gaucho
good judge of horses (a)	un buen entendido de caballos
groom	mozo de caballos, cuidador de caballos, caballerizo
harness maker	talabartero, guarnicionero
horse agent	agente de caballos
horse breaker	domador/a de caballos, caballerango, petisero (Arg)
horse breeder	criador/a de caballos
horse chiropractor	quiropráctico de caballos
horse dealer	comerciante de caballos, vendedor de caballos, negociante de caballos, tratante de caballos
horse dentist	dentista de caballos
horse guard	guardia montada
horse handler	caballerango, caballerizo
horse hauler	transportador de caballos
horse manager	manager de caballos
horseman/horsewoman	caballista, equitador/a
horse owner	dueño de caballo
horse person	persona a caballo, aficionado al caballerizmo
horse thief	cuatrero, ladrón de caballos

horse trader	comerciante de caballos, vendedor de caballos, negociante de caballos
horse trainer	entrenador, domador/a de caballos
horsey person	persona a caballo
hot walker	paseador, caminador
international competitor	concursante internacional
jockey	vaquerillo (Mex), jinete, jockey
landowner	terrateniente
absentee landowner	ausente
leather worker	talabartero
liveryman	propietario de caballo de alquiler
muleskinner	mulero, muletero, arriero
muleteer	mulero, muletero, arriero
novice/beginning rider	jinete novicio/a, jinete en entrenamiento
owner of horses	dueño de caballos
pack saddle maker	enjalmero
Peruvian trainer	chalán
professional rider	profesional, jinete profesional
rancher	ranchero
rider	jinete, equitador
riding instructor	instructor de equitación
riding master	maestro de equitación
riding student	estudiante de equitación, discípulo de equitación

saddle maker	guarnicionero, monturero
saddler	monturero, sillero
skilled rider	jinete, caballero, amazona, equitador de experiencia
student	estudiante
tailor	sastre
teacher	profesor, maestro
trainer	domador/a de caballos, entrenador
English trainer	entrenador de inglesa
dressage trainer	entrenador de adiestramiento
hunter trainer	entrenador de caza
jumper trainer	entrenador de salto
western trainer	entrenador de vaquero
trick rider	jinete de circo
veterinarian	veterinario/a
working student	discípulo de maestro
wrangler	caballerango/a

equine words and phrases

palabras y expresiones equinas

bray	rebuzno, relinchar
cart rut	carril, rodada
Do not stand behind this horse.	No se paren detrás de este caballo.
equine insurance	seguro equino
equine race	raza de equina
harness shop	guarnicionería, talabartería
herd of colts	potrada

herd of horses	caballada
hoofbeat	ruido de cascos
horseback (on)	a caballo
horse-drawn	tirado por caballos
horse management	administración de los ca- ballos
horsemanship	equitación
horse trade/horse trading	comercio en caballos, cam- bio de caballos, ne- gocio de caballos
horse under saddle	caballo ensillado
horsey smell	un olor a caballo
leather shop	talabartería
mount (a)	un caballo
bad mount	mala monta (Mex)
beginner's mount	caballo de jinete novicio
good mount	buena monta (Mex)
poor mount	pobre monta (Mex)
mounted	a caballo, montado a ca- ballo, montado
mule track	camino carretero
neigh (the)	relincho
neigh (to)	relinchar
overhorsed	no puede con el caballo
pack saddle (to make a)	enjalmar
picket (to)	estacar
picket the horse (to)	atar un caballo a la estaca
pull a carriage (to)	arrastrar un carruaje
riding is easy	es fácil montar a caballo
riding style	estilo de montar
saddle repair	reparación de montura
saddle shop	tienda de monturas, mon- turía

stampede (the)	estampida, desbocamiento
stampede (to)	estampidar, provocar una espantada
tack shop	talabartería
Where is the tack shop?	¿Dónde está la talabartería?
tailor shop	sastrería
tour on horseback	viajar a caballo
trick riding	volteo
underhorsed	no tiene suficiente caballo
whinny (the)	relincho
whinny (to)	relinchar
whoa!	¡so!

Equestrian Facility Management

Administración de instalaciones ecuestres

the facilities	las instalaciones
aisle	pasillo
aqua tread	máquina con banda para ejercicio en el agua
arena	arena
covered arena	arena cubierta
enclosed arena	arena cerrada
practice arena	arena para ensayar, arena para practicar
automatic waterer	agua automática, abrevadero automático
barn	galpón, cuadril
grain barn	granero
grain silo	silo para granos
hay barn	galpón de forraje

hayloft	henil, galpón de forraje
horse barn	cuadril
training barn	cuadril de entrenamiento, centro hípico
bathroom	baño, cobertizo
Where is the bathroom?	¿Dónde está el baño?
bedding storage	galpón
buildings	edificios
bull pen	corral redondo, corral toril
cattle guard	guardavaca
corral	corral
cross-ties	amarraderos, amarras cruzadas
equestrian center	centro equestre
farmhouse	casa
feed room	granero, cuarto de alimento
feed trough	artesa, comedero
feed tub	tina de comida
feeding manger	pesebre
feeding rack	pesebre
fence	cerca, alambrado
barbed-wire fence	cerca de púas
board fence	cerca de tabla
chain-link fence	cerca de malla
concrete fence	cerca de concreto, cerca de material
electric fence	cerca eléctrica
nylon fence	cerca de nilón
pipe fence	cerca de pipa, cerca de tubo
rubber fence	cerca de hule, cerca de goma
wire fence	cerca de alambre

gate	puerto, paso
grounds	tierras
bridle path	senda, sendero, huella, caminito
field	campo
open field	campo abierto
grassland	pastizal
hard ground	terreno duro
meadow	prado
large meadow	pradera, pradería
small meadow	prado pequeño
paddock	potrero
pasture	pasto, pastizal, pastura
summer pasture	agostadero, veraneo
pond	charca
prairie	pradera
race track	pista de carrera
riding path	camino de herradura
trail	sendero, vereda, huella
hitching post	poste de amarre
hitching rack	amarradero, palenque
hot walker (device)	mecánica para pasear, caminante
horse swimming pool	alberca para caballos, piscina para caballos
manger	pesebre, comedero
office	oficina
barn office	oficina, oficina de establo
lock the office (to)	cerrar la oficina con llave
stable office	oficina de establo
unlock the office (to)	abrir la oficina con llave
Where is the office?	¿Dónde está la oficina?

practice area	área para ensayar, área para practicar, área de ensayo
riding school	escuela de equitación, picadero
ring	arena, pista de montar, picadero, cancha
covered ring	arena cubierta
dressage ring	arena de adiestramiento
jumper ring	picadero, cancha de salto, arena de salto
manege	manege, picadero de equitación
round ring	arena redonda
schooling ring	arena de entrenamiento, picadero de trabajo
saddle room	cuarto de monturas
saddling area	área para ensillar
sand	arena
snubbing post	poste para amarrar, poste de atar
stable	establo, caballeriza, cuadra
livery stable	establo de caballos de alquiler
rental stable	caballeriza para alquiler
training stable	establo entrenamiento, centro hípico
stall	caballeriza, chiquero
box stall	caballeriza cerrada, caballeriza
covered stall	caballeriza cubierta
in-and-out stall	caballeriza con corral

pipe stall	corral de tubo
temporary stall	caballeriza temporánea, caballeriza temporal
stall mats	pisos de hule, pisos de goma
sun pen	corral
swinging rail	tranca, tranquera
tack room	cuarto de equipo, cuarto de aperos, cuarto de arreos
telephone (the)	teléfono
Where is the telephone?	¿Dónde está el teléfono?
turn-out pen	corral
wash rack	lavadero
water bucket	balde de agua
water tank	aljibe, tanque de agua
water trough	abrevadero

the property

la propiedad

boarding facility	cuadril, instalación, edificio para mantener caballos
farm	finca, granja, fundo
breeding farm	yeguada, criadero, rancho de criadero
cooperative farm	finca cooperativa
lay-up farm	campo de descanso, rancho de descanso
stud farm	yeguada
hacienda	hacienda
holding	propiedad

plot	parcela
ranch	rancho
horse ranch	rancho de caballos
riding school	escuela de equitación, picadero
station (large operation)	estancia
training facility	instalación de entrenamiento

maintenance equipment

equipo de mantenimiento

barbed wire	alambre de púas
bolt	cerrojo
broom	escoba
car	carro, auto, máquina, coche
disc harrow	rastra de discos
extension cord	extensión eléctrica, cordón eléctrico
electricity	electricidad
gasoline	gasolina, petróleo, bencina
hose	manguera, manga
irrigation system	sistema de riego
light bulb	bombilla, eléctrica, ampolleta
rake	rastrillo, rastra
pitchfork	horqueta, horca, yeldo (Mex)
plow	arado
power mower	motosegadora, segadora motorizada
shovel	pala
sprinkling system	sistema de aspersión
tools	herramientas
crowbar	palanca

hammer	martillo
nail	clavo
saw	serrucho, sereta
screwdriver	desatornillador
sledgehammer	combo
wirecutter	corta alambre
wrench	llave para las tuercas
tractor	tractor
trash can	balde de la basura
truck	camión, troqué
water truck	camión aguador
wheelbarrow	carretilla
Where is the wheelbarrow?	¿Dónde está la carretilla?

facility maintenance

mantenimiento de la instalación

bedding	cama
dirt floor	piso de tierra
peat moss	viruta
replace the bedding (to)	reemplazar el aserrín, cambiar la cama
rice hulls	cáscara de arroz
shavings	aserrín, viruta
give more shavings (to)	dar más aserrín, poner más viruta
The shavings are wet.	El aserrín está muy mojado.
The shavings are dirty.	El aserrín está muy sucio. La cama está sucia.
straw	paja

clean (to)   limpiar
  clean the stall (to)   limpiar la caballeriza
  clean the stall later (to)   limpiar la caballeriza
                                      más tarde
  clean the tack room (to)   limpiar el cuarto del
                                      equipo
closed   cerrado
  Always keep the door   Mantengan siempre la
    closed.   puerta cerrada.
close the door (to)   cerrar la puerta
dirty   sucio
fence   cerca, barda, valla, pared,
                                      alambrado

  check the fences (to)   revisar las bardas
  paint the fence (to)   pintar la cerca, pintar la
                                      pared

  repair the fence (to)   reparar la cerca, reparar
                                      la pared

  set the fences/jumps (to)   poner los saltos
fix (to)   arreglar, componer
  fix this (to)   arreglar esto/a, componer
                                      esto/a

garbage bag   bolsa de basura
garbage can   lata para basura, cubo de
                                      la basura, basurero
  empty the garbage cans (to)   vaciar los basureros
hose down the barn aisles   regar los pasillos de cuadril
    (to)   para limpiar
maintain the rings (to)   mantener las arenas, man-
                                      tener los picaderos

  drag the rings (to)   emparejar las arenas
  groom the rings (to)   limpiar las arenas
  rake the rings (to)   rastrillar las arenas
  seal the rings (to)   sellar las arenas

water the rings (to)	regar las arenas
maintain the track (to)	mantener la pista
manure	abono, cagajón, estiércol, mierda
droppings	cagajones, estiércol
dung	cagajón, bosta, mierda
manure heap	estercolero
pitchfork	horca
Can I use your pitchfork?	¿Podría yo, usar su horca? ¿Puedo usar su horca?
repair (to)	reparar
repair this (to)	reparar esto/a
stall	caballeriza
check the stalls at night (to)	chequear los establos por la noche
close the stall door during the night (to)	cerrar la puerta de la caballeriza durante la noche
lay the stall mats (to)	extender los pisos
muck out the stall (to)	vaciar el aserrín, limpiar el guano, limpiar la caballeriza
open the stall door during the day (to)	abrir la puerta de la caballeriza durante el día
remove the horse from the stall (to)	sacar el caballo de la caballeriza, sacar el caballo del box
The stall door is broken.	La puerta de la caballeriza está quebrada.
The stall smells.	La caballeriza heule.
sweep (to)	barrer
sweep later (to)	barrer más tarde
turn off (to)	apagar

turn on (to)	encender
turn on the ring lights (to)	encender las luces de la arena
urine	orina, orín, meado
vacuum (to)	limpiar con aspiradora, aspirar
vacuum the office (to)	limpiar con aspiradora la oficina, aspirar la oficina
wash (to)	bañar
water the grass (to)	regar el pasto, regar el sácate
wet	mojado

staff management	**administración de personal**
alien	extranjero, ajeno
Call me if you cannot work.	Llámame si no puede trabajar.
citizenship	ciudadanía
Are you a U.S. citizen?	¿Es Ud. ciudadano? ¿Es Ud. ciudadano de los Estados Unidos?
Do you have papers?	¿Tiene Ud. papeles?
have papers (to)	tener papeles, tener mica
deport (to)	deportar
deported (to be)	ser deportado
deportation	deportación
discharge (to)	despedir, perforar su carta (Mex)
do good work (to)	trabajar bien, hacer buen trabajo
You do good work.	Ud. trabaja bien.

drink (to)	beber
driver's license	licencia para manejar, licencia de conductor
Do you have a driver's license?	¿Tiene Ud. una licencia para manejar?
drunk	borracho/a
drunkard	borracho/a
experience (to have)	tener experiencia
Do you know how to ride?	¿Sabe Ud. montar a caballo?
Have you worked with horses before?	¿Ha trabajado con caballos antes?
Do you have experience with horses?	¿Tiene experiencia con caballos?
Where have you worked before?	¿Dónde trabajó anteriormente?
family	familia
Do you have family here?	¿Vive aquí su familia? ¿Tiene Ud. familia aquí?
fire (to)	darle aire (Mex), despedir
fired (to be)	estar despedido/a
You are fired.	Está despedido/a.
hired (to be)	estar contratado/a
You are hired.	Está contrado/a.
How old are you?	¿Cuántos años tiene?
immigrant	inmigrante
immigrate (to)	inmigrar
immigration office	oficina de inmigración
immigration officer	oficial de inmigración
immigration service	la "migra"
In an emergency call . . .	En caso de emergencia llame . . . ; En emergencia llama . . .

My telephone number is . . .	Mi número de teléfono es . . . ; Mi teléfono es . . .
No sir.	No señor.
The stable is closed on . . .	El establo está cerrado en . . . ; El establo se cierra a las . . .
What is your address?	¿Dónde vive Ud.? Deme, por favor, su dirección.
What is your name?	¿Cómo se llama Ud.?
What is your telephone number?	¿Cuál es su número de teléfono? ¿Cuál es su teléfono?
When can you start work?	¿Cuándo podría comenzar su trabajo?
Where are you from?	¿De dónde es Ud.?
Where were you yesterday?	¿Dónde estabas ayer?
Yes sir.	Sí señor.
You finish work at . . .	Termina Ud. su trabajo a las . . .
You start work at . . .	Empieza Ud. su trabajo a las . . .
Your day off is . . .	Su día de descanso es . . . ; Su día libre es . . .
Your hours are . . .	Sus horas de trabajo son . . .

payroll management

administración de pagos

cash	dinero
cents	centavos

check	cheque
deductions	deducciones
dependents	dependientes
dollars	dólares
money	dinero
pay (the)	pago, dinero, sueldo, lana
pay plus room and board	sueldo más borde
take-home pay	sueldo neto
pay (to)	pagar
How much do you pay?	¿Cuánto paga Ud.?
How much do I owe you?	¿Cuánto le debo?
I will pay you . . .	Yo le voy a pagar . . . ; Le pagaré . . .
pay every . . . (to)	pagar ceda . . .
pay in cash (to)	pagar en efectivo
pay monthly (to)	pagar mensualmente
pay weekly (to)	pagar cada semana, pagar semanalmente
pay with a check (to)	pagar con cheque
Payday is . . .	El día de pago es . . .
rate per day	sueldo por día
rate per hour	sueldo por hora
rate per month	sueldo por mes
rate per week	sueldo por semana
rate per year	sueldo por año
salary	sueldo, salario
taxes	impuestos
tip (the)	propina
tip (to)	propinar, dar propina
split this tip with . . . (to)	dividir la propina con . . . ; compartir la propina con . . .
This tip is for you.	Esta propina es para Ud.

wages	salarios
minimum wage	salario mínimo
What do you charge to blanket?	¿Cuánto cobra para poner la manta?
What do you charge to feed a horse?	¿Cuánto cobra para alimentar un caballo?
What do you charge to turn out a horse?	¿Cuánto cobra para soltar el caballo?

Commonly Used Words and Phrases

Palabras y frases comunes

colors	**colores**
black	negro
blue	azul
brown	colorado, café, marrón
dark	oscuro
green	verde
light	claro
orange	naranja
pink	rosa, rosado
purple	morado
red	rojo
white	blanco
yellow	amarillo

communication

comunicación

Do you speak English?	¿Habla inglés? ¿Habla Ud. inglés?
Do you speak Spanish?	¿Habla español? ¿Habla Ud. español?
Do you understand?	¿Comprende Ud.?
Help me, please.	Ayúdame por favor. Ayúdeme por favor.
How do you say . . . ?	¿Cómo se dice . . . ?
I do not speak English.	No hablo inglés.
I do not speak Spanish.	No hablo español.
I do not understand.	No comprendo.
Speak slowly, please.	Hable despacio, por favor.

expressions of time

expresiones de tiempo

day
  afternoon
    in the afternoon

  daybreak
  evening
    this evening
  midnight
  morning
    in the morning

    this morning
night
  at night

  last night

día
  tarde, medio día
    por la tarde, en la tarde

  amanecer alba
  tarde, anochecer
    esta tarde
  medianoche
  mañana
    por la mañana, en la mañana
    esta mañana
noche
  por la noche, en la noche
  anoche

nightfall	anochecer, crepúsculo
noon	mediodía
sunrise	salida del sol
sunset	puesta de sol, ocaso
today	hoy
tomorrow	mañana
day after tomorrow	pasado mañana
tomorrow morning	mañana por la mañana
tonight	esta noche
yesterday	ayer
day before yesterday	anteayer
yesterday afternoon	ayer por la tarde, ayer en la tarde
yesterday morning	ayer por la mañana, ayer en la mañana
days of the week	días de la semana
Monday	lunes
Tuesday	martes
Wednesday	miércoles
Thursday	jueves
Friday	viernes
Saturday	sábado
Sunday	domingo
week	semana
last week	la semana pasada
next week	la semana entrante, la semana que viene
this week	esta semana
weekend	fin de semana
next weekend	próximo fin de semana
this weekend	este fin de semana
months of the year	meses del año
January	enero

February	febrero
March	marzo
April	abril
May	mayo
June	junio
July	julio
August	agosto
September	septiembre
October	octubre
November	noviembre
December	diciembre
year	año
last year	el año pasado
next year	el año entrante, el año que viene
this year	este año
years	años
seasons	estaciones
spring	primavera
summer	verano
Indian summer	veranillo de San Martín
fall	otoño
winter	invierno
time	tiempo
a little later	un poco después
a little while ago	hace un poco, hace un momento
again	otra vez
At what time?	¿A qué hora?
each time	cada vez
from time to time	de vez en cuando
hours	horas

How long ago?	¿Hace cuánto tiempo? ¿Cuándo ha? ¿Hace cuándo?
How many times?	¿Cuántas veces?
in a little while	dentro de un momento, dentro de poco
It is one o'clock.	Es la una.
minutes	minutos
now	ahora
once	una vez
What time is it?	¿Qué hora es? ¿Qué hora son?
When?	¿Cuándo?

expressions of the weather

expresiones del clima

changeable weather	tiempo variable
cloud	nube
cyclone	ciclón
dew	rocío
drought	sequía
fine weather	buen tiempo
freeze	helada
frost	escarcha
hail	granizo
humidity	humedad
It is humid.	Hay humedad. Está húmedo.
hurricane	huracán
lightning	relámpago
rain	lluvia
downpour	aguacero

Is it raining?	¿Está lloviendo?
It is about to rain.	Está para llover.
snow	nieve
snowfall	nevada
snowflake	copo de nieve
sun	sol
temperature	temperatura
cold (to be)	hacer frío
It is very cold.	Hace mucho frío.
hot (to be)	hacer calor
warm (to be)	hacer calor
It is very warm.	Hace mucho calor.
thunder	trueno
weather conditions	condiciones atmosféricas
weather permitting	si el tiempo no lo impide, si el tiempo lo permite
whirlwind	torbellino, manga de viento
wind	viento
breeze	brisa
gust of wind	ráfaga de viente
What is the weather like?	¿Cómo está el tiempo?
	¿Cómo está el clima?
	¿Qué tiempo hace?

fractions   fracciones

one-eighth	un octavo
one-quarter	un cuarto
one-third	un tercio
one-half	una media

three-quarters	tres cuartos
seven-eighths	siete octavos

measures

medidas

measures of length	medidas de longitud
1 inch = 0.025 m	1 pulgada = 0,025 metros
1 foot = 0.03 m	1 pie = 0,03 metros
1 yard = 0.91 m	1 yarda = 0,91 metros
1 meter = 3 ft. 3 in.	1 metro = 3 pies 3 pulgadas
1 mile = 1760 yds. = 1609 m	1 milla = 1760 yardas = 1609 metros
measures of surface	medidas de superficie
acre	acre
1 acre = 40.468 ares	1 acre = 40,468 áreas
measures of volume	medidas de capacidad, medidas de volumen
bale	bala, fardo
cup	taza
gallon	galón
1 gallon = 3.785 liters	1 galon = 3,785 litros
liter	litro
10 liters = 2.2 gallons	10 litros = 2,2 galones
1 liter = 1.057 quarts	1 litro = 1,057 cuartos de galón
pint	pinta
quart	cuartos de galón, un cuarto
scoop	pala
tablespoon	cucharada
measures of weight	medidas de peso

gram	gramo
kilogram	kilógramo
1 kilogram = 2.204 pounds	1 kilógramo = 2,204 libras
ounce	onza
1 ounce = 28.35 grams	1 onza = 28,35 gramos
pound	libra
1 pound = .4536 kilograms	1 libra = 0,4536 kilógramos
ton	tonelada

numbers

números

one	uno
first	primero/a
two	dos
second	segundo/a
three	tres
third	tercero/a
four	cuatro
fourth	cuarto/a
five	cinco
fifth	quinto/a
six	seis
sixth	sexto/a
seven	siete
seventh	séptimo/a
eight	ocho
eighth	octavo/a
nine	nueve
ninth	noveno/a
ten	diez

tenth	décimo/a
eleven	once
twelve	doce
thirteen	trece
fourteen	catorce
fifteen	quince
sixteen	dieciséis
seventeen	diecisiete
eighteen	dieciocho
nineteen	diecinueve
twenty	veinte
twenty-five	vienticinco
thirty	treinta
forty	cuarenta
fifty	cincuenta
sixty	sesenta
seventy	setenta
eighty	ochenta
ninety	noventa
one hundred	cien

salutations

saludos

Congratulations!	¡Enhorabuena!
	¡Felicitaciones!
Good afternoon.	Buenas tardes.
Good evening.	Buenas noches.
Good morning.	Buenos días.
Good-bye.	Adiós.
Happy New Year.	Feliz año nuevo.
Happy Birthday.	Feliz cumpleaños.
Happy Thanksgiving.	Feliz día de dar las gracias.
	Feliz día de gracias.

Hello.	Hola. ¿Qué hubo?
How are you?	¿Cómo está Ud.?
How do you do?	¿Cómo ha estado?
Merry Christmas.	Feliz Navidad.
See you later.	Hasta luego.

other words

otras palabras

after	después de, después que
all	todo/a, todos, todas
at last	finalmente, al fin, por fin
at once	al instante, enseguida
backward	hacia atrás
Band-Aid	vendita, curita (Mex)
because	porque
because of	a causa de, a causa por, debido a
before (in front of)	adelante de, por delante de
before (time)	antes de
belong to	pertenecer
Do you have . . . ?	¿Tiene Ud. . . . ?
enough	bastante, suficiente
everybody	todo el mundo, todos
everything	todo, todo lo que
everywhere	por todas partes
forward	hacia adelante
here	aquí
I'm sorry.	Lo siento.
in front of	en frente de
left	izquierda
Let's go over there.	Vamos hacia allá.
many	muchos/as

My name is . . .	Me llamo . . . ; Mi nombre es . . .
next	próximo
no	no
now	ahora
over there	por allá
please	por favor
right	derecho
someone	alguien
sorry	perdone, perdón
thank you	gracias
No thank you.	No gracias.
Thank you very much.	Muchas gracias.
that	eso, esa, ese
there	allá
this	esta
this way	hacia acá
Wait a minute.	Horita.
What?	¿Cómo? ¿Qué?
What's that?	¿Qué es eso?
What's the matter?	¿Qué pasa?
What's this?	¿Qué es esto?
When?	¿Cuándo?
where	donde
Where is . . . ?	¿Dónde está . . . ?
Who?	¿Quién?
Why?	¿Por qué?
Would you please?	¿Si es Ud. tan amable?
yes	sí
You're welcome.	De nada. Por nada.

Illustrations

Ilustraciones

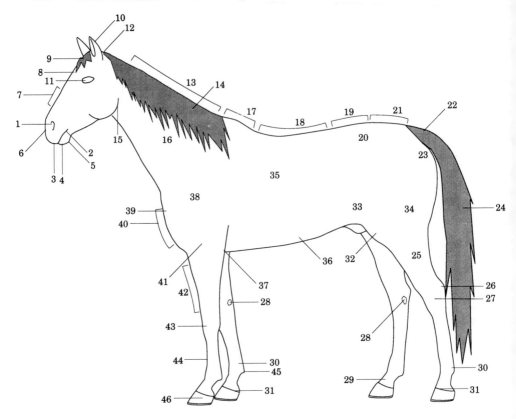

Points of the Horse/Puntos del Caballo

1. Nostril, *Ollar, Nariz*
2. Mouth, *Boca*
3. Upper Lip, *Labio Superior*
4. Lower Lip, *Labio Inferior*
5. Under Lip, *Labio Bajo*
6. Muzzle, *Hocico, Boca*
7. Bridge of the Nose, *Puente de la Nariz*
8. Forehead, *Frente*
9. Forelock, *Copete, Chasca, Mechón, Tupe*
10. Ear, *Oreja*
11. Eye, *Ojo*
12. Poll, *Nuca*
13. Crest, *Cresta, Cresta del Cuello*
14. Mane, *Crin, Crinera, Tuse/a*
15. Throatlatch, *Friador, Ahogador, Gargantilla*
16. Neck, *Cuello, Pescuezo*
17. Withers, *Cruz*
18. Back (Upper), *Espalda*
19. Loin, *Lomo, Ijada*
20. Point of the Hip, *Punta de la Cadera*
21. Croup, *Grupa, Rabadilla*
22. Dock, *Maslo, Maslo de Cola*
23. Buttock, *Nalga, Grupa*
24. Tail, *Cola, Rabo*
25. Gaskin, *Muslo de la Pierna, Muslo*
26. Point of the Hock, *Punto del Corvejón, Punto del Garrón*
27. Hock, *Corvejón, Garrón*
28. Chestnut, *Ergot, Castaña, Espejuelo*
29. Pastern, *Cuarta, Cuartilla*
30. Fetlock, *Nudo, Nudillo*
31. Coronet, *Corona del Casco, Corona, Margen Superior del Casco*
32. Stifle, *Babilla*
33. Flank, *Flanco*
34. Thigh, *Muslo*
35. Barrel/Ribs, *Costilla*
36. Belly, *Barriga*
37. Elbow, *Codo, Codillo*
38. Shoulder, *Hombro*
39. Point of the Shoulder, *Punto del Hombro, Punto del Pecho*
40. Chest/Breast, *Pecho*
41. Arm, *Brazo, Paleta*
42. Forearm, *Antebrazo, Brazuelo, Brazo*
43. Knee, *Rodilla*
44. Cannon, *Caña*
45. Ergot, *Ergot*
46. Hoof, *Casco, Pezuña*

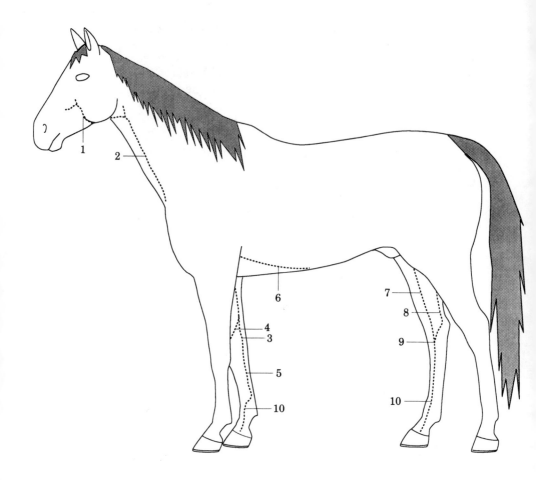

Primary Veins of the Horse/Venas Principales del Caballo

1. Facial Vein, *Vena Facial*
2. Jugular Vein, *Vena Yugular*
3. Cepahlic Vein, *Vena Cefálica*
4. Accessory Cephalic Vein, *Vena Cefálica Accesoria*
5. Metacarpal Vein, *Vena Metacarpiana*
6. External Thorasic Vein, *Vena Torácica Externa*
7. Saphenous Vein, *Vena Safena*
8. Posterior Tibial Vein, *Vena Tibial Posterior*
9. Metatarsal Vein, *Vena Metatarsiana*
10. Digital Vein, *Vena Digital*

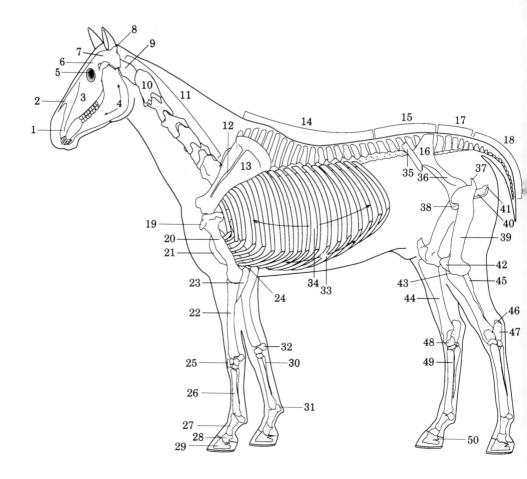

Bone Structure of the Horse/El Esqueleto del Caballo

1. Premaxillary, *Premaxilar*
2. Nasal, *Nasal*
3. Maxillary, *Maxilar Superior*
4. Mandible, *Mandíbula*

5. Orbit, *Porción Orbitaria del Frontal*
6. Frontal, *Frontal*
7. Temporal Fossa, *Escama del Temporal*

8. Occipital, *Cresta Occipital*
9. Atlas, *Atlas*
10. Axis, *Axis*
11. Cervical Vertebra (7), *Vértebras Cervicales (7)*
12. Scapular Spine, *Espina de la Escapula*
13. Scapula, *Escapula*
14. Thoracic Vertebra (18), *Vértebras Toracicas (18)*
15. Lumbar Vertebra (6), *Vértebras Lumbares (6)*
16. Tuber Sacrale, *Tuberosidad Sacra*
17. Sacral Vertebra (5), *Vértebras Sacras (5)*
18. Coccygeal Vertebra (17–20), *Vértebras Coccígeas (17–20)*
19. Tuberosity of Humerous (Point of the Shoulder), *Tuberosidad Húmero*
20. Humerous, *Húmero*
21. Sternum, *Esternón*
22. Radius, *Radio*
23. Ulna, *Cúbito*
24. Olecranon, *Olécranon*
25. Carpus, *Carpo*
26. Large Metacarpal, *Gran Metacarpiano*
27. 1st Phalanx (Pastern), *I Falange, (Cuarta)*
28. 2nd Phalanx, Middle Phalanx (Short Pastern), *II Falange*
29. 3rd Phalanx, Distal Phalanx (Pedal Bone), *III Falange*
30. Proximal Sesamoid, *Sesamoideo Proximal*
31. Small Metacarpal, *Pequeño Metacarpiano, Metacarpiano Externo, II Metacarpiano*
32. Accessory Carpal, *Accesorio*
33. Costal Cartilages, *Cartílagos de la Costilla*
34. Ribs (18), *Costillas (18)*
35. Tuber Coxae, *Tuberosidad Coxal*
36. Ilium, *Ilión*
37. Greater Trochanter of the Femur, *Trocanter Mayor*
38. Pubis, *Pubis*
39. Femur, *Femer*
40. Ischium, *Isquión*
41. Tuber Ischii, *Tuberosidad Isquiática*
42. Patella, *Rótula*
43. Femoral Trochlea, *Troclea Femoral*
44. Tibia, *Tibia*
45. Fibula, *Peroné*
46. Tuber Calcanei (Point of the Hock), *Tuberosidad Calcánea (Punto del Corvejón)*
47. Calcaneus, *Tarsoperoneo*
48. Talus (Tibial Tarsal), *Tarsotibial*
49. Large Metatarsal, *Gran Metatarsiano (III Metatarsiano)*
50. Distal Sesamoid Bone (Navicular Bone), *Hueso Navicular, Sesamoideo Distal*

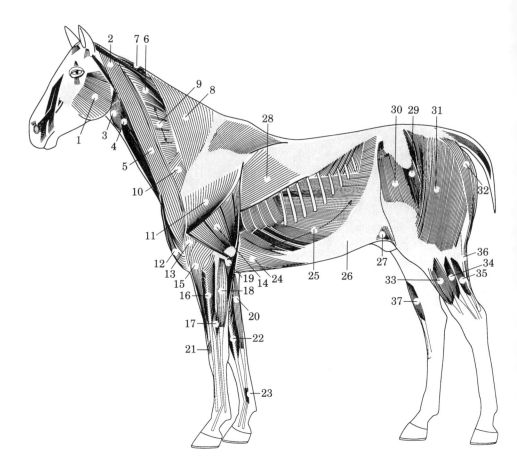

Muscles of the Horse/Músculos del Caballo

1. Masseter M., *M. Masetero*
2. Wing of the Atlas, *M. ala del Atlas*
3. Sternothyrohyoid/ Omohyoid M., *M. Omohioideo*
4. Sternocephalic M., *M. Esternofalico*
5. Brachiocephalic M., *M. Braquiocefálico*
6. Splenius M., *M. Esplenio*
7. Rhomboid M., *M. Romboides*
8. Trapezius M., *M. Trapecio*
9. Ventral Serate M., *M. Serrato Cervical*
10. Cranial Deep Pectoralis M., *M. Pectoral Profundo Anterior*
11. Deltoid M., *M. Deltoides*
12. Cranial Superficial Pectoral M., *M. Pectoral Superficial Anterior*
13. Brachialis M., *M. Braquial*
14. Triceps M., *M. Triceps*
15. Radial Carpal Extensor M., *M. Extensor Carporradial*
16. Common Digital Extensor M., *M. Extensor Digital Común*
17. Lateral Digital Extensor M., *M. Extensor Digital Lateral*
18. Lateral Carpal Flexor M., *M. Flexor Carporlateral*
19. Deep Digital Flexor M., *M. Flexor Digital Profundo*
20. Middle Carpal Flexor M., *M. Cubital Lateral*
21. Oblique Carpal Extensor M., *M. Extensor Oblícuo del Carpo*
22. Medial Carpal Flexor M., *M. Flexor Carpormedial*
23. Digital Flexor Tendon, *Tendón Flexor Digital*
24. Pectoral M., *M. Pectoral Profundo*
25. External Abdominal Oblique M., *M. Oblicuo Abdominal Externo*
26. Aponeurosis of External Abdominal Oblique M., *Aponeurosis de M. Oblícuo Abdominal Externo*
27. Cutaneous M., *M. Cutáneo Abdominal*
28. Latissimus Dorsi M., *M. Gran Dorsal*
29. Superficial Gluteal M., *M. Glúteo Superficial*
30. M. Tensor Fasciae Latae, *M. Tensor de la Fascia Lata*
31. Biceps Femoris M., *M. Biceps Femoral*
32. Semitendinous M., *M. Semitendinoso*
33. Long Digital Extensor M., *M. Extensor Digital Largo*
34. Lateral Digital Extensor M., *M. Extensor Digital Lateral*
35. Long Digital Flexor M., *M. Flexor Digital Profundo*
36. Achilles Tendon, *M. Tendón de Aquiles*
37. Anterior Tibial M., *M. Tibial Anterior*

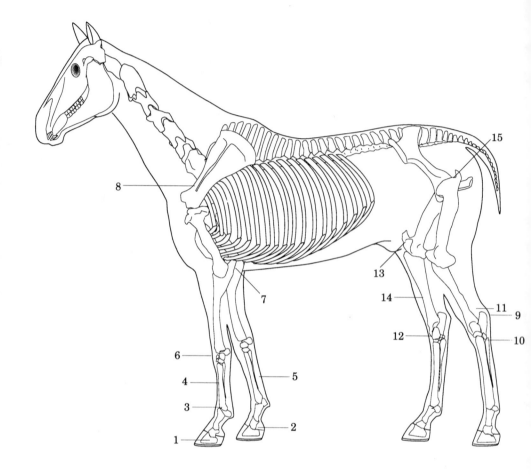

Sites of Lameness in the Horse/Puntos de Cojera en el Caballo

1. Bruised Sole, *Contusión de la Suela, Planta Contusa*
   Corns, *Callos*
   Contracted Heel, *Talón Encogido, Talón Contraído*

Cracked Heels, *Talones Encogidos, Talones Contraídos (Arg)*
Cracked Hoof, *Casco Rajado, Vaso Partido, Fisura del Casco*

1. (CONTINUED)
   Dropped Sole, *Suela Caída*
   Founder/Laminitis,
   Aguado, Laminitis,
   Infosurado
   Gravel, *Arenilla*
   Keratoma, *Queratoma*
   Navicular Disease, *Enfer-*
   medad Navicular, Navicular
   Pedal Osteitis, *Osteitis*
   Podal
   Pumiced Hoof, *Casco*
   Pómez
   Pyramidal Disease, *Enfer-*
   medad Piramidal
   Quarter Crack, *Cuarto*
   Rajado, Fisura del Cuarto
   Sand Crack, *Rajadura de*
   Arena, Fisura del Casco
   Seedy Toe, *Separación del*
   Casco, Hormiguillo, Sepa-
   ración de la uña
   Sesamoid Fracture, *Frac-*
   tura Sesamoideo
   Scratches, *Rasguños, Ras-*
   paduras
   Side Bones, *En-*
   durecimiento de los Cartí-
   lagos Laterales de las
   Patas
   Stone Bruise, *Contusión*
   de Piedra
   Thrush, *Afta, Enfermedad*
   del Pie del Caballo con
   Descarga Fétida
2. Ring Bone, *Sobrehueso,*
   Sobrehueso de la Cuartilla,
   Sobrehueso de la Corona
3. Wind Puffs, *Bolsas de Aire*
   Osselets, *Osteitis, Huese-*
   cillos
   Sesamoiditis, *Sesamoiditis*
   Stocking Up, *Hinchando*
4. Bucked Shins, *Periostitis*
   de los Huesos
   Metacarpianos
   Splints, *Sobrehuesos*
5. Bowed Tendon,
   Tendinitis, Tendón Botado
   (Arg, Ch, Ven), Tendón
   Arqueado
6. Carpitis, *Carpitis, Rodilla*
   Dislocada
   Epiphysitis, *Epifisitis*
7. Capped Elbow, *Capelet*
   (Sp, Arg), Higroma del
   Codo, Bursitis del Codo
8. Sweeny, *Atrofia de los*
   Músculos del Hombro
9. Capped Hock, *Higroma*
   del Corvejón, Bursitis del
   Corvejón
10. Curb, *Corva, Corvaza*
11. Thoroughpin,
    Hinchazón Tarsal
12. Occult spavin,
    Esparaván Oculto
    Bog Spavin,
    Esparaván Falso
    Bone Spavin,
    Esparaván Oseo
13. Gonitis, *Gonitis*
14. Stringhalt, *Mioclonia de*
    las Patas Traseras
15. Coxitis, *Coxitis*

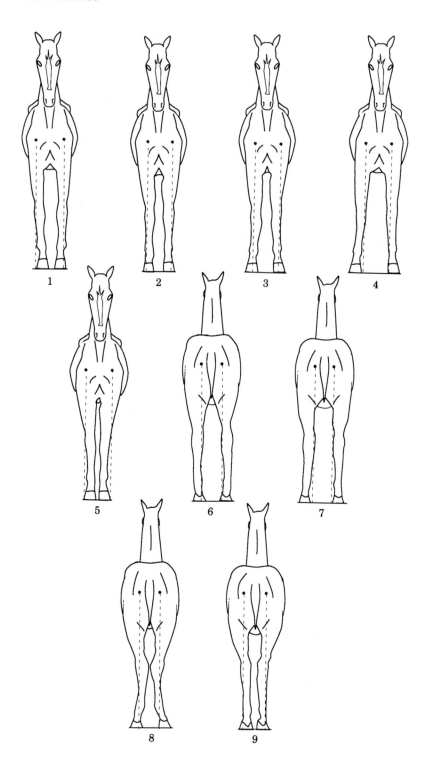

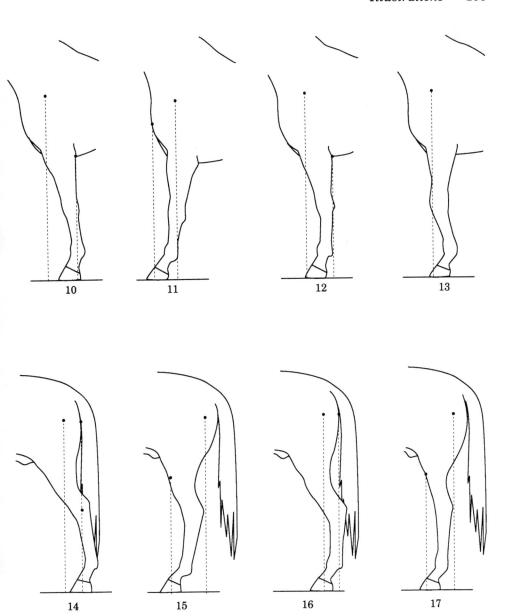

18   19   20

21   22

Set of the Legs/Aplomos, Conformacion de Las Piernas

1. Pigeon-toed, *Pie de Paloma*
2. Crooked Legs, *Piernas Chuecas*
3. Knock-kneed, *Patizambo*
4. Open in Front, *Abierto de Adelante*
5. Closed in Front, *Cerrado de Adelante*
6. Bowlegged, *Curvada, Rodilla Arqueada*
7. Open Behind, *Piernas Abiertas de Atrás*
8. Cow-Hocked, *Patizambo, Corva de Vaca*
9. Closed Behind, *Cerrado de Atrás, Piernas Cerradas de Atrás*
10. Camped-Under in Front, *Remitido de Adelante*
11. Camped-Out in Front, *Plantado de Adelante*
12. Hollow Kneed, *Rodilla Transcorta, Rodilla Hueca*
13. Sprung Kneed, *Transcorto*
14. Camped-Out Behind, *Plantado de Atrás*
15. Camped-Under Behind, *Remitido de Atrás*
16. Sickle Hock, *Pata de Sable*
17. Straight Hock, *Corvejón Derecho, Corvejón Erguido*
18. Stumpy Pastern, *Corto de Cuartilla*
19. Broken-Forward Foot, *Inclinación Excesiva Hacia Adelante*
20. Broken-Back Foot, *Inclinación Excesiva Hacia Atrás*
21. Sloping Pastern, *Corto Angulada*
22. No Heel, *Destalonado*

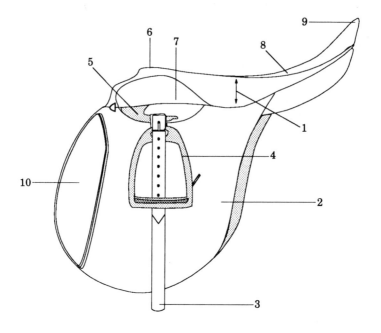

Parts of the English Saddle/Partes de la Silla Inglesa

1. Waist, *Cintura*
2. Saddle Flap, *Falda*
3. Leathers, *Arciones*
4. Irons, *Estribos*
5. Stirrup Bar, *Barra de Estribo*
6. Pommel, *Cabecilla*
7. Skirt, *Falda*
8. Seat, *Asiento*
9. Cantle, *Cantileja, Borren*
10. Knee Roll, *Rollo*

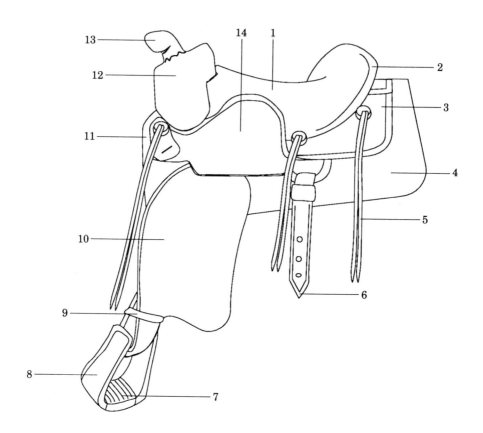

Parts of the Stock Saddle/Partes de la Montura Vaquero

1. Seat, *Asiento*
2. Cantle, *Cantileja, Borrén, Copa, Teja*
3. Back Jockey, *Sobrefalda*
4. Skirt, *Falda*
5. Saddle Strings, *Correas*
6. Flank Clinch, *Barriguera*
7. Stirrup Tred, *Piso del Estribo*
8. Stirrup, *Estribo*
9. Hobble Strap, *Porta Manea, Porta Cuarta, Portamanea*
10. Fender, *Falda, Arción*
11. Front Jockey, *Cobrefalda*
12. Swell, *Borrén, Delantero, Hombro*
13. Horn, *Cacho, Cuerno, Cabeza*
14. Side Jockey, *Sobrefalda*

Index

Indice